The Cuban Economy

The John Hopkins
Studies in Development

Vernon W. Ruttan and
T. Paul Schultz,
Consulting Editors

To our parents   Dorothy Zimbalist and,
in memoriam,
Sam Zimbalist,
Aina Brundenius,
and Anders Brundenius

Contents

Tables

Acknowledgments

This book represents a culmination of our individual and joint efforts during the past six years. These efforts have taken Brundenius to the United States and Zimbalist to Sweden on several occasions and both of us to Cuba over ten times since 1982. None of our work would have been possible without financial support from the Jean Picker Fellowship Fund, Smith College, Swedish Agency for Research Cooperation with the Developing Countries (SAREC), and the Research Policy Institute of the University of Lund, Sweden.

In Cuba, we received immeasurable support from Fidel Vascós, Minister-President of the State Statistical Committee, and members of his staff, particularly Jesus Molina, Ramón Martínez, and Carlos Estrada. We also benefited from ongoing conversations and exchange of materials with several Cuban economists, including José Luis Rodríguez, Miguel Figueras, Armando Santiago, Regino Boti, Eugenio Balari, Juan Valdés Paz, Alfonso Casanova, Ernesto Ortega, Miriam Fernández and Gonzalo Rodríguez. Travel to Cuba, especially for Zimbalist, was never easy, but patient assistance from Ariel Ricardo, Manuel Davis, Juan Carlos Martínez Triana, and Nestor Garcia of the Cuban Foreign Ministry made it both possible and more fruitful.

Many colleagues in the United States and Europe have provided us with invaluable commentary on drafts of our work. In particular, we would like to mention Archibald Ritter, Wayne Smith, Jorge Domínguez, Arthur MacEwan, Carmen Diana Deere, Susan Eckstein, Jean Stubbs, Eva Ehrlich, Joe Brada, Bill Moskoff, Debbie Milenkovitch, Nelson Valdés, Marifeli Pérez-Stable, Abram Bergson, Steve Marglin, Frank Holzman, Joe Berliner, Howard Wachtel, Carol Benglesdorf, Roger Kaufman, Deborah Haas-Wilson, Steve Goldstein, Charles Staelin, Nola Reinhardt, Tom Riddell, Mieke Meurs, Sinan Koont, Stuart Brown, Anju Joglekar, and Jean Sussman. We are grateful to Carsten Blennow of the Research Policy Institute, who provided us with important documentation and insights on the economy of Taiwan. We have also benefited from the consistently excellent computer and research assistance of Mary Ann Coughlin, Betty Nanartonis, Gretchen Iorio, Nina Huffman, Ophelia Yeung, Linda Tay, and Holly Jones.

Andy Richter, senior editor at Johns Hopkins University Press, encouraged and guided us through the final months of the project. He provided detailed commentary on style and substance. Although some of his wisdom was not always immediately apparent, in the end it was and our book is much improved for his efforts.

Finally, as all authors know well, writing a book not only takes a lot of time but it is often emotionally distracting and exhausting. Lydia and Helle not only endured this, but they somehow bolstered us in the process. Jeffrey, Michael, Katarina, Tomas, and Peter provided the humor and unquestioning love to re-energize us daily. Our never-ending gratitude to our families.

Several of this book's chapters are revised and updated versions of articles that previously were published in professional journals. We would like to acknowledge permission for the right to include such material in this book. The articles are the following: "Cuba's Statistical and Price Systems: Interpretation and Reliability," *Latin American Perspectives* 15, 2 (Spring 1988); "Cuban Industrial Growth: 1965–84" and "Development and Prospects of Capital Goods Production in Revolutionary Cuba," *World Development* 15, 1 (January 1987); "Using Physical Indicators to Estimate GDP Per Capita in Cuba: An Estimate and a Critique," *Journal of Comparative Economics* 13, 1 (March 1989); "Incentives and Planning in Cuba," *Latin American Research Review* 23, 1 (January 1989).

The Cuban Economy

CHAPTER 1   *Introduction*

Few people in the United States are indifferent about Cuba. As the first socialist country in the Western Hemisphere, ninety miles from Key West, Florida, Cuba has been perceived for thirty years as a threat to U.S. political hegemony. Cuba's independent and assertive foreign policy has represented an ideological and political challenge to U.S. control. Many members of an active community of some one million Cuban exiles resident in the United States have done their best to assure that Cuba receives abiding antagonistic attention from the U.S. government. Cuba is blamed for inspiring radical insurgency movements and aiding left-wing governments throughout the world and for grossly violating basic human rights of its own people. U.S. policy toward Cuba has been hostile and offensive since the spring of 1959 (see Szulc 1986 and Morley 1987). Overt measures against Cuba have included breaking of diplomatic relations; an economic blockade initiated in 1960 and pressure on U.S. trading partners to follow suit; a U.S.–sponsored invasion in April 1961; financial and logistical support for dissident and rebellious groups; ongoing efforts at economic and political destabilization; and the establishment in 1985 of Radio José Martí, an anti-Cuban propaganda station.

On the other end of the political spectrum is a group of individuals who are appalled by what is perceived as hypocritical U.S. policy toward Cuba, who have hurdled the inconveniences and traveled to Cuba and who, to one degree or another, have been moved by the energy, enthusiasm, and apparent commitment displayed by the Cuban people to their government. The polarization of views is reinforced by the general ban on travel to Cuba by U.S. citizens, the restrictions on travel by Cubans to the United States, and the the trade embargo—all of which have limited the flow of information between the two countries.

Almost ineluctably, any writing on Cuban society is judged to be tainted by the political blinders of one group or the other. To be sure, some writers are more dispassionate than others, but even the relatively more objective observers cannot avoid criticism for being politically biased.

Ideological prejudice and passion are not good foundations for serious scholarship. The foundations are further weakened by travel impediments and, for the tenacious few U.S. investigators who make it to Cuba, by research impediments in Cuba itself. Cuba does not have the resources to accommodate, or the practice of opening up to, foreign social scientists. Obtaining approval for on-site visits or for survey work is difficult, as is access to policymakers or to some data. The resulting empirical base has been thin and this has only solidified the initial biases of investigators.

With the brief period of opening between Cuba and the United States during the Carter administration, however, travel restrictions were eased and dozens of researchers were able to set the groundwork for study projects. At the same time, the Cuban revolution was undergoing a process of institutionalization and the economy was in the midst of an extended boom. The Cubans, thus, were better equipped and more ready to open aspects of their revolution to outside scrutiny. A new wave of scholarship, with a deeper empirical base, was initiated and has begun to bear fruit in the mid- and late-1980s.[1]

INTERPRETING THE CUBAN ECONOMY

The Cuban-born economist Jorge Salazar-Carrillo published an article in 1986 entitled "Is the Cuban Economy Knowable?" (Salazar-Carrillo). This is a good question. Salazar-Carrillo's answer is no because, he says, Cuban statistics are indecipherable. This, in our judgment, is the wrong answer. Cuba's national income accounting conventions are those of the Soviet trading bloc (Council of Mutual Economic Assistance CMEA). Once apprehended, these conventions yield entirely fathomable statistics. It is not clear, however, whether most people who have written about the Cuban economy have taken the trouble to learn the CMEA accounting system.

In a lengthy series of articles (Brundenius and Zimbalist 1985a, 1985b, 1985c), we have provided detailed examples of how the mainstream interpreters of Cuban economic reality misinterpreted and distorted the meaning of Cuban economic data. Many of the errors of interpretation continue to be repeated by the same authors (Mesa-Lago 1986, 1988; Pérez-López 1987b). Some of these issues are discussed in the next four chapters of this book.

The failure of professional economists to assemble a rigorous picture of Cuban economic structure and performance has left a tabula rasa for political prejudice. The range of evaluation of the Cuban economy, even from U.S. official sources, has been quite broad. Consider, for instance, the remarkable assessment in the U.S. Senate's Foreign Relations Committee Staff Report of 1975 that "per capita income in Cuba is by far the highest in Latin America with the possible exception of Venezuela where everthing is distorted by oil" and that "the Cubans are on the verge of constructing a socialist showcase in the Western Hemisphere" (U.S. Senate 1975: 2).

Not surprisingly, during the Reagan administration it was much more fashionable to adopt the opposite interpretation. Indeed, a passing condemnation of the Cuban economy seemed to become almost mandatory, a kind of litmus test of professionalism, for journalistic accounts of Cuba. Thus, Susan Kaufman Purcell of the Council on Foreign Relations wrote in the the *New York Times*

Book Review in October 1986 that Castro had presided over no less than "the destruction of the Cuban economy." And one month later, in the same publication, Stanley Hoffman asserted that "the [Cuban] economy is in a wretched state." Official pronouncements, of course, were equally derogatory and severe. Former Vice President Bush, for instance, was quoted in the *Miami Herald* (December 11, 1986) as saying "Castro has taken one of the hemisphere's strongest, most productive economies and ruined it."

The stridency and ubiquity of these negative assessments in the first half of the 1980s reflected more accurately developments in the United States than they did developments in the Cuban economy. While the rest of Latin America was experiencing an acute recession, Cuba was in a period of robust growth. It was not until 1987 that the effects of the debt crisis brought negative economic growth to Cuba.

One reason why the impact of the debt crisis was mitigated and delayed for Cuba was Cuba's special trading relationship with the Soviet Union and the CMEA. This relationship has entailed stable and very favorable terms of trade, direct project and payments aid, and a seventeen-year moratorium of debt service obligations.

Many who have acknowledged positive aspects of Cuban economic performance have attributed this success solely to massive doses of Soviet aid. For instance, Lawrence Theriot, in a U.S. Department of Commerce study prepared for the Joint Economic Committee, wrote that "the genuine socioeconomic and political accomplishments of the Cuban revolution have attracted much international attention . . . [but they] have been possible only because of massive economic assistance provided by the Soviet Union" (Theriot 1982: 3,5). Another example of this line of interpretation is from Carmelo Mesa-Lago, a prominent interpreter of Cuban economic affairs, who was quoted in an article in *Fortune* magazine (September 16, 1985) as saying that "without a phenomenal Soviet subsidy, the Cuban economy would be a disaster." In fact, while Soviet assistance has been instrumental to Cuban economic development, its magnitude has not been rigorously determined nor its impact systematically analyzed.

In short, the basic facts of Cuba's economic record have yet to be agreed upon. Before interpreting Cuban development structures and strategies, then, it is necessary to comprehend the methodology of Cuban statistics, to appraise their reliability, to rigorously identify shifts in branch and sectoral shares in the economy, and to quantify branch, sectoral, and aggregate rates of growth.

PLAN OF THE BOOK

This study proceeds in two basic parts: Part One endeavors to establish the record of Cuban economic performance, and Part Two attempts to interpret the dynamics of sectoral and aggregate economic development. In chapter 2 we introduce Cuba's system of national income accounting. The consistency and reliability of official statistics are discussed. Since the interpretation of Cuban economic statistics cannot be divorced from the Cuban price system, the latter is also explained. In chapter 3 we discuss official and independent estimates of Cuban industrial growth and, then, offer a new estimate.

Building on this, in chapter 4 we estimate output shares for all economic sectors, a consumer price index, and constant price gross domestic product (GDP) growth. We estimate growth rates in terms of value added and constant 1981 Cuban prices. We also use relative prices and sectoral shares from other Latin American economies where possible in order to discern their impact on measurements of Cuban economic performance. Structural change and sectoral shares are identified in terms of gross value of output and net value added, as well as with and without turnover taxes. Our resulting best growth estimates, although somewhat below official figures, confirm the pattern suggested in the official statistics of slow growth from 1959 to 1970 and rapid growth from 1970 to 1985. In chapter 5, we employ several variants of the physical indicator methodology to estimate Cuban GDP per capita in 1980 U.S. dollars.

Having reconstructed a record of branch, sectoral, and aggregate output in the Cuban economy, we then proceed in Part Two to analyze the strategies, the strengths, and the weaknesses of Cuba's economic development. In chapter 6, we offer a case study of the emergence and rapid growth of Cuba's capital goods sector. With the exception of the East Asian newly industrializing countries (NICs), India, Brazil, and, to a lesser extent, Mexico and Argentina, developing economies have had little growth in capital goods production. Many analysts, including Hirschman (1968), Rosenberg (1976), and Bruton (1988), have emphasized the constructive role that can be played by this sector. Capital goods production can not only provide import substitution, but, more importantly, it can promote learning and autonomous technological development.

In chapter 7 we discuss the evolution of Cuban agricultural policy and the relation of this sector to Cuba's development strategy. Agriculture is often considered to be the Achilles heel of socialist economies. Whereas the Cuban agricultural sector has been plagued with inefficiencies and a traditional concentration on sugar, it has also played a key role in the economy's growth. A flexible and noncoercive policy toward agriculture has facilitated this sector's contribution. The share of sugar in national income and exports has decreased gradually and the development of sugar byproducts has spurred dynamic growth in new areas.

Perhaps most significantly, Cuba's land reforms of 1959 and 1963 succeeded in integrating rural areas into the modern economy and in providing reciprocal markets and resources for the industrial sector. Substantial land reform and capital goods development are common ingredients to the Cuban, South Korean, and Taiwanese experiences. Another common ingredient to the economic growth process in these three countries is the major role played by the state in mobilizing and directing capital resources for development.

In chapter 8 we assess Cuba's system of economic management and central planning. Throughout the 1960s, while Cuba's political institutions were still in flux, economic management was unsteady and poorly coordinated. Since the early 1970s, however, a trend toward institutionalization has produced stable five-year plans and development strategies. After introducing a Kosygin-type reform in 1976, Cuba found the earlier Soviet model to be too centralized for the Cuban environment. A ten-year period of growing decentralization and increasing use of material incentives ensued but came to a halt with the "rectification" drive beginning in April 1986. Common to all centrally planned economies (CPEs), Cuba has struggled with finding the best balance of centralized versus decentralized management and material versus moral incentives. Also common to other CPEs, Cuban central planning has suffered from serious problems of coordination and inefficiency. Nonetheless, through central planning the state has been able to play an instrumental role in promoting the country's economic development.

In chapter 9 we explore several issues pertaining to Cuba's external economy. First, we compare Cuban dependence on sugar and the United States prior to 1959 to its dependence on sugar and the Soviet Union since 1959. Second, we evaluate the role of Soviet subsidies in supporting the Cuban economy. Third, we discuss the evolution of Cuba's foreign trade and debt and their impact on macroeconomic performance in the 1980s.

Finally, in chapter 10, we conclude our study by appraising the Cuban development experience in comparative perspective. Despite its manifold problems, the Cuban economy has outperformed most developing countries in terms of both economic growth and equity. We cautiously attempt to identify the successful features of Cuba's economic institutions and development policies and to draw some more general lessons.

This book will not put an end to interpretational disagreements about Cuban economic performance. If we are successful, however, the book will bring us closer to a scholarly consensus regarding Cuba's economic record and will allow for more openmindedness in assessing the strengths and weaknesses of Cuban socialism.

PART I

*Quantifying
Economic Growth
and Structural
Change*

CHAPTER 2

Statistical Methods and Meanings

One of the things that interpreters of the Cuban economy agree upon is that one must make recourse to statistics to fathom economic performance. Production statistics, a commonly used measure of performance, record the *value* of output in various branches and sectors of the economy as well as for the economy as a whole. Such data enables the researcher to discern not only the structure of production (e.g., the share of the sugar products branch in the economy, the size of capital goods relative to consumer goods output, etc.) but also the rate of growth of the economy and its parts.

The ambiguity and the dispute in interpreting Cuban economic statistics are rooted in two problems. First, the Cubans use the so-called Material Product System (MPS) to compute the value of their economy's production. The MPS system of national income accounting is common, with some local variations (R. Martínez 1985), to all countries of the Soviet trade bloc. The MPS differs in important ways from the national income accounting system employed in the West, the so-called System of National Accounts (SNA).

Second, to obtain a single output measure based on the physical production of heterogeneous commodities (over one million different goods are produced or consumed in Cuba), it is necessary to use prices. That is, how does one know if ten tons of raw sugar and five tons of nickel is worth more or less than five tons of raw sugar and ten tons of nickel? Some system of valuing these commodities is needed. The value could be expressed in ounces of gold, pesos, dollars, rubles, etc., as long as it is a unit applicable to all goods produced in the country. Here again, the method of price setting in Cuba differs fundamentally from that in the West, prompting many economists to question the meaning of Cuban output statistics. The problem is compounded when one tries to compare the output values in two countries, expressed in two different currencies. Let us consider each of these problems in turn.

MPS AND SNA ACCOUNTING SYSTEMS

One commonly used measure of an economy's total output in the Soviet bloc is gross social product (GSP). There are two basic and important differences between GSP and the Western concept of gross domestic product (GDP). GDP is based on value added and includes "nonproductive services," and GSP is based on gross value and excludes "nonproductive services."

To understand the difference between value added and gross value, let us consider an example: the production of a cotton shirt. Suppose this is accomplished in four stages before the final product reaches the consumer: cotton farming; spinning and weaving (textile factory); designing, cutting, and sewing (garment factory); and retailing. The distinction between value added and gross value can be depicted as follows:

	Value added	Gross value
Cotton farming	$ 1	$ 1
Textile	3	4
Garment	3	7
Retail	4	11
TOTAL	11	23

The cotton farmer combines land and labor to produce enough raw cotton to make one shirt and sells this cotton to the textile factory for one dollar. The textile factory transforms this cotton into cloth, which it sells to the garment factory for four dollars; it has added three dollars of value to the product in process. The garment factory adds an additional three dollars to the value of the cloth and sells the shirt to the retail store for seven dollars, which, in turn, sells it to the consumer for eleven dollars. According to the SNA system, which uses value added, the shirt in this hypothetical illustration contributes a value of eleven dollars (the sum of the value added at each stage or the retail price) to GDP. According to the MPS system, however, which uses gross value, this same shirt would contribute a value of twenty-three dollars to GSP. Under the MPS method the output value of earlier stages of production is counted anew at each successive stage. Economists refer to this as "double counting" since it gives an inflated value (a value greater than the retail price) to final output.

The second major difference between the concepts GDP and GSP is that the latter does not include "nonproductive services," e.g., arts and culture, government, military, sports, banking, housing, health, education, personal services, etc. The fact that the Soviet bloc countries do not include these items in their measurement of national output should not be construed to mean that these activities are undervalued. To be sure, the activities of the Politbureau itself are not counted as output. Rather, this practice is a vestige from the early years of the Soviet revolution, when it was decided that they would not be included since, according to orthodox Marxian value theory, these activities did not produce surplus value.

The presence of double counting and the exclusion of nonproductive services, then, complicates the interpretation of the Soviet bloc accounting category of GSP. Fortunately, the problem of double counting can be sidestepped by reference to other national income concepts of the MPS method.

GSP − Intermediate consumption = Gross material product (GMP)

GMP − Depreciation = Net material product (NMP) or National income

The concept of gross material product or GMP theoretically eliminates double counting and represents a national income measure based on value added.[1] When depreciation (wearing down of machinery, plant, and equipment) is deducted from GMP, net material product results. If an accurate estimate could be made of nonmaterial services (NMS),[2] this figure could be added to GMP to estimate the SNA concept of GDP (or to NMP to estimate NNP[3]).

How important are these distinctions and what difference do they make in interpreting Cuban economic performance? Let us consider this question in three parts: impact of the distinction on measuring the absolute level of economic activity and income per capita; impact on measuring economic growth rates; and impact on measuring economic structure and its transformation.

According to Cuban official statistics, GSP in 1984, measured in constant 1981 prices, was 25.92 billion pesos, and NMP was 13.7 billion pesos. That is, the value of all intermediate consumption (including depreciation) in 1984 was the difference between these two figures, 12.22 billion pesos; or, NMP was just over half (52.9 percent) of GSP, a rather substantial difference!

If we add nonmaterial services to NMP, we can arrive at an estimate for net domestic product (NDP), and adding depreciation to NDP, we can get an estimate for GDP. The principal problem here is that the Cubans to date have not calculated an official statistic on the value of nonmaterial services. Independent estimates have ranged from 13 to 35 percent of national income, depending on the year and the methodology. Since the average ratio of nonmaterial services to GDP in Latin America is approximately .25, and our own estimates for this ratio in Cuba lie between .25 and .30, let us assume that in Cuba in 1984 nonmaterial services amounted to 25 percent of (estimated) NDP. In this case, by simple algebraic manipulation, we can calculate that nonmaterial services (NMS) would equal 33 percent of NMP, or 4.57 billion pesos in 1984.

NNP = NMP + NMS = 13.7 + 4.57 = 18.27 billion pesos

GDP = NDP + Depreciation = 18.27 + 2.25 = 20.52 billion pesos[4]

Hence, according to this rough estimate, in 1984 GSP was 25.92 billion pesos while GDP was 20.52 billion (each measured in 1981 prices); that is, the Western SNA concept of GDP had an estimated value 20.8 percent below the official value of the MPS concept of GSP. Again, the difference is appreciable.[5]

Another way such figures are often used is to assess comparative levels of economic development by calculating GDP per capita. With a population of just over ten million in 1984, estimated Cuban per capita GDP (in 1981 pesos)

in that year is 2,052 pesos. To compare this figure with other countries it is necessary to convert this peso figure into a common currency, usually dollars. If we used the official exchange rate in January 1981 of 1 peso = $1.36, then we would conclude that Cuban per capita GDP in 1984 (measured in constant 1981 prices) was $2,792. Since this exchange rate is fixed by the Cuban government and not by the supply and demand for the peso internationally, most Western economists believe that the use of the official rate for conversion into dollars is highly dubious. To be sure, since Cuba has run chronic balance of trade and current account deficits, Western economists would argue that the peso is overvalued at the official rate. On the other hand, a standard practice employed for converting national income in local currencies into dollars, the so-called purchasing power parity or ppp method, consistently yields much higher GDP per capita estimates than when converted at the official exchange rate for both centrally planned and developing economies. If Cuba's adjusted ppp followed the same pattern as Hungary's, for instance, the estimate for Cuba's GNP per capita in 1984 would exceed $4,000. This result has to do with relative price structures in centrally planned versus market economies and developed versus less developed economies (see chapter 5). Finally, another method that by-passes the knotty issue of conversion into dollars (as well as the problem of different national income accounting methodologies), the so-called physical indicators or PI method, has been applied to Cuba and also yields higher estimates of GNP per capita than those derived from conversion at official exchange rates (Mesa-Lago and Pérez-López 1985b). We shall return to this elusive issue of exchange rate conversion and dollar per capita GDP estimates for Cuba in chapter 5.

The impact of the different national income accounting systems can also be seen with respect to economic growth. Does Cuban GSP grow faster or slower than (an estimate of) Cuban GDP? This will depend on two factors: one, if the growth rate of GSP is above or below the growth rate of NMP; and, two, if the growth rate of NMP is above or below the growth rate of nonmaterial services (NMS).

The Cubans published data on constant price GSP and NMP in their 1984 statistical yearbook (*Anuario Estadístico de Cuba*, AEC) for the years 1975 through 1984. Over this period the average annual growth rate of GSP was 5.4 percent and of NMP was 5.9 percent. NMP, which deducts intermediate consumption from GSP and, hence, does not double count, grows more rapidly because less and less input was employed per unit of output.[6] Put differently, factor productivity increased (or efficiency in the use of inputs improved) over these years. That is, although GSP gives a higher absolute level of output due to the double counting it embodies, GSP yields a lower rate of growth when factor productivity is increasing (the case for most countries).

The issue of whether NMS grows more or less rapidly than NMP is very complicated, and we shall return to consider it in more detail in chapter 4. For

Table 2.1. Industrial Share (percentages)

	1975 (with turnover taxes)	1984 (with turnover taxes)	1984 (without turnover taxes)
Gross value[a]	—	43.8	54.2
Value added[b]	30.4	33.6	—

Source: CEE/AEC 1984 and data from the State Statistical Committee.
[a]Gross value of industrial output divided by gross social product
[b]Value added of industrial output divided by net material product

the time being, let us assume that the growth rates of NMS and NMP have been approximately equal since 1975.[7] If this is true, then it is also true that *the growth rate of GDP in Cuba would be higher than the growth rate of GSP.*

Finally, it remains to consider the impact of the different accounting systems on Cuban economic structure. This issue is rather involved, so we shall simply illustrate the scope of the problem at this point with a single example.

There has been a good deal of debate recently about the industrial share in Cuba's GSP.[8] The industrial share drops and the share of the commercial sector rises if turnover (sales) taxes are included in the calculation. This is because the incidence of such taxes is primarily on the commercial sector. When the calculation is made exclusive of these taxes, the industrial share rises over time.[9] We return to this matter in chapter 4.

The industrial share is also affected, however, by making the calculation in gross value (with double counting) or value added terms. A large share of Cuba's industrial output in gross value terms counts imported intermediate inputs as part of the output. These inputs are not produced in Cuba and properly should not be included as part of Cuban industrial output. When the calculation is made in value added terms, these inputs are in fact excluded. Since industrial intermediate inputs are proportionately larger than those for other sectors, the industrial share in GSP (gross value measurement) is larger than the industrial share in NMP (value added measurement).

It is evident from Table 2.1 that the industrial share reckoned in gross value is greater than in value added. It is also clear that the industrial share is larger without turnover taxes and is increasing since 1975. Separately, it can be observed that the industrial share increases more rapidly in value added than gross value terms, other things being equal, and that the industrial share, by any measure that neutralizes the distorting effect of turnover taxes, has increased since 1959.[10]

THE SETTING AND INTERPRETATION OF PRICES

As already mentioned, Western economic theory questions the meaning of prices set by the government as well as any value of production estimates predicated on such prices. According to this approach, market prices that are determined by the interaction of supply (costs of production) and demand (consumer preferences) properly represent the scarcity value and utility of the product to the society, with a few exceptions. This approach would also maintain that government-fixed prices do not represent consumer preferences; rather, they register the preferences of the planners or of those who set the prices. As such, they do not record the utility of the product to the society even if the prices are rooted in production costs. Thus, if product prices do not represent utility from the consumption of the product, aggregating national output values with these prices will yield figures for national income that do not bear a clear relationship to society's welfare. National income in this circumstance could go up, but social welfare could go down.

The socialist response to this critique would point out, *inter alia*, that consumer preferences in capitalist societies are registered in direct proportion to one's wealth, and in planned economies the planners are responsive to consumer preferences and are able to take into account indirect costs (e.g., externalities) that the market ignores.

How, in fact, do the Cubans set prices and how do these prices affect estimates of growth rates for the Cuban economy? The Comité Estatal de Precios (State Price Committee) is in charge of fixing prices for Cuba's one million plus products.[11] To be sure, some prices are set by local governments when the good only circulates locally (e.g., artisan production), and other prices fluctuate freely according to the conditions of supply and demand (e.g., perishable consumer goods toward the end of the marketing period).

The State Price Committee was formed in 1976 with the introduction of the SDPE (Sistema de Dirección y Planificación de la Economía, the Cuban system of management and planning[12]). The committee is housed in an old, ten-story building in Old Havana and employs some 200 professional workers in its central office. The committee is divided into groups that deal with different types of products and other functions of the committee. One group in charge of price setting for most nonperishable consumer goods has fourteen employees. It is responsible for over 250,000 individual products, each having at least two prices—one wholesale and one retail. Each year the group will consider adjusting approximately 15,000 prices as cost conditions and inventory levels change. Such adjustments, however, are generally minor. The large and comprehensive adjustments are saved for periodic price reforms.[13]

The first major price reform occurred in 1981. According to the Cuban authorities, prices prevailing prior to this reform were the same as 1965 prices in the material production sectors.[14] (Of course, products introduced after 1965—and there were many—carried the price assigned to them in the year they were first produced.) The 1981 reform was based on an assessment of prices, costs, and structures existing in 1978. New wholesale prices were introduced in January (400,000 prices were changed) and new retail prices in December 1981. The next comprehensive reform is scheduled for January

1989[15] and will be based on prices, costs, and structures of 1985.

The key to a successful price reform is to identify a new structure of prices that is internally consistent. If the prices of inputs used in producing widgets are increased, then the price of widgets must also be increased (unless there was a previous imbalance). If not, then widget producers will not be able to turn a profit and there will be no enterprise bonus to share with their workers. Workers, in turn, will generally lose incentive and productivity will lag. If widget prices do increase, then other goods that use widgets as an input will also have to receive higher prices. And so on. This problem of consistency is extraordinarily complex, but extremely important for the proper functioning of Cuba's economic mechanism as it has been designed. The complexity of the problem is compounded when price reforms are implemented only every eight years. In the interim, domestic conditions of supply and demand change and international prices change, sometimes dramatically. Such changes engender inconsistencies in the existing price structure; hence the yearly modifications, due to extensive interdependencies, often create as many new inconsistencies as they resolve old ones.

The actual setting of prices takes place more or less as follows. The enterprises producing a particular product (sometimes disaggregated to include style detail, sometimes at the level of generic product, e.g., cotton shirt, adult male) send a price proposal along with information on production cost to the State Price Committee. The relevant group within the committee analyzes the cost data it receives from each of the producers and, if it finds no irregularities, proceeds to take an average of the estimated costs of production for all of the enterprises in the branch. To this estimate of average cost of production in the branch is added a percent markup for profit[16]; in the textile branch of industry, for instance, this markup is 4 percent, while in construction it is 6.1 percent and the economywide average is 9.2 percent.

Consider a simple example. Suppose there are two enterprises producing guayabera shirts. One of them, the more efficient, estimates costs per shirt at $4.85, and the other at $5.15.[17] The State Price Committee takes the average, $5.00, and adds 4 percent, to arrive at the wholesale price or $5.20. The more efficient enterprise, assuming the cost estimates were correct, earns 35 centavos profit per shirt; the less efficient enterprise earns only 5 centavos. If to this wholesale price the turnover (sales) tax is added, or the state subsidy deducted, the resulting figure is the retail price (excluding retail margins and transportation costs).

Recall that the nonperishables group in the State Price Committee has 14 workers and is in charge of some 250,000 products. What if a particular product is produced by only one enterprise in Cuba or by two enterprises with very different technologies? What if some of the cost information is questionable? What if enterprise financial directors pressure to have prices changed? What if relatives call the head of the group to complain that prices are too high?

The imbroglio continues. There is a State Committee on Standards that, among other things, is in charge of classifying product quality into three grades. For products in the top grade (quality of international competitiveness) planned profits are allowed to rise by 30 to 50 percent; this increase is effected by a price increase of a couple of percentage points. The second grade is entitled to a profit increase from 10 to 30 percent, implying yet a different price increase. The third grade retains the base price. Further, there is also the possibility of a price increase for new product designs and styles, as an incentive to enterprises that innovate. All these price modifications are the responsibility of the State Price Committee.

It goes without saying that the State Price Committee uses many shortcuts to carry out its tasks and that the resulting structure of prices will be imperfect. The magnitude of this price-setting task is one of the strongest arguments on behalf of market socialism. Market socialism, however, brings on its own problems.[18]

To be sure, most advocates of central planning still prefer government- over market-determined prices for most products. This position holds that: 1) market prices respond disproportionately to the preferences of the wealthy and these prices, in turn, skew production decisions away from the social good; 2) market prices do not reflect social costs and benefits; 3) market prices are subject to manipulation by corporations with market power; 4) that market prices move erratically in response to speculators and ephemeral influences, causing instability and short-sightedness in the economy; and 5) market prices are subject to periods of instability and inflation that engender uncertainty, lower productive investment, and generally poor economic performance. So far, at least, such arguments seem to hold sway in the socialist economies, as extensive price fixing and price controls are still state prerogatives even in the most decentralized planned economies.

It remains to clarify that there are several different kinds of retail prices in Cuba. Many basic goods are still rationed and are heavily subsidized by the government, although the size of these subsidies was cut by over 60 percent as a result of the 1981 price reform. Consider the examples in Table 2.2.

These are the prices for rationed quantities of pasteurized milk and top-quality beef. The milk subsidy was reduced from 8 to 3 centavos per liter by the 1981 price reform, while the beef subsidy was lowered from 69 to 54 centavos

Table 2.2.   Price Subsidies (dollars)

Product	Cost	1980 price	1982 price	1982 subsidy
Milk (liter)	.28	.20	.25	.03
Beef (lb.)	1.24	.55	.70	.54

Source: Data from the State Statistical Committee.

per pound. Both milk and top-quality beef are available for purchase as well on the "parallel market." The parallel market, also controlled by the state, has fixed prices that are higher, often severalfold higher, than those for rationed quantities. For instance, a liter of rationed milk still sold for 25 centavos in 1988, but the parallel market price for purchases above the ration quota was one peso—four times as high.[19] In the case of some basic services (e.g., education, health, and some cultural and sports activities) the state subsidy is 100 percent; that is, the service is free. On the other hand, for luxury items and unhealthy products (tobacco, alcohol, fancy restaurants, cars, etc.) the state levies a turnover tax that significantly raises the retail price above production cost. Finally, there are special dollar shops for foreigners where prices are denominated in dollars, and there exists a black market for a variety of commodities (and currencies) where prices exceed the regulated prices set by the state.

As is the case for planned output, the state does not have sufficient information and personnel to perfectly control all prices. Some goods have no centrally set prices at all, and others have official prices that are violated. Prices are regularly checked by a network of popular and professional inspectors. Popular price inspection was begun in July 1978, and professional inspection has grown as more specialists have been trained. As of May 1985, there were 3,875 popular inspectors and 240 professional specialists (Padron 1985: 102). According to inspections carried out during 1982–84, there was a total of 32 million pesos of charges at below the official price and 40 million pesos of charges above the official price; there were 187 million pesos of transactions of goods with no official price (or one-quarter of 1 percent of GSP for these years) (Toledo 1985: 14). Although this is still a very small share of economywide transactions, it is notable that the number of registered price violations has increased in recent years. This reported increase may be a statistical artifact; that is, a function of more, better trained inspectors and wider dissemination of official price lists. It is likely, however, that with the expanding private economy until spring 1986 there was more incentive to violate official prices, and part of the reported increase is real. Most of the registered violations occurred in retail outlets and most of these in restaurants.[20]

However one judges the allocative and social impact of Cuban (as distinct from market) prices, the practical question of how these prices affect measurement of economic performance remains. If Cuban prices are higher than market prices for products and branches that are growing more rapidly, then Cuban prices would impart an upward bias to estimates of economic growth. If Cuban prices are lower for such products, then they impart a downward bias. There is little, if any, a priori basis to suspect the presence of either bias. In fact, as we shall see in chapter 3, when compared to Guatemalan prices Cuban prices exhibit no discernible growth bias in either direction. We shall return to this issue when considering the reliability of Cuban economic statistics.

Cuban Statistics: Their Scope, Consistency, and Reliability

On December 1, 1976, the Cuban State Statistical Committee (Comité Estatal de Estadísticas, CEE) was formed. Prior to this date, economic statistics were gathered, computed, and published through the Statistical Directorate of JUCEPLAN (the Central Planning Board). The establishment of a separate state committee to handle statistics represented a recognition by Cuban leaders of the vital importance of accurate and timely statistics to the efficient operation of a centrally planned economy. Prior to 1976 the generation of economic statistics was generally irregular and unsystematic, with methods and definitions changing every few years. This legacy has made it difficult for the CEE to establish consistent historical series of data going back to 1959.[21]

Since 1977, however, a consistent methodology has been applied in rigorous and systematic fashion. Each year the CEE has published more information on the economy, with more explanations of its procedures. Current data has been published in an increasingly timely manner, and historical series have been gradually reconstructed (although much still remains to be done). This significant and rapid improvement in the quality of Cuban statistics has been recognized even by harsh critics.[22] These critics, however, still in important ways misinterpret the meaning of many statistical categories as well as the method employed to generate the statistics. This misinterpretation has led them to underrepresent both the extent of the improvement in statistical publications and the gains in economic performance.

As already discussed, when critics challenge official growth rates, the basis for this challenge lies in the meaning of Cuban prices, not in the underlying physical output data, which has been accepted without question. There are many reasons for this, but three points in particular merit some discussion.

First, as any Western economist who has studied centrally planned economies would readily acknowledge, accurate, comprehensive, and timely information in a centrally planned system is essential for its effective operation. Ultimately, the supply of such information always falls short of the demand for it. The system, thus, is overburdened generating one set of reliable, consistent statistics. Those who claim that two sets of data books are maintained, one for internal use and one for public relations purposes, have too much faith in the information processing capabilities of the system.

Second, there is Alec Nove's well-known "law of equal cheating." The law states that once output statistics have been falsely inflated to make growth rates appear higher, it is necessary to inflate the lie more and more each year. That is, by this reasoning, it would be much more difficult to deceive the world about growth rates than about the standard of living at one point in time.

Third, when the Cubans do not want to reveal a statistic, their practice appears to be to classify rather than invent it. Presumably, a statistic might be classified because it is politically sensitive or because it is embarrassing. It is important to point out that the Cubans have not shrunk from publishing embarrassing economic and social data. It is equally important that the Cubans have declassified a substantial amount of information in recent years. Much remains classified, however, such as income distribution data, data on their debt to the Soviet Union,[23] studies on the cost of the U.S. blockade, and six-digit input-output tables.

Thus, official physical output data from Cuba has been accepted by the experts, including the revolution's critics. The critics, however, have alleged that there is hidden inflation in Cuba's constant price (adjusted for inflation) growth rates, and they have implied that Cuban relative prices have made growth appear to be higher than it really is.

In the next chapter, we explore this claim in detail by comparing different estimates of Cuban industrial growth, each based on relative prices from different countries for a particular year. Here it is useful to mention two of the conclusions from this comparison. First, as stated above, other things equal, Cuban prices do not impart an upward bias to the growth rate estimate. Second, our independent estimates based on wide product coverage, value added branch weights, and 1981 Cuban prices came very close to the Cuban official statistics.

It is important to emphasize that in these estimates the physical output of each year between 1962 and 1985 was valued using 1981 prices. Since the same prices were used throughout, it cannot be argued that hidden inflation is responsible for exaggerated real growth rates in these estimates.

The prominent Cubanologist, Jorge Domínguez, alleged in the September/October 1985 issue of *Problems of Communism* that "Cuba's statistical system has yet to generate credible data about the obviously economically troubled 1980–82 period, for which official figures unconvincingly suggest an economic boom." One year later in the same journal, a similar contention was made by Jorge Pérez-López: "More important, there is reason to believe that a significant portion of the reported GSP growth in 1981–85 may be attributable to inflation. . . ."[24] The official Cuban figure of real industrial growth in 1981, the year of the wholesale price reform, does appear excessive, and it is possible that an incomplete accounting for inflation in that year biased the official figure upward. But it must also be emphasized that our constant price estimate for 1981, which is downward biased due to inadequate coverage of new product groups, still suggests a very strong growth spurt in that year.

Domínguez has trouble reconciling strong growth with falling sugar prices, but the issue is much more complicated. First, the impact of sugar prices on economic activity may well be lagged. World sugar prices averaged record high levels in 1980, which permitted an accumulation of foreign exchange and an expansion of imports in that year. These imports were used, among other things, to buy materials to complete a large number of investment projects undertaken in the late 1970s. To be sure, Cuba's investment ratio and absolute investment spending were higher in the late 1970s than in any previous or subsequent period. Many of these projects were consummated in 1980 and 1981, leading to output spurts.

Second, when world sugar prices fall, the Cubans sell a larger share of their sugar to CMEA countries at heavily subsidized prices. Third, a variety of policy measures such as the opening of free peasant markets and the expansion of parallel markets greatly increased the availability and variety of consumer goods. This, in turn, provided workers with a greater incentive to work harder for prizes and bonuses.

In short, we believe a careful, dispassionate review of Cuban statistics would show them to be fundamentally reliable and of high quality.[25] It is interesting that many of Cuba's antagonists criticize Cuban data, claiming it overstates performance, and then compare it with selected data from other Latin American countries, which goes unscrutinized. Irregularities and shoddy methods in statistical offices throughout Latin America abound, and many countries have been known to deliberately distort the reporting of economic data (Cohen 1987a: 32; 1987b: 22). Should Cuban statistics be compared with those of most other countries in Latin America, they would stand the test very well.

Nevertheless, much remains to further improve Cuban statistics. Historical series must be made consistent. Some classified information is not politically sensitive and should be declassified. Other information should be published with greater regularity, timeliness, and accessibility. Anomalies, to be discussed in subsequent chapters, still remain. It must be remembered, however, that Cuba is still a developing country with scarce resources to lavish on the perfection of its statistical system. Cuban statistics should be judged by the same standards applied to other developing economies. Lastly, the accessibility and verifiability of Cuban statistics will always be a problem to U.S. citizens and scholars as long as the U.S. blockade of Cuba endures.

CHAPTER 3   *Industrial Growth*

According to official figures, industrial value added growth in Cuba has been strong since 1965, averaging 7.3 percent per annum in constant 1981 prices between 1965 and 1985. During 1980–85 the industrial growth rate accelerated to 11.5 percent per annum.[1]

If the official Cuban industrial growth statistics could be accepted at face value, they would suggest a rather impressive performance, at least through 1985. However, as discussed in chapter 2, methodological differences, administered prices, procedural irregularities and opaqueness, double counting, and new product pricing practices, among other things, have engendered caution and suspicion among Western specialists when interpreting official national income figures from centrally planned economies. Many comparative economists have employed techniques such as Bergson's adjusted factor cost pricing to make the national income estimates of the MPS methods compatible with those of the Western SNA methods.[2] Another widely used technique to estimate growth and levels of national income is based on physical indicators (Marer 1985a, 1985b).

As part of the recent World Bank International Comparisons Project, two economists, Carmelo Mesa-Lago and Jorge Pérez-López, were asked to analyze Cuban economic performance. In their report, however, not only did they cite a lack of sufficient data to generate their own estimates of Cuban national income and its growth, but they cast a broad doubt on existing independent estimates of Cuban economic performance (Mesa-Lago and Pérez-López 1982). Whereas their criticisms of these studies were on the whole well taken, their own discussion of Cuban national income methodology and statistics was amply flawed.[3]

Subsequent to his participation in the World Bank project, Pérez-López was hired by Wharton Econometric Forecasting Associates (WEFA), itself under contract to the U.S. State Department, to develop estimates of Cuban economic growth. This WEFA study was completed in November 1983 and then updated in a 1985 paper and a 1987 book by Pérez-López (Pérez-López 1983, 1985, 1987b).[4] Both the initial WEFA study and its updates present a vigorous challenge to the rosy figures of the Cuban government. The WEFA estimates have, in turn, been published by the CIA in its *The Cuban Economy: A Statistical Review* (CIA 1984) and have been cited extensively in U.S. press coverage of the Cuban economy.

In this chapter, after briefly summarizing the WEFA and other studies, we shall present and evaluate new estimates of Cuban industrial growth. These estimates are based on more comprehensive price data and more meaningful branch weights than those used in the WEFA study. Although the results correspond more closely with the official record for the entire period than do the WEFA estimates, they fall considerably below the official statistics for 1980–85. This deviation, as we shall elaborate below, is largely attributable to a bias in our commodity set that underrepresents new product groups.

THE WEFA STUDY

In January 1981 a major wholesale price reform was put into effect in Cuba. According to data derived from the 1984 Cuban statistical yearbook, the implicit rate of wholesale price inflation in 1981 was 9.9 percent (CEE/AEC 1984: 89–91). WEFA argues, however, that the official figures, which report a real GSP increase of 16.0 percent in 1981, do not fully account for the price increases occasioned by the reform. Thus, the use of constant year prices would provide a truer measure of the increase in real output in 1981.

Due to the absence of sufficient Cuban price data and questions about the meaningfulness of Cuba's administered prices, WEFA employs a set of Guatemalan prices from 1973 and supplements this set with U.S. prices. WEFA chose Guatemalan prices because "the structure of the [Guatemalan] economy shared important features with Cuba: small, predominantly agricultural and eminently open" (Pérez-López 1983: 93). Some skepticism regarding the appropriateness of this price set is warranted. Among other things, as a member of the Central American Common Market, Guatemalan industry in 1973 enjoyed average tariff protection in excess of 25 percent. Through the National Agricultural Market Institute, the Guatemalan government at the time played a significant role in agricultural price formation and regulation, affecting the prices of milk, cream, butter, cheese, cereals, and meat, among other products. Interest rate controls and ceiling prices on medicines, dyes, basic clothing items, and other goods further distorted Guatemalan prices away from free, competitive market prices. Moreover, with 55 percent of Guatemala's labor force in agriculture in 1980 (compared to 23 percent in Cuba), secondary school enrollment of 16 percent of the relevant age cohort in 1981 (compared to 75 percent in Cuba), an illiteracy rate of 53.9 percent in 1973 (compared to 5 percent in Cuba), and a 1981 manufacturing share of GDP of 16.2 percent (compared to roughly 30 percent in Cuba), it is hard to see how Guatemalan factor endowments could be construed to be representative of those in Cuba. Acknowledging the difficulties of data collection, however, let us look further into the methods and results of the WEFA study.

WEFA used the so-called bottom-up method and applied its Guatemalan/U.S. price set to the 206 industrial products whose physical output is reported in the Cuban statistical yearbook for each of Cuba's 21 industrial branches.[5] More precisely, Laspeyres quantity indexes were calculated as follows:

$$I_{b_i} = \frac{\sum\limits_{j=1}^{n} (p_{j0})(q_{jt})}{\sum\limits_{j=1}^{n} (p_{j0})(q_{j0})} \tag{1}$$

where I_b is the output index for branch b_i, n is the number of products in WEFA's sample for the branch, p_{j0} is the base period price for the jth product in branch b_i, q_{jt} is the physical output of product j in the year t (where t runs from 1965 through 1980), and q_{j0} is the physical output of product j in the base year. Thus, activity indexes were estimated for each branch dating back to 1965.

The branch indexes were then aggregated by using hybrid estimates for branch value added. The majority of these estimates were generated roughly as follows: Economic Commission for Latin America estimates for branch value added (VA) in 1963 (based on JUCEPLAN figures for branch gross value added in 1961) were divided by estimated branch gross value of output (GVO) for that year; assuming the branch VA/GVO ratios to be constant between 1963 and 1975, the 1963 ratio was multiplied by branch GVO in 1975, yielding an estimate for value added in that year.[6] Specifically,

$$I = \sum\limits_{j=1}^{21} (I_{b_i})(W_{b_i}) / \sum\limits_{j=1}^{21} W_{b_i} \tag{2}$$

where I is the activity index for industry and W_b is the value added estimate for the ith branch.

There are significant problems both with WEFA's intra- and interbranch weighting procedures. WEFA's price set covers only 128 out of the 206 products for which it has yearly physical output data, or 62.1 percent of their product sample. Since the Guatemalan economy is significantly less industrialized than the Cuban economy, the 1973 Guatemalan price sample appears to systematically leave out many of Cuba's newest and most dynamic industrial product groups. In fact, this observation also holds for the 206 products included in Cuba's statistical yearbook, since this list has only incorporated eight new products since 1970 and none since 1978. This double sampling bias produces a downward skewing in the WEFA estimates of branch activity indexes.

In Table 3.1 we reproduce a comparison of the WEFA output index for five branches with an index we have generated based on 1981 Cuban wholesale prices (Brundenius and Zimbalist 1985b). In four of the five cases, the increased product coverage allowed by the Cuban price set resulted in signifi-

Table 3.1. Comparison of Estimated Growth Indexes for Selected Branches (1974 = 100)

	1965	1970	1974	1980	1984
Construction materials					
(12 products in sample)					
WEFA (8 of 12 products)	22	27	100	111	—
Brundenius and Zimbalist (12 of 12)	36	37	100	131	150
Metal products					
(8 products in sample)					
WEFA (2 of 8 products)	16	31	100	46	—
Brundenius and Zimbalist (8 of 8)	22	38	100	184	283
Nonelectrical machinery					
(11 products in sample)					
WEFA (5 of 11 products)	10	21	100	74	—
Brundenius and Zimbalist (9 of 11)	2	21	100	205	258
Electrical machinery					
(8 products in sample)					
WEFA (6 of 8 products)	58	34	100	129	—
Brundenius and Zimbalist (8 of 8)	60	45	100	162	216
Chemicals					
(29 products in sample)					
WEFA (11 of 29 products)	57	77	100	92	—
Brundenius and Zimbalist (23 of 29)	50	64	100	188	197

Source: Brundenius and Zimbalist 1985a.

cantly higher estimates for branch output growth. In the fifth case, the construction materials branch, the expanded coverage estimate for post-1974 growth is markedly higher. The nature of this bias can be illustrated by detailed reference to a particular branch, metal products. According to WEFA, this branch had a 1980 output index of .46 in relation to 1974 (=1.00); that is, output of metal products would be less than half in 1980 what it was in 1974. WEFA's estimate for this branch is based on only two of the eight products in the Cuban yearbook, namely pressure cookers and nails. The physical output of these two products declined by 75 percent and 7 percent, respectively, between 1974 and 1980. WEFA does not have prices for steel structures (whose output increased 480 percent), stainless steel tanks (whose output increased 46 percent), bottle caps (output up 13 percent), electrodes (up 5 percent), steel cans (down 4 percent), or aluminum cans (down 12 percent). When 1981 Cuban prices for all eight products are applied, the branch output index increases by 84 percent, instead of falling by 54 percent as in the WEFA estimate.[7]

Questions remain, of course, as to whether 1) this higher growth is due to product coverage or to a growth bias in the Cuban price set and 2) a similar tendency prevails in the other industrial branches. We shall return to these questions.

WEFA's interbranch weights also present a series of problems, ranging from the assumption of constant VA/GVO over 1963–75 to their hybrid fabrication.

The most significant source of bias in these weights, however, appears to be in the use of weights based on *precios del productor* (inclusive of turnover taxes) for certain branches instead of on *precios de empresa* (exclusive of turnover taxes). A stunning example of the resulting distortion is the 26 percent weight assigned to the beverages and tobacco branch in the WEFA estimate. This weight, over a quarter of all industrial output in Cuba, is approximately three times the weight assigned to the food industry, three times the weight given to chemicals, and four times the weight given to the sugar products branch.

As can be readily appreciated in Table 3.2, 76 percent of all industrial turnover taxes fall on the beverages and tobacco branch. In fact, the 1981 net value added weight for this branch, exclusive of turnover taxes, is 4.5 percent, that is, the WEFA weight is 5.8 times too high, given the Cuban price structure.

Table 3.2. Turnover Taxes as a Share of Gross Output in Industry, 1981 (million pesos)

Branch	Turnover taxes[a]	Gross value of output at enterprise prices	Share of turnover taxes in GVO (%)	Share of turnover taxes in GVO in U.S.S.R. 1972[b] (%)
Electrical energy	0	452.2	0	4.1
Fuel	0	512.6	0	15.1
Mining and ferrous met-allurgy	0	108.5	0	0.2[c]
Mining and nonferrous metallurgy	0.3	135.7	0.2	
Nonelectrical machinery	0.2	553.4	0.04	3.7
Electric machinery	0	100.6	0	
Metal products	0	141.4	0	0.2[c]
Chemicals	196.8	427.0	46.1	3.7
Paper products	0	136.0	0	
Graphics	0	81.1	0	0.9
Wood products	2.0	126.6	1.6	
Construction materials	0	369.1	0	1.4
Glass and ceramics	0.1	32.2	0.3	
Textiles	0	163.4	0	18.0
Apparel	0.8	195.2	0.4	
Leather	0.4	152.9	0.3	
Sugar	9.0	1,421.5	0.6	
Food	213.8	1,653.8	12.9	20.8
Fish	0	211.8	0	
Drink and tobacco	1,359.6	350.3	388.1	
Other	6.1	403.2	1.5	7.6

Sources: Pitzer 1982:35; CEE/AEC 1984.

[a]Calculated by the authors as the difference between official net value added in *precios del productor* and *precios de empresa*.

[b]From Pitzer 1982 (35). Although not specified, we assume Pitzer's measure of gross output is in enterprise prices, i.e., exclusive of turnover tax.

[c]The average turnover tax of these two branches is 0.2 percent.

Since according to WEFA's limited product coverage the output in this branch decreased between 1965 and 1980, this weighting distortion produces a powerful downward bias in the WEFA estimate of industrial growth.

METHOD FOR NEW ESTIMATE

We employ, as did WEFA, the bottom-up method. That is, we begin with the 206 industrial products whose physical output is reported in the Cuban statistical yearbook for each of Cuba's twenty-one industrial branches. The physical output data, for reasons provided by Nove (1977: ch. 13) and the findings of Grossman (1960), are taken to be reliable. This assumption is also made in the WEFA study.

To this output data we apply a set of 1981 Cuban wholesale prices provided by the Cuban State Statistical Committee. In Cuba, as elsewhere in the CMEA, there are two types of wholesale prices: *precios del productor*, which include turnover taxes, and *precios de empresa*, which do not. We use the latter. More precisely, Laspeyres quantity indexes were calculated as in equation (1) above. Activity indexes were estimated for each branch from 1963 to 1985.[8]

The branch indexes were then aggregated by using Cuban net value added figures from 1981 for each branch, as indicated in equation (2). We received no price data at all for six of the twenty-one industrial branches. For the remaining fifteen branches, which accounted for 77.4 percent of total net industrial value added in 1981, we obtained data for 79.4 percent of the products listed in the statistical yearbook. The estimates of Method A are based on this restricted sample of fifteen branches.

The six omitted branches with their share of net industrial value added are: fuel (2.8 percent); mining and nonferrous metallurgy (2.3 percent); graphics (1.2 percent); apparel (3.2 percent); sugar (10.2 percent); and fish (2.9 percent). Their exclusion could impart a significant bias to the estimate of Method A. Given the absence of Cuban prices for these branches, we sought other industrial price sets and were able to procure price sets from Peru (for 1967) and Chile (for March 1986).[9] The Chilean price set is far more complete for Cuban products than is either the Peruvian set, the Guatemalan set used by WEFA, or the U.S. industrial price sets published by the U.S. Bureau of Labor Statistics in *Producer Prices and Price Indexes*.

The main deficiencies of the Chilean price set are: one, poor coverage for the mining and nonferrous metallurgy branch and, two, the lack of correspondence between categories of fish product groups in the Chilean and Cuban data. As a consequence of the latter, we have no usable price data for Cuban fish products. Our procedure, then, for Method B was to use ton weights (equal price weights) for the seven fish products listed in the Cuban statistical yearbook.[10] To adjust for the fact that only one of five products in the nonferrous metallurgy branch was covered,[11] we calculated and applied 1981 Cuban export prices for four of the five products.[12] For the remaining four branches, we employed the 1986 Chilean price data. These prices represent late (actually post) year weights and, if anything, impart a downward bias to the growth estimates for these five branches.[13]

A further downward bias exists in the graphics branch. The slow growth of graphics production since 1976 suggested by the figures in the statistical yearbook is misleading, since it only includes output by economic units in the material production sphere. Thus, official government publications, journals of academic institutions, magazines, reports, and newspapers issued by public organizations—all of which have experienced a boom since 1975—are excluded.[14]

Output indexes for these six branches are then added to the fifteen branches covered in Method A, again using branch net value added weights from 1981. The result appears in the estimate of Method B.

Each of the new estimates presented in Table 3.3 lie in between the higher Cuban official figure and the lower WEFA estimate for industrial growth. This observation holds true for the entire period under study, 1962–85, as well as for each of the subperiods depicted in the table. The new estimates, however, lie closer to the official than to the WEFA figures.

According to these new estimates, industrial growth rates over the period under study are healthy, particularly since 1970. As indicated above, several authors have questioned the accuracy of the official figures, which suggest a growth spurt in 1981 (J. Domínguez 1985; Pérez-López 1986b). The new estimates do indicate very rapid industrial growth in 1981, even though they lie below the official real growth rate of 14.7 percent (in gross value terms, *precios de empresa*).[15]

Table 3.3. Estimates of Annual Rates of Real Industrial Growth (percentages)

	1962–85[a]	1965–85	1970–85	1980–85	1981
Method A	7.2	6.5	7.3	4.9	10.7
Method B	6.4	5.7	6.1	4.8	11.5
WEFA	na	2.3[b]	3.3[c]	n.a.	7.0[d]
Official[e]	7.0	7.3	7.5	7.3	14.7

Sources: Author's calculations; CEE/AEC, various years; Pérez-López 1983.

[a]The data for 1962–65 is less reliable due to less comprehensive product coverage. For 8 products, output estimates for 1962–64 were made by extrapolating backward their average growth rate from 1965 to 1970.

[b]For 1965–80; the original WEFA study covers the period 1965 through 1980 only.

[c]For 1970–80.

[d]From the updated WEFA studies, Pérez-López 1986a (162) and 1987b (120). These studies end with the year 1982. The updated growth estimate for 1980 is −2.6 percent and for 1982 is −2.5 percent. Alternatively, the yearly average growth estimate for 1980–82 in the updated WEFA studies is 0.5 percent; the official rate for 1980–82, GVO at *precios de empresa*, is 7.0 percent.

[e]Refers to gross value of industrial output (GVO), not value added. The data prior to 1975 involves putting together two different series, and must be treated as a rough estimate. The post-1975 data is based on *precios de empresa*.

EVALUATION OF NEW ESTIMATE

Sources of Upward Bias

There are two sources of potential upward bias in our estimate. The first source is the possibility of distortions arising from new product pricing.[16] It appears to be a standard practice in the Soviet Union to price new products (which are sometimes new only in a cosmetic sense) high enough to fully and immediately recover all research and development costs. Further, it has been claimed that Soviet pricing authorities are too overwhelmed with the enormity of their task to pay close attention to most new products and, hence, simply ratify the prices requested by the producing enterprises. In theory, this new price should be lowered once the initial R & D costs are recovered. In practice, the price is generally maintained. The resulting distortion to growth rates is twofold. First, price increases for products tend to exceed quality increases, and this biases upward growth estimates based on Soviet prices. Second, new products, which tend also to be more dynamic and faster growing, receive higher price weights, also biasing the growth rate upward.

Neither pricing regulation documents, nor published articles, nor discussions with Cuban pricing authorities has revealed any theoretical inclination to price new products in this way in Cuba. Cuban price officials clearly feel overwhelmed, and they too receive price proposals and exhortations from enterprises, but we have no evidence that they simply ratify enterprise requests for higher prices. Should such practices be in effect, they could affect our measure indirectly through the branch value added weights, which are based on Cuban prices. Since we are using constant year prices, however, there is no danger that the same product (only cosmetically altered) is assigned a higher price in the middle of the series. Again, we have no evidence to suggest a distortion of this type, but it is nevertheless appropriate to acknowledge this potential problem.

The second possible source of upward bias resides in our use of late year branch weights. As we shall explain below, late year *price* weights for individual products (intrabranch weights) would tend to impart a downward growth bias if Cuban prices behave conventionally. The employed value added branch weights, however, are a multiplicative function of both 1981 prices and 1981 quantities, tending to impart a higher weight *for any given price set* to branches with more rapid growth than would the use of branch value added weights from an earlier year. This is true because the 1981 quantities of the faster growing branches will be greater relative to other branches than the quantities from previous years. This observation, suggesting a reverse Gerschenkron effect, runs counter to the price bias in the conventional index number problem and holds only because a constant price set is stipulated. This possibility of late year branch weights imparting an upward bias to the estimate, not heretofore acknowledged in the literature, can be tested with data provided for the first time

Table 3.4. Industrial Growth with Branch Weights from 1975 and 1981 (average annual rates of growth, percentages)

	1965–85	1980–85
1975 weights	5.3	4.5
1981 weights	5.7	4.8

in the 1985 Cuban statistical yearbook. This yearbook contains the branch distribution of net value added at 1981 enterprise prices for the industrial sector in 1975 (CEE/AEC 1985: 144). When these 1975 branch weights are applied and compared to the results when 1981 branch weights are applied, using 1981 prices for product weights in both cases, the 1975 weights do indeed yield lower growth estimates, as depicted in Table 3.4. The difference, however, is not of large magnitude. (Estimates in Table 3.4 are based on twenty-one branches, as in Method B above.)

Sources of Downward Bias

There are several reasons to suspect a downward bias in our growth estimate. First, in using 1981 prices and value added weights we are applying late year weights. If Cuban prices behave in conventional ways, then according to the standard index number formulation the use of prices from the end of the period would bias the resulting growth estimate in a downward direction. On the other hand, the often-cited bias of the bottom-up procedure in underestimating quality improvements would be minimized by the use of late year prices if Cuban prices are adjusted to reflect quality gains over time.

Second, there appears to be little question that the products reported in the Cuban statistical yearbook, which form the basis for both our estimate and the WEFA estimate, seriously underrepresent new products. As mentioned above, only eight new products have been added to the list since 1970—and none since 1978. New products and product groups tend to grow more rapidly and their exclusion from the sample, therefore, engenders a downward bias. This bias becomes stronger in later periods. We were able to explore this impact in detail for three branches on the basis of additional output and price information supplied by the State Statistical Committee. In Table 3.5, four different estimates of capital goods production in the metal products, electrical machinery, and nonelectrical machinery branches are reported. The WEFA estimate is based on a total of thirteen goods in these three branches and 1973 Guatemalan prices. The Brundenius/Zimbalist (1) and (2) estimates use 1981 Cuban prices and are based on twenty-five products (appearing in the statistical yearbook) and over two hundred products, respectively. The official Cuban estimate is of course based on all products in these branches and 1981 prices. The underlying

Table 3.5. Comparison of Estimated Growth Indexes for
Engineering Goods Branches[a] (1980 = 100)

	1980	1981	1982	1983
WEFA (projected using				
WEFA methodology)	100	123	86	91
Brundenius/Zimbalist (1)	100	120	111	127
Brundenius/Zimbalist (2)	100	122	138	163
Official Cuban	100	124	139	164

Source: Brundenius and Zimbalist 1985a.
[a]These data refer to three branches: metal products, electrical machinery, and nonelectrical machinery. The B/Z(2) estimate includes only the
capital goods (excluding all consumer durables) in these three branches.
In value terms it accounts for approximately 37 percent of the production
in these three branches according to the official statistics.

tendency is clear: The more products included in the estimate, the higher the
growth rate. The contrast between the second and third estimates is sharp and is
based on the inclusion of products not listed in the statistical yearbook.

Two additional inferences are pertinent: First, the Cuban State Statistical
Committee does not select products for yearbook listing in order to give the
impression of higher economic growth; and, second, the similarity of Brun-
denius/Zimbalist (2), measured in constant 1981 prices, and the official Cuban
estimates suggests that there is no hidden inflation buttressing the official figures for these branches.

It remains to emphasize that the limited product sample engenders an increasing downward bias over time. Cuba's product mix has been shifting
rapidly over the last twenty years, but the list of products in the yearbook has
scarcely changed. Hence, the later the period, the more new products are
excluded. The 1980–85 period, according to official figures, was one of very
rapid growth and witnessed the introduction of hundreds of new, dynamic
product groups. These groups are not represented in the product base of our
estimate. It is, therefore, not surprising that our estimate deviates most significantly from the official figures during the 1980–85 period (see Table 3.3). In the
next chapter, we shall attempt to correct for that bias in building our estimates
for Cuban gross domestic product and its growth.

A third reason our estimate might be biased downward lies in the nature of
Cuban value added weights. Cuban capital goods prices are notoriously low.
Since capital goods output grew at 16.4 percent in real terms between 1965 and
1983,[17] the low relative prices denote low value added weights for the three
related branches and, hence, would create a downward bias in the overall
industrial growth rate.

There is also reason to suspect that the use of net value added weights (net of
capital consumption allowance) instead of gross value added might impart a
downward bias if the faster growing branches also tended to be more capital

intensive. As is common in the MPS system, value added is defined in net terms, and this was the only data available to us. Efforts to estimate depreciation from branch capital stock statistics were frustrated by irregular and, we believe, unreliable data. Running our estimates for branch capital/output ratios on branch growth rate yielded insignificant correlation coefficients. Should better capital stock series data become available, it would be interesting to explore this relationship further.

A fourth source of downward bias is that the physical output series employed represents gross (double counted) output. According to official Cuban statistics, net material product or national income has grown more rapidly than gross social product (by 0.42 percentage points per year for the whole economy and by 2.71 percentage points per year for the industrial sector) during the period 1975–85 (CEE/AEC 1985: 109, 124, 133, 148). Since the same, constant prices are used in each series, this implies that gross output has grown more slowly than net output; put differently, the use of intermediate and/or imported

Table 3.6. Branch Weights and Regression Growth Rates

Branch	(1) Branch weight,[a] percent of GVO	(2) Branch weight,[a] percent of value added	(3) Annual rates of growth 1962–85	(4) Annual rates of growth 1965–85
Electrical energy	5.9	12.2	7.6	7.6
Fuel	6.3	2.8	3.3	3.2
Mining and ferrous metal- lurgy	1.4	1.5	8.7	9.2
Mining and nonferrous met- allurgy	1.8	2.3	8.1	6.2
Nonelectrical machinery	7.2	14.8	25.4	24.1
Electrical machinery	1.3	2.3	8.5	9.3
Metal products	1.8	3.1	9.6	9.2
Chemicals	5.5	4.3	5.6	5.4
Paper products	1.8	2.8	5.7	5.7
Graphics	1.0	1.2	13.9	11.3
Wood products	1.6	3.7	1.1[c]	−0.5[c]
Construction materials	4.8	6.0	7.9	8.3
Glass and ceramics	0.4	0.4	5.9	6.2
Textiles	2.1	2.0	2.7	3.1
Apparel	2.5	3.2	3.6	3.4
Leather	2.0	4.3	−0.3[b]	−1.2[b]
Sugar	18.4	10.2	2.0	1.6
Food	21.4	10.2	4.7	3.3
Fish	2.7	2.9	8.4	8.5
Drink and tobacco	4.5	4.5	−0.0[c]	−0.4[c]
Other	5.2	5.4	5.4	6.4

[a]Using *precios de empresa.*
[b]Significant at .05 level.
[c]Not significant at .10 level, all others significant at .01 level.

Table 3.7. Impact of Cuban Prices, Product Coverage, and Branch Weights on Industrial Growth Rates

	1965	1966	1969	1970	1971	1974	1975	1976	1980
Estimate A 1981 Cuban prices, WEFA branch weights, WEFA product coverage	77	85	99	87	79	100	110	106	114
Estimate B 1973 Guatemalan prices, WEFA branch weights, WEFA product coverage	81	83	91	82	82	100	109	106	113
Estimate C 1981 Cuban prices, WEFA branch weights, extended coverage	76	83	97	85	78	100	108	108	134
Estimate D (method A) 1981 Cuban prices, Cuban net value added branch weights, extended coverage	52.5	58.9	63.5	65.3	77.5	100	112.3	112.2	149.4

Source: Zimbalist 1987a.

inputs per unit of output has declined. The use of gross physical output, then, would create a downward bias as well. Here again, the deviation between industrial growth in value added and in gross output is greater during 1981–85 (3.03 percentage points higher in value added) than during 1975–80 (2.4 percentage points higher in value added) (CEE/AEC 1985: 109, 124, 133, 148). This reinforces the stronger downward bias in our estimates for later periods.

In Table 3.6, branch weights net of turnover tax in both GVO and VA terms are presented, along with branch regression growth rates.[18] The simple correlation coefficient between column three (branch growth rates) and the difference of column 2 minus column 1 is .47, significant at the .06 level, denoting that the use of net value added weights results in higher growth estimates than gross output weights.

SOURCES OF DIFFERENTIALS IN GROWTH ESTIMATES

In this section we follow the lead of Stanley Cohn[19] and endeavor to quantify the impacts of 1) Cuban prices, 2) product coverage, and 3) branch weights on the various estimates for Cuban industrial growth. In Table 3.7, four separate estimates are presented. Estimate A is based on 1981 Cuban prices, WEFA branch weights, and WEFA's restricted product coverage. Estimate B differs in method from Estimate A only in its use of Guatemalan, instead of Cuban, prices. Estimate C departs from Estimate A only in its extended product coverage, corresponding to the greater coverage of the Cuban price set. Finally, Estimate D differs from Estimate C in its use of Cuban net value added weights from 1981.

Table 3.8 depicts the average annual growth rates of each estimate. By comparing the incremental change with the difference between the highest and lowest estimates, Table 3.9 shows the contribution of the various factors to explaining the variation in growth rates. The use of Cuban rather than Guatemalan prices has virtually no impact. Indeed, if it were possible to adjust for the fact that the Cuban prices are from 1981 and the Guatemalan prices are from 1973, one might find that, if anything, the Cuban prices produce a downward growth bias. This would be consistent with the previous discussion of low prices for capital goods. Extended product coverage accounts for 26.1 percent

Table 3.8. Components' Rates of Growth

	Average annual growth rate, 1965/66–1980
Estimate A	2.3
Estimate B	2.2
Estimate C	3.5
Estimate D	6.8

Table 3.9.   Incidence of Components in Industrial Growth

	Percent difference between low and high estimate accounted for by
Cuban prices	2.2[a]
Product coverage	26.1[b]
Branch weights	71.7[c]

[a]Equals (Est. A − Est. B) ÷ (Est. D. − Est. B).
[b]Equals (Est. C − Est. A) ÷ (Est. D. − Est. B).
[c]Equals (Est. D − Est. C) ÷ (Est. D. − Est. B).

of the growth estimate differential, and the choice of branch weights accounts for nearly three-quarters of the differential. Again, this latter finding is to be expected given the rapid and substantial transformation of Cuba's product mix since 1965. The divergence in branch growth rates as well as in branch gross and net output weights shown in Table 3.6 illustrates the potential sensitivity of the estimate to the underlying weighting system.[20]

CONCLUSION

In this chapter we have employed the bottom-up method with Cuban late year prices and value added weights to generate a new, independent estimate of Cuban industrial growth from 1962 to 1985. On the whole, the estimates of this study are close to, albeit below, the official growth figures, with the discrepancy increasing for later periods. In our judgment, this result lends heightened credibility to the implicit price deflators used in the official Cuban statistics, as well as to the overall presentation of economic data in the Cuban statistical yearbook. We retain, however, some skepticism regarding the official deflator used for 1981 itself, the year of the wholesale price reform.

Due to a lack of data on industrial subsidies, inadequate data on capital stock, and no access to an input-output table, we were unable to develop adjusted factor cost prices. Adjusted factor cost prices would have been desirable to use to weight product groups, branches, or end-use categories in measuring changes in Cuba's industrial production potential. We were able, however, to directly compare the growth bias of Cuban and Guatemalan prices, and in some cases the comparison was also made with 1967 Peruvian and 1972 U.S. prices.

Our estimate is that real annual Cuban industrial growth during 1962–85 was 6.4 percent (Method B).[21] This is a very healthy, if not impressive, rate of growth and compares favorably with the industrial growth experience in the rest of Latin America. The structure of industrial growth has also deviated from the typical pattern in Latin America. This fact will be addressed in the next chapter and discussed at length in chapter 6, on Cuba's capital goods industry.

CHAPTER 4   *Gross Domestic*
                   Product: Rate of
                   Growth

As explained in preceding chapters, for a variety of reasons there is no straight-forward, problem-free method of estimating growth rates and comparable GDP statistics for centrally planned economies. The best one can do is to apply the most rigorous and least biased methods used by practitioners in the field. In the last chapter we attempted to execute such an estimate for Cuban industrial growth. In this chapter we tackle yet more complicated estimates of Cuban GDP growth.

GDP GROWTH RATE, 1962–85

Method and Estimates of Sectoral Growth

There are no official estimates of GMP or NMP in constant prices covering the entire period 1962–85. Preliminary GDP estimates have been made by the Cuban State Statistical Committee for several years in the 1970s, and new time series estimates of GDP are being prepared through 1986 but have not yet been published. Beyond sectoral growth indexes, then, it is not feasible to rely on official aggregate statistics for constructing GDP estimates.

Efforts to estimate real economic growth in Cuba have been frustrated by a number of factors, many of which have already been discussed. One central problem in making estimates for Cuba is the lack of consistent time series since 1959, as well as gaps in the available data. The only official national income aggregate that has been published for all years since 1962 is gross social product (GSP), the gross value of output of all sectors in the "productive sphere." Yet over the years the Cubans have changed their method of evaluating gross output. In 1977, for instance, they changed from *circulación completa* (gross turnover) to *a la salida de empresa* (enterprise exit), thereby eliminating the double counting of inputs produced within a given enterprise. No consistent series has been reconstructed using either methodology, although GSP for 1974 was estimated with each method. The new methodology, enterprise exit, pro-duced a 1974 GSP estimate that was 7.6 percent below the estimate using the gross turnover method (CEE 1982). The Cubans have also changed how they delineate economic sectors as well as branches within sectors. Further, GSP data for several years is constructed from a mixture of current and constant prices. Thus, between 1962 and 1966 official figures are given in constant 1965 prices; between 1967 and 1974 prices are reportedly in constant 1965 prices, except for the trade sector, which is in current prices; and since 1975 GSP and other aggregates are reported in both constant 1981 and current prices.

As discussed in chapter 2, there are basic differences in the concepts of GSP in the material balances system of the CMEA and of GDP in the national accounts system of the West. The two most important differences are that GSP is based on gross value of output (GVO) rather than value added, and that GSP excludes "nonmaterial services."[1] Fortunately, with the 1985 statistical yearbook the Cubans have begun to publish not only current and constant price time series but also data on gross value and value added of output in economic sectors and economywide. This improvement in statistical reporting, along with additional information provided by the Cuban State Statistical Committee and gleaned through numerous interviews and seminars held at the Statistical Committee to elucidate methodology, make it possible to elaborate reliable estimates of Cuban GDP growth since 1962.

This is how we have proceeded. First, we estimated constant price growth in value added by main economic sectors (industry, construction, agriculture, forestry, transportation, communications, trade, and "nonproductive" services). Since information is more readily available in some sectors than in others, we relied here on a mix of techniques and assumptions. The Cubans, for example, have not published data on the value of output in the "nonmaterial services" (NMS) sector. Second, we estimated the sectoral distribution of GDP in our benchmark year, 1981. We then aggregated the indexes of real sectoral growth using this estimated 1981 distribution as sectoral weights.

Step One: Construction of Sectoral Growth Indexes

As already indicated, the most reliable statistics are from the 1975–85 period, and this was our starting point. Official data on the net material product (NMP) (that is, aggregate net value added[2] in the sphere of material production) for this period are available in both current and constant 1981 prices. This data was first published in the 1984 statistical yearbook, but only in *precios del productor*, which include turnover taxes. These taxes affect certain branches and sectors disproportionately and, hence, do not give a reliable portrait of growth and structure. In the 1985 yearbook, however, constant price, net value added data by branch and sector was also given in *precios de empresa* for the 1975–85 period. *Precios de empresa* are the prices received directly by the producing enterprise before the levying of turnover taxes. In our view this is the best data available, and we used it as the basis for our sectoral growth indexes for the 1975–85 period.[3] As an alternative for the industrial sector, we also used our own estimates of industrial growth for this period (Method B outlined in the last chapter).

As stated in chapter 3, we believe that our estimate of industrial growth incorporates an increasing downward bias over time, which becomes particularly severe after 1980. The major reason for this is that our estimate is based on a sample of products that fails to incorporate any new products after the late 1970s, and only does so minimally for earlier years. The physical output data we employed also represents gross output, which grew more slowly than net output due to increasing productivity and materials savings in industry from 1975 to 1985. Nevertheless, while our estimate confirms the impression of a growth spurt in 1981, the official figure of real industrial growth of 25.1 percent in that year seems excessive and potentially influenced by inadequate adjustment for the price reform of 1981. While we regard the official figure for industrial growth during the 1975–85 period as basically reliable, we view it more as an upper bound estimate. Hence, as an alternative lower-bound estimate, we made a second calculation using our estimated index of industrial growth during 1975–85.

To estimate nonmaterial services growth during 1975–85 we, took the total wage bill in the "nonproductive" sphere and deflated it by our estimated consumer price index. Theoretically, such an estimate would only distort the true growth record if depreciation or surplus in this sphere grew at appreciably different rates than in the productive sphere. Even so, since services tend to be relatively labor intensive, the distortion would probably be small. Further, we have no evidence to suggest differential growth trends in these factor components. The trick here, then, is to produce a reasonable price index.

There is no official consumer price index in Cuba, but in the 1985 yearbook there does appear an official implicit deflator for "personal consumption" as well as an implicit deflator for "social consumption." The "personal consumption" deflator purportedly includes price increases in the free peasant markets (defunct as of May 1986), which in 1985 accounted for less than one percent of total retail sales according to official statistics (CEE/AEC 1985: 152). We combined these two deflators by weighting them proportionately to the shares in total consumer expenditures in 1981: personal consumption, .7865, and social consumption, .2135. It was then necessary, to obtain a comprehensive deflator for consumer purchasing power and make it parallel to the Western concept of the consumer price index (CPI), to factor in the effect of gratuitous consumer services—in particular, to take account of the fact that medical services, educational services, and many housing services are provided free of charge. Other housing services are not free, but they have not experienced price increases for the most part.

How does one weight these gratuitous or constant price services that are not figured into the official deflators? One possibility was to consider the weights of these services in the U.S. CPI, which in December 1986 were as follows: medical care, 5.42 percent; education, 3.37 percent; and housing, 42.9 percent (0.4 percent of which was for maintenance and should be excluded). Together these services accounted for 51.29 percent of the U.S. CPI! Naturally, relative

Table 4.1. Indexes of Real Output by Sectors, 1975–85 (1981 prices, 1981 = 100)

	Industry[a] (Alt. 1)	Industry[b] (Alt. 2)	Construction	Agriculture	Forestry	Transport	Communications	Trade	Net material product[a]	Gross material product[a]	Nonmaterial services
1975	57.3	69.9	65.6	82.3	72.7	49.2	53.0	104.6	71.3	70.8	68.6
1976	58.6	69.5	69.1	84.8	72.7	52.0	55.7	114.8	74.9	74.3	72.8
1977	60.2	75.4	76.5	88.9	74.5	63.6	53.9	130.8	81.2	80.4	72.2
1978	66.4	84.6	80.4	95.8	78.2	65.6	64.3	137.4	86.8	86.2	78.6
1979	74.4	90.2	72.9	93.8	72.7	73.9	76.7	125.6	87.4	87.2	84.1
1980	79.9	89.7	79.9	84.0	83.6	77.7	89.6	96.8	82.8	83.6	88.0
1981	100.0	100.0	100.0	100.0	100.0	100.0	100.0	100.0	100.0	100.0	100.0
1982	103.6	98.9	101.1	95.0	105.5	102.8	108.7	124.3	105.1	105.4	105.9
1983	114.6	103.3	115.4	86.4	130.9	103.3	119.1	132.7	110.8	111.6	110.2
1984	130.0	108.6	141.4	87.7	147.3	115.2	127.8	119.7	119.1	119.8	114.9
1985	143.2	113.1	142.0	83.6	145.5	110.4	133.0	126.8	124.5	125.7	116.9

[a]Based on official figures, constant 1981 prices.
[b]Our estimate, from chapter 3.

prices, consumer preferences, and resource endowments in the United States and Cuba are very different, and such a weight would be too high for Cuba. Instead, given the unavailability of such information for countries similar to Cuba in factor endowments, we reduced the U.S weight for these services by more than half, to 25 percent, assigning the remaining 75 percent proportionately to the personal and social consumption deflators. Although this reduction to 25 percent was somewhat arbitrary and may seem excessive, we thought it preferable to err on the side of producing an inflation estimate that was too high, rather than one that was too low.

The resulting CPI estimates for Cuba averaged 0.5 percent annually for 1975–80 and 3.1 percent annually for 1980–85. These estimates were used to deflate the nominal wage bill in the "nonproductive" sphere. Our estimate, then, for average annual real growth in the nonmaterial services sector between 1975 and 1985 is 5.47 percent, which appears to be conservative if one considers that expenditures on public health grew from 304.2 million pesos in 1975 to 860.1 million pesos in 1985, and expenditures on education grew from 808.5 million pesos in 1975 to 1,696.8 million pesos in 1985 (both in current pesos). On the other hand, this estimate appears reasonable given the yearly average increase in employment in this sector of 3.9 percent during 1975–85 and a yearly productivity increase in services generally assumed to be around 1.5– 2.0 percent (Marer 1985b: 170).

The next step was to link our estimates of sectoral growth for 1975–85 with estimates for the period 1962–75. There already exists official real output data for the same sectors (measured in constant 1965 prices) for the period 1962–66, again except for nonmaterial services. We used this official data to construct our sectoral growth indexes for these years. For 1966–75 the total wage bill in each sector, except industry, served as our proxy for growth. In industry we used our estimate from chapter 3 for these years. Since there is no official price deflator for 1966–75, we were forced to rely on the nominal wage bill. Although an appreciable monetary surplus did build up during the late 1960s, consumer goods prices during this period were frozen and actual price inflation was negligible. There was, however, a price increase for some nonbasic consumer items sold on the parallel market during the early 1970s, which might inflate slightly our nominal wage bill proxy.

Another perspective on this matter is gained by comparing the growth in the wage bill with worker productivity. Between 1965 and 1970 the annual growth rate of the average wage exceeded that of worker productivity by 6.4 percentage points.[4] However, this trend was reversed during 1970–75 as the annual growth rate of worker productivity exceeded that of the average wage by 7.4 percentage points.[5] This data suggests that productivity growth exceeded wage growth over the entire 1965–75 period and, hence, that the nominal wage bill would understate the growth in real output. Further, it should be recalled that in the case of the industrial sector our output estimates use late year (1981) prices and

Table 4.2. Indexes of Real Output by Sectors, 1962–75 (1981 = 100)

	Industry[a] (Alt. 1)	Industry[b] (Alt. 2)	Construction	Agriculture	Forestry	Transport	Communications	Trade	Net material product	Gross material product	Nonmaterial services
1962	30.1	29.4	28.8	63.9	25.5	21.3	31.3	58.6			23.1
1963	29.7	30.6	27.2	60.4	12.7	24.4	32.2	65.5			28.5
1964	30.8	35.2	32.7	63.8	12.7	24.8	30.4	76.6			30.3
1965	32.0	37.3	40.6	72.0	14.5	25.2	30.4	64.2			32.6
1966	31.5	38.4	40.3	67.7	14.5	25.8	28.7	61.0			33.9
1967	36.2	44.1	40.9	69.4	21.8	30.6	31.3	63.5			36.1
1968	34.8	42.5	41.4	66.9	81.8	34.1	33.0	69.9			43.3
1969	34.1	41.6	40.8	65.4	54.5	37.0	35.7	76.7			43.6
1970	38.4	46.9	40.5	72.5	36.4	37.9	38.3	86.7			44.3
1971	41.1	50.1	37.4	66.7	50.9	43.2	40.9	86.5			46.3
1972	42.0	51.2	44.2	70.7	58.2	43.0	46.1	91.1			50.4
1973	48.2	58.8	51.0	73.7	72.7	44.6	48.7	98.3			55.3
1974	51.5	62.9	55.3	76.7	78.2	46.7	51.3	104.7	71.3		61.4
1975	57.3	69.9	65.6	82.3	72.7	49.2	53.0	104.5	71.3	70.8	68.6
1981	100.0	100.0	100.0	100.0	100.0	100.0	100.0	100.0	100.0	100.0	100.0

[a]Based on official figures for 1962–66 and 1975–85, and on our estimate for 1966–75.
[b]Our estimate, from chapter 3.

do not incorporate most new product groups, engendering a probable downward bias to our estimate for that sector. In the final analysis, there is a priori no reason to expect a systematic bias in our estimate in either direction. The results of this linking exercise are shown in Table 4.2.

Step Two: Estimating Sectoral Weights for 1981

The next task in building our estimate was to find a weighting method to aggregate the sectoral growth indexes in a benchmark year. We selected 1981 as our benchmark year for a number of reasons. First, this is the benchmark year for the new official accounts of Cuba. Second, 1981 is the most recent year for which there is an input-output table of the economy.[6] Third, 1981 is the year of the most recent wholesale (and retail) price reform, and the prices used in the chapter on industrial growth are from that year.

Estimation of sectoral weights for 1981 (or any other year) is complicated by the absence of compatible official data. There are several problems with the official data. First, almost all of the sectoral breakdowns are given inclusive of turnover taxes. This provides a substantial upward bias to the share of the trade sector. Second, most breakdowns are given in gross value of output rather than value added, and this provides an upward bias to the industrial share. (When net value added calculations are made, an upward bias is imparted to the estimated trade share, since the imputed value is the same as under the gross value method.) Third, the breakdown published recently in the 1985 yearbook in net value added exclusive of turnover taxes lumps the sectors of trade, communication, and transportation together, as it does with the agriculture and forestry sectors. Further, there is a discrepancy in the published figures that makes the estimates questionable.[7] Finally, the CMEA system for measuring the contribution of foreign trade seems to inflate significantly the relative size of the trade sector given international and domestic prices for Cuban tradeables. In particular, the contribution of foreign trade to national income is reckoned as follows:

value of foreign trade = commercial margin + foreign trade differential

where,

commercial margin = expenditures of foreign trade organizations +
                    commission (a percentage of sales)

and,

foreign trade differential = international price converted − domestic
                             wholesale price − commission

Imports are valued cost, insurance, and freight (c.i.f.), and exports are valued free-on-board (f.o.b.). Depending on whether or not trade is subsidized, the foreign trade differential can be either positive or negative for a particular commodity and for all traded items together. If we consider the situation for sugar, however, which has accounted for 75–77 percent of Cuban exports in recent years, there must be a strong presumption that the overall trade differential is significantly net positive. The domestic wholesale price for raw sugar has been approximately .12 pesos per pound since the 1981 reform. In 1985, the Soviet Union purchased 82.5 percent of Cuba's sugar exports in value terms, paying an average price per pound of .447 pesos (CEE/AEC 1985: 433). For this Soviet-purchased sugar, then, the foreign trade differential, even allowing a ten percent commission, would be .283 pesos or 63.2 percent of the export value. Together the differential plus the commission would represent 73.2 percent of the export value. This magnitude is simply too great to begin to be offset appreciably by negative differentials on other commodities. This presumption is confirmed by a 1986 article in the journal of the State Finance Committee that reported that the share of total budgetary receipts generated by the net foreign trade differential was positive and large in each year between 1981 and 1984: 19.1 percent in 1981, 17.3 percent in 1982, 15.3 percent in 1983, and 15.9 percent in 1984 (Chaviano et al. 1986: 78).[8] The officially reported share of the trade sector, then, is inflated very significantly by this accounting practice and is clearly unusable for our purposes.

Our skepticism about official sectoral weights compelled us to devise our own estimating procedure. We did this as follows: We began by taking Cuban employment shares by sector for 1981 and then constructed an index of relative productivity per worker across sectors, based on 1982 data from Chile, a country with approximately the same GDP per capita as Cuba in the early 1980s (see chapter 5). The Chilean weights are, of course, based on the SNA concept of value added.[9] The relative productivity index was then multiplied by each sector's employment share in Cuba's productive sphere, yielding our estimates for 1981 sectoral shares in Cuban GMP (see Table 4.3).

Finally, once sectoral shares in GMP were established it was necessary to estimate the share of nonmaterial services (NMS) in GDP and to convert the other sectors accordingly to portions of GDP. We did this by estimating value added (labor payments + depreciation + profits) in the NMS sector. First, we took the 1981 wage bill for the NMS sector as reported in the statistical yearbook, which amounted to 1,621.4 million pesos, or 28.2 percent of the wage bill for the entire economy. We then estimated depreciation. According to official figures, fixed capital formation in the NMS sphere came to 18.2 percent of fixed capital formation in the whole (state sector) economy (CEE/AEC 1985: 165). We estimated depreciation in NMS to be 18.2 percent of economywide depreciation, or 79.6 million pesos in NMS. Then, considering these proportions in other economies and following the spirit of Bergson's adjusted factor cost method, profits were assumed to be equal to twice depreciation in all sectors, or 159.2 million pesos in the NMS sector. NMS value added came to 1,860.2 million pesos in 1981. Using the same procedure for the entire economy and taking the NMS share, we arrived at the estimate of 26.5 percent for NMS in GDP.

There has been a wide range of estimates of the size of Cuba's service sector in the past.[10] We regard the present effort as the most reliable, and, if anything, a bit conservative. Using Cuban employment figures and Chilean relative sectoral productivity weights, the Cuban service sector would come to 28.2 percent of its GDP. Given the advanced state of Cuba's health industry and electronic data processing, it is improbable that applying Chilean weights would overstate the relative productivity of Cuba's service sector. Further, if we note the size of the service sectors in other Latin American economies during the early 1980s, our estimate for Cuba is clearly on the lower end. In particular, in 1982 the service sector (including transportation, communication, and trade) as a share of GDP was: 53 percent in Peru, 42 percent in Colombia, 60 percent in Chile, 59 percent in Uruguay, and 55 percent in Mexico (World Bank 1986: 222–23). According to our estimates, the size of the service sector in Cuba in 1981 (including the "productive" services of transportation, communication, and trade) was 46.6 percent. Whereas the development of consumer services in Cuba is below that in most Latin American countries, the development of other services such as health and education is superior. In our judgment, cultural and sports activities in Cuba have attained at least average levels for Latin American countries with similar living standards. Finally, the government sector in Cuba is larger than elsewhere in the region. It seems, then, that our estimate for nonmaterial services is, if anything, too low. The results of our sectoral weighting exercise are shown in Table 4.3.

Table 4.3. Sectoral Distribution of GMP and GDP, 1981 (percentages)

	Share of gross material product	Share of gross domestic product
Industry	43.8[a]	32.2
Construction	12.7	9.3
Agriculture and forestry	21.7	16.0
Transport	7.1	5.2
Communications	0.9	0.7
Trade	13.8[b]	10.1
Gross Material Product	100.0	73.5
Net Material Product	—	26.5
Gross Domestic Product	—	100.0

Source: CEE/AEC, 1985: 177; author's calculations.

[a]In the 1985 statistical yearbook, the estimated share of industry in net material product (NMP) was 45.7 percent for 1981 (CEE/AEC 1985: 177). It is based on the 1981 Cuban input-output table and purports to neutralize the effect of turnover taxes.
[b]The employment share of Cuba's trade sector in the entire productive sphere in 1981 was 15.5 percent. Hence the 13.8 figure implies that productivity in the trade sector was .89 of the average productivity in the productive sphere.

Step Three: Aggregating Sectors, Estimates of Growth

The last step in obtaining estimates for GMP and GDP growth is to combine the sectoral growth indexes with the corresponding sectoral weights. In Table 4.4, we present two different sets of estimates, based alternately on the adjusted official industrial growth index (as described in the text) and on the estimated industrial growth index (Method B from chapter 3).

Both estimates suggest real annual GDP growth on the order of 5 percent over the 1962–85 period. GDP2, based on the estimate of industrial growth from chapter 3, results as expected in slower growth estimates for later periods than GDP1 (3.6 percent versus 4.0 percent for 1975–80 and 5.4 percent versus 7.9 percent for 1980–85). Again, this is because of the GDP2 underrepresentation of new industrial product groups with faster growth for later years. Because of slower growth since 1975, GDP2 also yields a slower growth over the entire 1962–85 period. As reported in the official figures, economic growth in both estimates is more rapid during 1970–75 and 1980–85 than during 1965–70 and 1975–80.

There is a literature on investment cycles in centrally planned economies (see, for instance, Neuberger and Tyson 1980). It appears, however, that these five-year Cuban cycles have more to do with changes in the prices of Cuban exports (principally sugar) and changes in domestic policy. It is interesting to note, nevertheless, that the pattern of alternating periods of fast and slow growth is continuing, as the Cuban economy has entered a period of (very) slow growth once again during 1985–90. Changes in the external economy (see chapter 9) seem to be primarily responsible, but the accumulation of unfinished investments from the previous quinquennium is also an influence.

Overall, our GDP growth estimates lie below the official estimates for GSP

Table 4.4.   Estimated Annual Growth Rates of
Real Gross Domestic Product (percentages)

	GDP1[a]	GDP2[b]
1962–65	5.4	7.1
1965–70	3.6	3.8
1970–75	6.6	6.7
1975–80	4.0	3.6
1980–85	7.9	5.4
1962–80	4.9	5.1
1962–85	5.5	5.2

Source: Table 4A.1.
[a]Based on the adjusted official industrial growth index (explained in text). Figures rounded off to nearest decimal.
[b]Based on the estimated industrial growth index from chapter 3.

growth, but above the GDP growth estimates produced for Wharton Econometric Forecasting Associates by Jorge Pérez-López. In the next chapter we elaborate on this comparison and estimate absolute dollar levels of Cuban GDP per capita.

APPENDIX

Table 4A.1. Indexes of GMP and GDP, 1962–85

Measure	1962	1963	1964	1965	1966
Index GMP1	40.43	40.44	43.88	45.48	43.90
Index GDP1	35.84	37.27	40.28	42.07	41.25
Index GMP2	40.12	40.83	45.81	47.81	46.92
Index GDP2	35.62	37.56	41.69	43.78	43.47
	1967	1968	1969	1970	1971
Index GMP1	47.13	47.44	47.79	52.55	52.53
Index GDP1	44.21	46.34	46.68	50.35	50.87
Index GMP2	50.59	50.81	51.08	56.27	56.47
Index GDP2	46.75	48.82	49.09	53.09	53.77
	1972	1973	1974	1975	1976
Index GMP1	55.34	60.74	64.45	69.65	72.83
Index GDP1	54.02	69.29	63.63	69.36	72.80
Index GMP2	59.37	65.39	69.44	75.17	77.60
Index GDP2	59.98	62.70	67.30	73.42	76.31
	1977	1978	1979	1980	1981
Index GMP1	78.36	84.20	85.38	83.05	100.00
Index GDP1	76.70	82.70	85.03	84.36	100.00
Index GMP2	85.02	92.18	92.30	87.34	100.00
Index GDP2	81.60	88.56	90.12	87.51	100.00
	1982	1983	1984	1985	
Index GMP1	104.30	110.49	120.01	125.67	
Index GDP1	104.71	110.40	118.64	123.33	
Index GMP2	102.24	105.54	110.64	112.49	
Index GDP2	103.20	106.76	111.75	113.64	

CHAPTER 5

Gross Domestic Product: Dollar Level

A variety of methods have been used to estimate GDP per capita in centrally planned economies. Most methods are data and computationally very intensive. These do not produce obviously superior results. One method, developed by the Hungarian economist Ferenc Janossy in 1963 and elaborated by the United Nations Economic Commission for Europe, Hungarian economist Eva Ehrlich, and others, is more modest—albeit not trivial—in its data and computational requirements. It is most commonly known as the physical indicators (PI) method. The recently concluded World Bank international comparisons project, headed by Paul Marer, gave the PI method a good review: "A detailed examination of the physical indicators [method] . . . suggest[s] that its use should once again be seriously considered" and "the physical indicators approach has much to recommend it for comparing CPEs with each other and with MTEs [market-type economies]" (Marer 1985b: 97–98).

Given our inability to obtain sufficient data to reliably implement other methods, and the recommendation of the World Bank project, we decided to perform PI estimates for Cuban GDP per capita in 1980, the most recent year for which we were able to obtain sufficient data for our selected 28 reference countries and 29 physical indicators.

The method is premised on the assumption that per capita GDP is associated with the consumption of certain commodities (inputs as well as outputs), the stock of certain assets, and various social indicators (intended as proxies for expenditure levels). Basically, in the method's most rudimentary form, GDP per capita in dollars (converted at the prevailing exchange rate) for a particular year is run in a simple regression[1] on each of the "physical indicators" across a sample of reference countries. The estimated equations are then used to estimate GDP per capita in the target country (Cuba in this case), using that country's indicators. The various estimates (one for each indicator) are then averaged geometrically to obtain the desired estimate.

Other than its convenience, the method has to recommend it the fact that it relies on physical rather than value measures of each indicator. Thus, the resulting estimate stands independent of the country's national income accounting system. relative prices, adjusted factor cost weights, and exchange rate. The various physical indicators are supposed to represent different parts of the economy and of the development process. The specific indicators employed are selected because they have been found to be close correlates of GDP per capita.

The original Janossy study was based on 24 indicators. The Economic Commission for Europe ECE initially used 36 indicators, but later discarded 15 and subsequently added 9. A study on Cuba by Mesa-Lago and Pérez-López used the 24 indicators from the revised ECE study that were available for Cuba as well as the reference countries for 1965, 1970, 1975, and 1977 (Economic Commission for Europe 1970; Mesa-Lago and Pérez-López 1985b). We used the 24 indicators from the latter study supplemented by an additional 5 indicators suggested by the new project of Eva Ehrlich (1985). We could not obtain 1980 data for one of their indicators (persons per room in urban areas), so this was dropped. Another indicator, school enrollment ratio with first and second levels combined, was not statistically significant, but when the first and second levels were separated and tested, each was significant at the .01 level. Our indicators are reported in Table 5.1.

We employed the same group of reference countries as in the Mesa-Lago and Pérez-López study. It is important that the sample of reference countries be at a relatively similar stage of development as the target country for the regression coefficients to be meaningful for estimating GDP per capita.[2] In 1980, the 28 reference countries used in our estimate had GDPs per capita (converted at the official exchange rate) that varied between $5,973 (Trinidad and Tobago) and $292 (Haiti). Table 5.2 gives the list of reference countries used, along with reported and purchasing power parity (ppp) dollar per capita GDP levels in 1980.

The simple regression PI method is hardly eloquent, but the consensus holds it to be efficient and to produce realistic estimates. Nonetheless, several questions and critiques have been raised about the method. First, in the simple regression format each indicator receives equal weight (although when the geometric rather than the arithmetic mean is used, outliers receive less weight). Thus, there is a question about whether different GDP activities are being properly represented. Marer reports that the traditional response to this criticism has been that more elaborate weighting schemes have been used without "obviously superior results, and with a large number of indicators, slight changes in the weighting system cease to be important" (Marer 1985b: 96). A priori it would seem desirable to employ multiple regression analysis with all the physical indicators, thereby allowing the indicators to weight themselves. However, since the number of physical indicators (independent variables) is normally equal to or greater than the number of countries (observations) in PI exercises, this procedure is unworkable. An obvious and workable alternative is to apply factor analysis, grouping the indicators into linear combination clusters orthogonal to each other. In our view, factor analysis better approximates a correct specification of the underlying model, and we have employed it as one of our techniques. A frequent problem with factor analysis, the interpretation of the phenomena represented by the factors, is not a primary issue here since our interest is in obtaining estimates of the dependent variable, GDP per

Table 5.1.   Physical Indicators for Estimating Per Capita GDP in Cuba, 1980

I. Industry and energy
   1. Steel consumption per capita (STEEL)
   2. Cement production per capita (CEMENT)
   3. Electricity consumption per capita (ELECT)
   4. Energy consumption per capita (ENERGY)
   5. Percent labor force in industry (LFIND)

II. Agriculture
   6. Milk yield per cow (MLKCO)
   7. Fertilizer consumption per hectare (FERT)
   8. Tractors per 1,000 agricultural population (TRACT)
   9. Percent labor force in agriculture (LFAGR)

III. Food consumption
  10. Daily animal protein intake per capita (ANPROT)
  11. Daily animal and vegetable protein intake per capita (AVPROT)
  12. Sugar consumption per capita (SUGAR)
  13. Daily calorie intake per capita (CALOR)

IV. Clothing and consumer durables
  14. Industrial consumption of cotton per capita, metric tons per
      1,000 population (COTTON)
  15. Televisions per 1,000 population (TELEV)
  16. Radios per 1,000 population (RADIO)
  17. Passenger vehicles in use per 1,000 population (CARS)

V. Communications and transportation
  18. Newsprint consumption per capita (NEWSP)
  19. Telephones in use per 1,000 population (TELEPH)
  20. Commercial vehicles in use per 1,000 population (COMVEH)

VI. Services
  21. School enrollment ratio, first level (SCH1)
  22. School enrollment ratio, second level (SCH2)
  23. School enrollment ratio, third level (SCH3)
  24. Percent labor force in services (LFSER)
  25. Infant mortality rate (IMORT)
  26. Population per hospital bed (POPHB)
  27. Population per physician (POPPH)
  28. Population per dentist (POPDNT)
  29. Population per nurse (POPNUR)

capita in dollars, through tightly fitted equations.[3] The results of our factor analysis exercise are discussed below.

A second criticism is that indicators are not qualitatively comparable. The number of cars or televisions per capita might be equal in two countries—but both products might be superior in the same country. Physical indicator estimates will not capture this quality differential. Since it is commonly believed

Table 5.2. Reference Countries with Reported GDP Per Capita in 1980 (dollars)

	Exchange rate converted (K_v scale)		Purchasing power parity (K_x scale)
	1980 prices and exchange rate[a]	1978–80 prices and exchange rate[b]	international dollars, 1980[c]
1. Costa Rica	$2,147	$1,730	$3,173
2. Dominican Republic	1,219	1,160	1,980
3. El Salvador	751	660	1,417
4. Guatemala	1,139	1,080	2,333
5. Haiti	292	270	547[d]
6. Honduras	647	560	1,212
7. Jamaica	1,226	1,040	2,248[d]
8. Mexico	2,687	2,090	3,414[d]
9. Nicaragua	798	740	1,506
10. Panama	1,816	1,730	3,185
11. Trinidad and Tobago	5,973	4,370	5,085
12. Argentina	5,453	2,390	3,843
13. Bolivia	937	570	1,632
14. Brazil	2,059	2,050	3,349
15. Chile	2,484	2,150	3,650
16. Colombia	1,233	1,180	2,838
17. Ecuador	1,445	1,270	2,586
18. Paraguay	1,403	1,300	2,131
19. Peru	1,120	930	2,508
20. Uruguay	3,482	2,810	4,259
21. Venezuela	3,942	3,630	5,432
22. Philippines	733	690	1,740
23. Thailand	720	670	1,438
24. Turkey	1,267	1,470	2,410
25. Greece	4,165	4,380	5,097
26. Ireland	4,793	4,880	5,480
27. Spain	5,658	5,400	6,353
28. Portugal	2,532	2,370	3,832
Arithmetic mean	$2,219		$3,024
Standard deviation	1,677		1,481

[a]Converted at average 1980 prices and exchange rate, as reported in the United Nations' Statistical Yearbook. These are the figures used for the physical indicator analysis (K_v scale) in this study.

[b]Converted at average 1978–80 prices and average 1978–80 exchange rates, as reported in the World Bank's *World Development Report*. These figures have the advantage of exchange rate smoothing and are used for the interpolations descibed in note d below. They, however, are not used in the physical indicator analysis because they are not in 1980 prices.

[c]Calculated in international dollars of 1980 by the repricing method of the International Comparisons Project, as reported in United Nations Commission of the European Communities 1986.

[d]Rank interpolated, according to the ratio between the figure in column 3 and the figure in column 2 (or exchange rate deviation index) of the country with nearest GDP per capita in column 2.

that product quality is inferior in LDCs and CPEs, this would bias upward the estimate for these countries. Comparisons within each group, however, would still be unbiased. Regarding our estimate for per capita GDP in Cuba, it is not clear that a serious bias exists. For one thing, the differential quality issue is reduced because the sample of reference countries excludes advanced, industrial economies. For another, within the sample it is arguable that for many indicators Cuban quality is at or above average. This observation would apply, for instance, to physicians, dentists, nurses, and hospital beds per capita, among others. For several additional indicators the commodity in question is homogeneous (e.g., electric power), and for yet others (e.g., infant mortality), quality is either not an issue or it takes on a different dimension, namely, the accuracy of the government statistics. In this case at least, there is good reason to believe that Cuban statistics are more accurate than those of most, if not all, the other reference countries.[4] It remains, of course, to point out that capturing quality differentials is a problem in any GDP comparison, either within a country over time or across countries.

Third, pertaining to the indicators that represent intermediate consumption, relatively inefficient production methods (using more inputs per unit of output) will not be captured by the PI method. Hence, there again will be an upward bias in the GDP estimates of LDCs and CPEs, generally held to employ more wasteful production methods. This bias is likely to affect our Cuba estimate, but the magnitude of the upward bias here might not be very significant given production inefficiency in the reference countries.[5]

Fourth, as the method is based on initial exchange rate converted dollar GDPs, it incorporates rather than solves the exchange rate bias. As stated this criticism is valid, but it is also easily circumvented by beginning with ppp-based GDP estimates, where such estimates are available. If this alternative is not used, for whatever reason, it has been claimed that a new wrinkle in the PI methodology developed by Eva Ehrlich can be used both to obtain better fits and to minimize the exchange rate bias. This modified PI method, which we dub "elaborated PI," adds a new procedure to the rudimentary PI method. It is described by Marer as follows:

> Next comes a series of iterations intended to obtain a tighter fit between each indicator and the successively adjusted per capita dollar GDP estimates. The iteration consists of repeating [the earlier steps] while substituting the latest adjusted per capita dollar GDP estimate for the original dollar GDP estimate. The iteration ends when the nth adjusted dollar per capita GDP estimate coincides with estimate labeled (n-1). This last value is taken to be the corrected GDP estimate for each country. The final per capita dollar GDP estimate so obtained . . . is in effect valued not at domestic U.S. dollars but in a currency unit that reflects the dollar's realistic international purchasing power. The difference between the original and the "corrected" U.S. per capita GDP estimate in any given year is due largely to the temporary

overvaluation or undervaluation of the U.S. dollar in terms of other currencies. (Marer 1985b: 94)[6]

Neither Marer nor Ehrlich provide a theoretical explanation of this claim. In our view, there is no theoretical reason why the repeated iterations should be correcting for an exchange rate bias. Indeed, our empirical results from the "elaborated PI method," which are discussed in the appendix to this chapter, confirm this observation.

RESULTS

Rudimentary PI Method

Table 5.3 reports the best fit simple regressions for each of the estimated relationships between 1980 exchange rate converted (the so-called K_v scale) GDP per capita and the 29 physical indicators. The double logarithmic form most often yielded the tightest fit, followed by the semi-logarithmic and linear specifications.[7] All of the equations are significant at the .01 level, save that for fertilizer consumption, which is significant at the .0276 level.

The GDP per capita estimate for Cuba in 1980 that results from the rudimentary simple regression method is $2,325. Despite the statistical significance of all the equations, it might be objected that some of the R^2s are quite low for this method. If we consider only the 23 equations with R^2s above .40, the GDP per capita estimate for Cuba rises to $2,384. If we follow the lead of Mesa-Lago and Pérez-López and include only the 19 equations with R^2s equal to or above .50,[8] the estimate for Cuba would increase further to $2,485. Although it is desirable to obtain as high R^2s as possible in this method, it does not seem justifiable to eliminate any equations that are statistically significant at a predetermined level. Hence, we shall treat the (lowest) estimate of $2,325 based on all 29 indicators as our best estimate on the K_v scale using the rudimentary method.

Table 5.4 reports the best fit simple regressions for each of the estimated relationships between 1980 GDP per capita in international dollars (the so-called K_x scale) and the 29 physical indicators.[9] The international dollar is a purchasing power parity measure that is estimated by comparing the domestic prices of a set commodity basket across countries. It offers the prospect of eliminating errors in comparative income estimates that arise from exchange rate distortions and divergent relative prices.

The exchange rate distortion has two aspects. First, exchange rates do not always adjust in the short run according to a country's current account situation. While there are a number of reasons for this, the most glaring is that many countries (particularly low-income countries) still employ government-fixed exchange rates. When rapid inflation is not accompanied by commensurate

Table 5.3. Estimating Equations for 1980 (Exchange Rate Converted, K_v Scale)

Equations	Number of observations	R^2	Predicted per capita GDP, Cuba
1. GDPPC = 728.53 + 20.107 STEEL	28	.697	$1,754
2. LnGDPPC = 7.00 + 1.735 CEMENT	28	.362	1,818
3. LnGDPPC = 2.27 + .7863 LnELECT	24	.749	2,235
4. LnGDPPC = 3.01 + .6678 LnENERGY	28	.795	2,555
5. LnGDPPC = 1.84 + 1.827 LnLFIND	28	.857	2,957
6. LnGDPPC = 7.26 + .8236 LnMLKCO	28	.398	1,937
7. 1/GDPPC = .0021 − .00022 LnFERT	28	.173	2,342
8. LnGDPPC = 6.84 + .3471 LnTRACT	28	.730	3,060
9. GDPPC = 11425.43 − 2653.309 LnLFAGR	28	.740	3,126
10. LnGDPPC = 3.36 + 1.258 LnANPROT	26	.818	2,766
11. LnGDPPC = −1.91 + 2.228 LnAVPROT	26	.671	2,427
12. −1/GDPPC = −.0048 + .0011 LnSUGAR	27	.382	3,539
13. LnGDPPC = 6.10 + .00056 CALOR	28	.476	2,267
14. 1/GDPPC = .00041 + .00045 1/COTTON	24	.678	1,870
15. GDPPC = 95.41 + 22.962 TELEV	28	.817	3,103
16. 1/GDPPC = .0034 − .00051 LnRADIO	28	.434	1,895
17. LnGDPPC = 8.12 + .2778 LnCARS	28	.449	1,075
18. LnGDPPC = 2.77 + .5887 LnNEWSP	28	.608	1,869
19. LnGDPPC = 5.12 + .6121 LnTELEPH	26	.712	1,655
20. LnGDPPC = 10.75 + .7834 LnCOMVEH	27	.710	1,652
21. −1/GDPPC = −.012 + .0025 LnSCH1	28	.343	1,603
22. LnGDPPC = 6.27 + .0246 SCH2	28	.456	3,181
23. 1/GDPPC = .0022 − .00056 LnSCH3	26	.388	1,890
24. LnGDPPC = 5.36 + .0510 LFSER	28	.594	2,469
25. LnGDPPC = 10.62 − .8420 LnIMORT	28	.516	3,341
26. LnGDPPC = 13.44 − 1.013 LnPOPHB	28	.609	2,773
27. LnGDPPC = 13.78 − .8661 LnPOPPH	23	.691	3,609
28. 1/GDPPC = .00034 + .000000033 POPDNT	24	.570	2,229
29. GDPPC = 9979.52 − 1158.46 LnPOPNUR	26	.497	3,138

Geometric mean, Cuba = $2,325

devaluation, the real exchange rate appreciates and GDP conversions at official rates overstate a country's living standards. In instances of galloping inflation—for example Argentina—this distortion can be rather large. Thus, in Argentina the rate of inflation was 159.5 percent in 1979 and 100.8 percent in 1980, but the Argentinean peso was only devalued by 39 percent on average between 1979 and 1980.[10] Not surprisingly, Argentina's current account balance went from positive $1,836 million in 1978 to negative $535 million in 1979, negative $4,774 million in 1980, and negative $4,057 million in 1981. Hence, when Argentina's GDP per capita is converted to dollars at the average

Table 5.4. Estimating Equations for 1980 (PPP-based, K_x Scale)

Equations	Number of observations	R^2	Predicted per capita GDP, Cuba
1. GDPPC = 1648.2 + 18.57 STEEL	28	.761	$2,595
2. LnGDPPC = 7.57 + 1.282 CEMENT	28	.384	2,803
3. LnGDPPC = 4.39 + .5343 LnELECT	24	.807	3,261
4. LnGDPPC = 4.69 + .4824 LnENERGY	28	.804	3,581
5. LnGDPPC = 3.93 + 1.290 LnLFIND	28	.830	3,944
6. LnGDPPC = 7.76 + .5899 LnMLKCO	28	.396	2,929
7. 1/GDPPC = .0012 − .00012 LnFERT	28	.216	4,019
8. LnGDPPC = 7.46 + .249 LnTRACT	28	.726	4,064
9. GDPPC = 10701 − 2213.195 LnLFAGR	28	.659	3,781
10. LnGDPPC = 5.11 + .860 LnANPROT	26	.751	3,738
11. LnGDPPC = 1.85 + 1.443 LnAVPROT	26	.552	3,380
12. −1/GDPPC = −.0024 + .00055 LnSUGAR	27	.372	4,994
13. LnGDPPC = 6.997 + .00037 CALOR	28	.413	3,232
14. 1/GDPPC = .00025 + .00023 1/COTTON	24	.727	3,184
15. GDPPC = 1169.12 + 20.063 TELEV	28	.799	3,797
16. 1/GDPPC = .0017 − .00023 LnRADIO	28	.377	3,046
17. LnGDPPC = 8.40 + .209 LnCARS	28	.492	1,892
18. LnGDPPC = 4.37 + .443 LnNEWSP	28	.668	2,865
19. LnGDPPC = 6.27 + .429 LnTELEPH	26	.783	2,637
20. LnGDPPC = 10.23 + .555 LnCOMVEH	27	.688	2,608
21. −1/GDPPC = −.0063 + .0013 LnSCH1	28	.370	2,746
22. LnGDPPC = 7.04 + .0180 SCH2	28	.471	4,214
23. 1/GDPPC = .0012 − .00029 LnSCH3	26	.438	3,237
24. LnGDPPC = 6.39 + .0367 LFSER	28	.598	3,490
25. LnGDPPC = 10.12 − .590 LnIMORT	28	.491	4,283
26. LnGDPPC = 12.15 − .719 LnPOPHB	28	.595	3,775
27. LnGDPPC = 12.06 − .568 LnPOPPH	23	.658	4,397
28. 1/GDPPC = .00022 + .000000016 POPDNT	24	.560	3,615
29. GDPPC = 10535.4 − 1109.298 LnPOPNUR	26	.512	3,985

Geometric mean, Cuba = $3,385

(overvalued) official exchange rate for 1980, it yields an inflated $5,453 (see Table 5.2, column 1). Yet when Argentina's GDP per capita is converted using average 1978–80 exchange rates, the distortion is smoothed over and the resulting estimate is $2,390 (see Table 5.2, column 2). This first bias of exchange rate conversions, then, operates generally in the short run and rather unstably.

Second, there is a long-run and systematic tendency for dollar GDP conversions at prevailing exchange rates to understate low-income countries' income.[11] This is true because productivity differentials across countries tend to be larger for tradeable goods than for nontradeable goods, and higher wages in more developed countries are translated into higher prices for nontradeables. There is also a tendency for nontradeable basic goods to be state-subsidized in lower-income countries, reinforcing this effect.

The per capita GDP estimates in Table 4.4, then, are based on purchasing power parity and are intended to minimize the exchange rate distortions just described.[12] Since the second distortion operates more systematically, the resulting adjustment yields higher GDP per capita estimates for low- and middle-income countries. Our ppp-based estimate for 1980 Cuban per capita GDP is $3,385 ($K_x$ scale, measured in 1980 international dollars), or 46 percent above the K_v scale estimate. We shall discuss the quality of these and other estimates in the last section of this chapter.

Factor Analysis

The PI method proceeds on the basis of very little theory. The physical indicators that are supposed to be correlates of the development process are weighted equally and averaged. If two indicators capture a similar aspect of the development process (e.g., infant mortality and physicians per capita), they will be highly correlated with each other. Since per capita GDP is regressed separately on each indicator, the underlying phenomenon will be counted twice in the average.

Without a specific theory that stipulates a functional form of the overall relationship between per capita GDP and the physical indicators, the preferred procedure would be to run per capita GDP on all the indicators in a multiple regression. The indicators would be allowed to weight themselves, and the "true" underlying model could be better approximated than with the simple regression method. The principal problem with this approach is practical. The number of observations (countries) rarely exceeds the number of indicators (independent variables) or exceeds them by a small amount. There are not enough degrees of freedom.

A standard circumvention of this problem is to use principal component/factor analysis, wherein the independent variables are linearly combined into composite variables or factors.[13] The first factor is constructed to reflect the maximum possible proportion of the total variation in the set of original variables. Additional factors can be constructed that are orthogonal to the previous factors and reflect the maximum possible proportion of the remaining variation in the original variables. The factors that explain a predetermined share of the variation in the original independent variables are then considered as potential regressors in an equation with the dependent variable. (The most common practice is to use factors with eigenvalues greater than one.)

Our set of independent variables yielded seven factors with eigenvalues over one. The first factor alone accounted for 41.9 percent of the variance of the set of all the independent variables (physical indicators), and the seven factors together accounted for 80.7 percent of the variance. Of these seven factors, however, only four lend themselves readily to economic interpretation, i.e., appear to represent identifiable sectors of economic activity. In Table 5.5 we present the rotated factor matrix where factor loadings by physical indicator are given. Focusing on those indicators with loadings above .60, the first factor appears to primarily represent industry in general with an emphasis on producer goods (high loadings obtain for steel, electricity, and energy consumption as well as for the percentage of the labor force in industry). The second factor appears to primarily represent agriculture, with high loadings for milk, animal and vegetable protein, and fertilizer consumption as well as for tractor use. The third factor again loads highly several industrial variables (cement, cotton, telephones, protein consumption, and nurses per population), with a possible emphasis on consumer goods. The fourth factor appears to primarily represent education with loadings over .74 for two of the three schooling variables, the other with a loading over .50 and no other indicator with a loading above .50. Factors five through seven do not cluster around any clear phenomenal pattern. The first four factors together accounted for 68.2 percent of the total variance of the initial set of all the independent variables.

Next, we ran a multiple regression of GDP per capita (both exchange rate converted and international dollars) on these four interpretable factors (F1 through F4). Equation 1 gives the results for the K_v scale and equation 2 for the K_x scale. The t-statistics are in parentheses below the coefficients.

$$\text{GDPPC} = 2219 + 1219\ F1 + 775.4\ F2 + 463.8\ F3 + 206.6\ F4 \quad (1)$$
$$(K_v) \qquad (15.9) \quad (8.6) \qquad (5.5) \qquad (3.3) \qquad (1.5)$$

$$\text{Adjusted } R^2 = .805$$

$$\text{GDPPC} = 3024 + 1137\ F1 + 605.6\ F2 + 407.5\ F3 + 382.6\ F4 \quad (2)$$
$$(K_x) \qquad (31.3) \quad (11.6) \qquad (6.2) \qquad (4.1) \qquad (3.9)$$

$$\text{Adjusted } R^2 = .881$$

There is an a priori basis for questioning whether the high coefficient on factor 1, which primarily represents industry, with an apparent concentration on producer goods, would bias the factor analysis prediction of GDP per capita in favor of centrally planned economies. Examining the country factor scores in Table 5.6, however, tends to diminish this concern. Cuba's scores for factors 2 and 4 actually have higher relative ranking than for factor 1, although the relative ranking of factor 1 for Cuba is above that for factor 3.

The results presented in Table 5.7 also diminish the concern regarding a relative upward bias in predicting Cuban GDP per capita. The standardized value (number of standard deviations from the mean) of Cuba's predicted per capita GDP from factor analysis is less than half of this value from rudimentary PI—and this holds for both the K_v and K_x scales.

Table 5.5. Rotated Factor Matrix

	Factor 1	Factor 2	Factor 3	Factor 4	Factor 5	Factor 6	Factor 7
STEEL	0.79098	0.16969	0.41135	0.11952	-0.05240	0.11439	0.09208
CEMENT	0.37877	0.22374	0.81538	0.19432	-0.03831	0.02912	-0.07883
ELECT	0.89380	0.09264	0.08280	0.14877	0.06124	-0.03050	0.12576
ENERGY	0.74709	0.29491	0.02185	-0.12275	0.15957	0.11986	-0.13971
MLKCO	0.33686	0.63540	0.26491	0.24698	-0.09675	-0.43470	-0.01593
TRACT	0.29997	0.88484	0.11264	0.10313	0.05167	0.06875	-0.04893
LFAGR	-0.69452	-0.32752	-0.02306	-0.25324	-0.24589	-0.43421	0.01134
ANPROT	0.34253	0.68829	0.35383	0.21058	0.14622	0.31544	-0.01618
AVPROT	0.35120	0.63359	0.53024	-0.00633	0.02306	0.30126	-0.08713
SUGAR	0.13669	-0.01014	-0.06543	0.23293	0.69590	0.32786	0.14689
COTTON	0.15129	0.04182	0.87577	-0.02627	-0.07699	-0.07012	-0.08226
TELEV	0.69994	0.51927	0.30772	0.16960	0.11721	0.17239	0.08719
CARS	0.33891	-0.06326	-0.00040	0.02193	0.02163	0.13321	0.75755
NEWSP	0.25611	0.85494	0.04093	0.16419	0.02482	0.18689	0.00575
TELEPH	0.50712	0.32212	0.62465	0.14299	-0.02802	-0.02254	0.00320
IMORT	-0.51802	-0.36658	-0.23942	-0.28689	-0.35016	0.17646	0.06566
POPHB	-0.39065	-0.38147	-0.28363	-0.42481	-0.42447	-0.07119	-0.13297
POPPH	-0.30093	-0.13596	-0.22163	-0.25122	0.07969	-0.74275	-0.05752
SCH1	0.23322	-0.04452	0.15096	0.74186	0.08167	0.13001	-0.24104
SCH2	0.40580	0.44473	0.34269	0.50227	0.16897	0.07354	-0.24494
SCH3	-0.02885	0.21287	-0.04580	0.89101	-0.04584	0.08691	0.07045
CALOR	0.46138	0.45670	0.46602	-0.20105	0.11795	0.17323	-0.09111
POPDNT	-0.17576	-0.10134	0.00627	-0.14763	-0.00839	-0.06712	0.86154
POPNUR	-0.09834	0.12055	0.76111	0.08618	0.12605	0.27301	0.20328
FERT	0.03987	0.85308	0.11055	0.00917	0.00855	-0.09047	-0.12754
LFSER	0.45281	0.23330	0.22553	0.40478	0.47128	0.41988	-0.07267
LFIND	0.73663	0.35520	0.26692	0.17355	0.06243	0.30028	0.02641
RADIO	0.17587	0.50411	0.03329	0.02449	0.40203	0.40346	0.00594
COMVEH	0.02814	-0.04672	-0.03426	-0.15597	0.84695	-0.22443	-0.10077

Table 5.6. Country Factor Scores

	FS1	FS2	FS3	FS4	FS5	FS6	FS7
Costa Rica	-0.12947	-0.16242	-0.40039	1.27139	0.75972	0.00381	-0.09853
Dominican Republic	-0.71204	-0.22167	-0.02389	0.65935	0.22783	-0.81067	1.25101
El Salvador	-0.82939	0.49089	-0.25736	-1.63275	0.29318	-0.01742	0.31420
Guatemala	-0.88544	-0.06999	-0.07496	-1.21913	-0.27143	-0.30916	1.38487
Haiti	-0.45114	-0.74595	-0.38142	-2.07254	-1.64036	0.05753	0.37908
Honduras	-0.89195	-0.54600	-0.11322	-0.69419	-0.31464	-0.35115	-0.34164
Jamaica	-0.12542	-0.29852	-0.34061	-0.85334	4.24229	-1.23297	-0.51817
Mexico	0.49588	-0.63836	-0.15184	-0.16476	-0.35497	0.85467	-0.35547
Nicaragua	-0.87968	-0.22616	-0.35131	-0.11082	0.37052	0.76618	-0.39867
Panama	0.27141	-0.68966	-0.02179	1.27129	0.16292	-0.02888	-0.58635
Trinidad and Tobago	2.71530	-0.20813	-0.73330	-1.48825	0.10127	0.32602	-0.75340
Argentina	-0.34722	1.07956	1.11778	0.55199	0.47730	1.61098	1.93699
Bolivia	-1.00990	0.03794	-0.52753	-0.50175	-0.24962	0.76237	-0.30666
Brazil	0.65945	-0.59364	-0.15056	-0.31637	0.35188	0.54539	3.68071
Chile	0.41804	-0.13651	-0.52758	0.44012	0.41017	0.62068	-0.50793
Colombia	0.17264	-0.72648	-0.32960	0.45861	-0.19183	0.24193	-0.87441
Ecuador	-0.94571	-0.15904	-0.60442	1.90238	-0.25904	0.20197	-0.36329
Paraguay	-0.48195	-0.08368	-0.06038	-0.50623	-0.82498	0.08260	-0.77384
Peru	-0.46062	-0.62627	-0.21347	0.71432	-0.54140	0.45998	-0.70751
Uruguay	0.05335	0.96177	-0.54746	0.19234	0.37701	1.31640	-0.57104
Venezuela	1.53861	-0.00344	-1.12770	0.25695	0.33193	0.86208	0.06871
Philippines	-0.95084	-0.53457	-0.67839	1.93969	-0.67958	-0.59853	-0.61305
Thailand	-0.39342	0.17455	-0.21713	-0.12722	-0.58472	-3.60865	0.32913
Turkey	-0.42899	-0.31837	0.73937	-1.11148	-0.95331	0.38617	-0.80185
Greece	-0.21175	-0.13783	4.29736	0.07420	0.49342	0.35842	-0.60692
Ireland	-0.0345	4.54977	-0.23679	0.00987	-0.38129	0.59853	-0.61305
Spain	2.74563	0.22520	0.47309	0.91161	-0.98967	-1.04956	0.44459
Portugal	1.09865	-0.39298	1.44351	0.14475	-0.36260	-1.01294	-0.46381
Cuba	0.09385	0.25502	-0.19201	0.72044	0.74279	0.59853	-0.61305

Table 5.7. Predicted Values of GDP Per Capita (1980 dollars)

	Rudimentary PI		Factor analysis PI[a]	
	K_v scale	K_x scale[b]	K_v scale	K_x scale[b]
1. Costa Rica	$1,960	$2,984	$2,012	$3,102
2. Dominican Republic	1,304	2,236	1,304	2,323
3. El Salvador	1,122	2,014	1,132	1,649
4. Guatemala	1,040	1,909	798	1,478
5. Haiti	505	1,132	485	1,111
6. Honduras	957	1,830	512	1,367
7. Jamaica	1,634	2,596	1,450	2,235
8. Mexico	1,814	2,826	2,224	3,076
9. Nicaragua	1,247	2,172	785	1,701
10. Panama	1,902	2,911	2,267	3,392
11. Trinidad and Tobago	2,404	3,395	4,720	5,117
12. Argentina	2,931	3,938	3,265	3,949
13. Bolivia	1,138	2,038	669	1,491
14. Brazil	1,806	2,813	2,427	3,232
15. Chile	2,071	3,088	2,469	3,370
16. Colombia	1,657	2,653	1,808	2,821
17. Ecuador	1,548	2,558	1,055	2,334
18. Paraguay	1,270	2,194	1,434	2,207
19. Peru	1,487	2,463	1,219	2,307
20. Uruguay	2,378	3,405	2,815	3,517
21. Venezuela	2,489	3,536	3,621	4,410
22. Philippines	1,015	1,950	731	2,085
23. Thailand	914	1,808	1,747	2,545
24. Turkey	1,373	2,314	1,562	2,219
25. Greece	3,220	4,264	3,862	4,479
26. Ireland	3,686	4,727	5,597	5,648
27. Spain	3,218	4,244	6,148	6,824
28. Portugal	2,393	3,422	3,953	4,679
Arithmetic mean	1,802	2,765	2,219	3,024
Standard deviation	793	860	1,531	1,404
Cuba	$2,325	$3,385	$2,691	$3,483
Cuba as percent of mean	129	122	121	115
Cuba, standardized score	.659	.721	.308	.327
Cuba rank	9	9	9	9
Implied ERDI		1.46		1.29

[a]Based on regression with first four factors.
[b]Measured in 1980 international dollars. For purposes of comparison, the U.S. GDP per capita is $11,447 on both scales.

Table 5.7 summarizes the results of our factor analysis-predicted values and compares these to our rudimentary PI estimates. Factor analysis-predicted GDP per capita for Cuba in 1980 is $2,691 on the K_v scale and $3,483 on the K_x scale.

When GDP per capita is regressed on all seven factors with eigenvalues greater than one, the predicted per capita GDPs for Cuba are $2,953 on the K_v scale and $3,756 on the K_x scale. That is, when seven rather than four factors are used in the predicting equation, the estimates for Cuba increase by 9.7 percent on the K_v scale and by 7.8 percent on the K_x scale. Similar percentage variations occur for many countries, though the estimates for some countries are lower since the mean predicted value is the same in each equation. We prefer the regression using only the four factors with identifiable economic patterns, but statistical criteria do not unambiguously commend a particular number of factors in the specification of the regression equation. The fact that the factor analysis-predicted values are sensitive to the number of factors included, then, is one drawback of employing factor analysis for physical indicator estimates.

It is noteworthy that in all four estimates, 1980 Cuban GDP per capita consistently ranks ninth in this group of 29 countries. Also, the arithmetic mean of the factor analysis predictions lies approximately $300 above the mean in the rudimentary PI methods. This discrepancy appears to be attributable to the use of geometric means for country estimates in the rudimentary PI method, since the largest positive displacements from the mean exceed the largest negative displacements in the raw data. The factor analysis results are not affected by this, and the means of the predicted values equal the means in the raw data (see Table 5.2).

Finally, the standard deviation of the predicted GDP values in the factor analysis corresponds much more closely to that in the raw data than does the standard deviation in the rudimentary PI predictions. In Table 5.7, it can be appreciated that the averaging or smoothing process of the rudimentary PI method has already begun in the first iteration. The standard deviation of the predicted country GDPs per capita is less than one half that in the raw data on the K_v scale and is .58 that on the K_x scale. The factor analysis method, however, basically preserves the variability of the raw data. Although the standard deviations of the factor analysis estimates are smaller than in the raw data, this discrepancy is negligible on both the K_x and K_v scales.[14]

The rudimentary PI and the factor analysis approaches can also be compared by examining the differences (the "residuals") between the initial GDP per capita values (on either scale) and the corresponding predicted GDP per capita values for the reference countries. (Note that such a comparison is particularly useful in our situation because the rudimentary PI approach, rather than providing an overall value of R^2, provides an R^2 value for each of the simple regressions done with each of the physical indicators.) We define the residual for each country as follows:

Residual = reported GDP per capita − predicted GDP per capita

For the K_v scale, let Resid1 and Resid2 denote the two sets of residuals obtained for all reference countries using the rudimentary PI and the factor analysis PI approaches, respectively. Similarly, let Resid3 and Resid4 denote

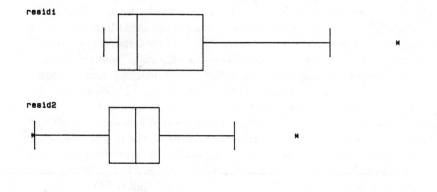

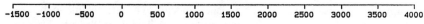

Figure 5.1.   Comparison of K$_y$ Scale Residuals

Note: resid1 and resid2, respectively, represent the rudimentary and the factor analysis PI residuals.

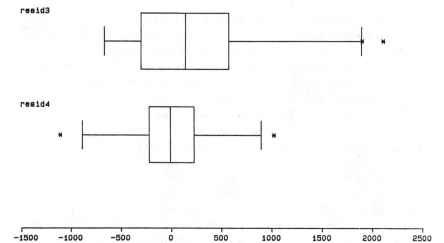

Figure 5.2.   Comparison of K$_x$ Scale Residuals

Note: resid3 and resid4, respectively, represent the rudimentary and the factor analysis PI residuals.

the corresponding sets of residuals on the K$_x$ scale. Figures 5.1 and 5.2 show a comparison of these residuals using a box plot of each set of residuals. A box plot for a set of numbers gives an indication of the center of the data (the median), the spread of the data (the difference between the upper and the lower quartiles), and the presence of outliers, and indicates the symmetry or asymmetry of the distribution of data values.[15] Both the figures show that the residuals associated with our factor analysis exercise are on the whole smaller than those associated with the rudimentary PI approach.

Before we discuss the plausibility of the different GDP per capita estimates for Cuba obtained in our exercise, we briefly summarize the three variants of the PI approach we have used. All three variants have the advantage that they rely on physical rather than value measures of each indicator. They all have the disadvantage that physical indicator estimates do not capture quality differences. The aspect in which the three variations differ is the statistical methodology employed. The rudimentary PI approach uses a set of simple regressions. That is, GDP per capita is regressed separately on each physical indicator to obtain as many estimates of GDP per capita for the target country as there are physical indicators, and these estimates are (geometrically) averaged to obtain an estimate of GDP per capita for the target country. This simple regression format has the advantage of having enough degrees of freedom for each regression, but we feel it ignores the correlations among the physical indicators themselves and arbitrarily weighs indicators equally. The elaborated PI approach is a modification of the rudimentary approach. It adds to the rudimentary approach an iterative process that has been claimed to correct for the exchange rate bias and to provide improved estimates. (We detail our reasons for rejecting the iterative procedure in the appendix to this chapter.) The factor analysis approach linearly combines the physical indicators into composite variables or factors and performs a multiple regression with GDP per capita as the dependent variable and some of the factors as independent variables. Through the use of factors and the methodology of multiple regression, this approach takes into account the correlation among the physical indicators and also circumvents the problem of not having enough degrees of freedom. Thus it differs from the rudimentary approach. It also differs from the elaborated PI approach that, in each iteration, performs a simple regression with a linear combination of physical indicators as the dependent variable (rather than GDP per capita), and each physical indicator as an independent variable. In summary, we feel that the factor analysis approach has much to recommend it, although the precise estimates it yields are sensitive to the number of factors included in the predicting equation.

DISCUSSION OF GDP PER CAPITA ESTIMATES FOR CUBA

The GDP per capita estimate for Cuba in 1980 using the rudimentary PI method is $2,325 on the K_v scale. Is this a reasonable estimate of Cuban per capita GDP in 1980? One way to explore the plausibility of this estimate is to compare it to the estimate of Oshima (1961), who calculated a Cuban GDP per capita of $430 in 1953, current dollars. Using the likely upper-bound estimate of per capita annual real growth of 1.77 percent between 1953 and 1958 (Brundenius 1984b: 145), we arrive at $470 per capita GDP in 1958 in 1953 dollars, or at $539 in 1958 dollars (using the U.S. GNP deflator). Now, if we compare $539 with $2,325, we get a nominal yearly per capita growth rate for GDP of 6.9 percent between 1958 and 1980, or a real growth rate of 2.0 percent (since the U.S. GNP deflator averaged 4.9 percent per annum over this period). If we add back in Cuban population growth (1.7 percent annual average between 1958 and 1980), the resulting estimate for average annual real GDP growth during the first 22 years of the revolution is 3.7 percent. The official Cuban estimate for real growth in gross material product over this period is 5.1 percent per year.

The GDP per capita estimate for Cuba in 1980, using the factor analysis method, is $2,691 on the K_v scale. If we compare this figure with $539, the per capita GDP estimate for 1958, the implied annual real growth rate is 2.7 percent in per capita GDP, or 4.4 percent in GDP. This latter growth rate estimate still lies below, but is closer to, the official annual growth rate of 5.1 percent for 1958–80. Since the sphere of nonmaterial services in post-1958 Cuba has grown more rapidly than the rest of the economy, the implied rate of (officially estimated) real GDP growth would be above 5.1 percent annually. By this standard, our PI estimates (both rudimentary and factor analytic) appear conservative. Allowing for some possible upward bias in the official figures or in the adjusted Oshima estimate for 1958, however, the PI estimates seem to fall into a plausible range. This conclusion receives additional support from the fact that Cuban GDP per capita consistently ranks ninth in the four distinct PI estimates.

Alternatively, we can make a rough comparison between the implied physical indicators growth rate estimate and our own estimates in Table 4.4 of chapter 4. Our estimates for real GDP growth per annum during 1962–80 were 4.9 percent and 5.1 percent, depending on the series of industrial output employed. Insufficient data prevent us from attempting a GDP estimate for 1958–62. While 1959 and 1960 appear to have been years of growth, 1961 and 1962 were years of stagnation. Reliable estimates for constant price total material product (TMP, i.e., gross value of output in agriculture, mining, manufacturing, and construction; or, roughly, GDP minus "productive" and "unproductive" services) are available for 1958–62 (Brundenius 1984b: 146–50), but these figures exclude services, which seem to have grown rapidly during the early years of the revolution. They therefore are likely to underestimate actual GDP growth. By chain-linking two constant price series, we derive the estimate for real TMP annual growth of 1.5 percent between 1958 and 1962. If we take this to approximate the GDP growth rate over these years and combine it with the average of our two GDP growth rate estimates for 1962–80 (5.0 percent), we arrive at 4.4 percent as our estimate for real annual GDP growth over 1958–80. This is slightly above the implied growth rate from our rudimentary PI estimate and the adjusted Oshima estimate, but it is precisely equal to the implied growth rate from our factor analytic PI estimate and the adjusted Oshima estimate.

In Table 5.8 we present our estimates of Cuban per capita GDP in constant 1980 dollars for the period 1962–85, inclusive. Estimate 1 ($GDP1A) is based on the simple regression PI method for determining per capita GDP in 1980. Estimate 2 ($GDP1B) is based on the factor analytic PI method.[16] Each estimate uses the GDP1 estimated growth rates from chapter 4.

In coming years, it is likely that new information will become available, allowing investigators to carry out ppp and repricing estimates for Cuba. The Cuban State Statistical Committee itself has undertaken work on presenting SNA national income estimates. The estimates presented in this chapter, then,

Table 5.8. Estimated Per Capita GDP, 1962–85 (in constant 1980 dollars, K_v scale)

Measure	1962	1963	1964	1965	1966
1 Index GDP1	35.8	37.3	40.3	42.1	41.3
2 Index Pop	75.0	77.0	79.1	81.1	82.7
3 GDP1 per cap	47.8	48.4	50.9	51.9	49.9
4 $GDP1A	$1308.5	1325.6	1395.1	1421.4	1366.5
5 $GDP1B	$1514.4	1534.2	1614.7	1645.1	1581.5
	1967	1968	1969	1970	1971
1 Index GDP1	44.2	46.3	46.7	50.4	50.9
2 Index Pop	84.2	85.7	87.0	88.2	89.7
3 GDP1 per cap	52.5	54.1	53.6	57.1	56.7
4 $GDP1A	$1437.7	1481.9	1469.0	1563.7	1552.9
5 $GDP1B	$1663.9	1715.1	1700.1	1809.7	1797.2
	1972	1973	1974	1975	1976
1 Index GDP1	54.0	59.3	63.6	69.4	72.8
2 Index Pop	92.0	93.0	94.7	96.0	97.3
3 GDP1 per cap	59.0	63.6	67.2	72.2	74.8
4 $GDP1A	$1616.3	1742.0	1841.3	1978.4	2048.8
5 $GDP1B	$1870.6	2016.1	2131.1	2289.7	2371.2
	1977	1978	1979	1980	1981
1 Index GDP1	76.7	82.7	85.0	84.4	100.0
2 Index Pop	98.4	99.3	100.0	99.4	100.0
3 GDP1 per cap	77.9	83.3	85.0	84.9	100.0
4 $GDP1A	$2134.3	2280.8	2328.8	2324.7	2739.0
5 $GDP1B	$2470.1	2639.8	2695.3	2690.5	3170.0
	1982	1983	1984	1985	
1 Index GDP1	104.7	110.4	118.6	123.3	
2 Index Pop	100.1	102.0	103.0	104.1	
3 GDP1 per cap	103.7	108.3	115.2	118.5	
4 $GDP1A	$2840.5	2965.2	3155.8	3245.1	
5 $GDP1B	$3287.5	3431.8	3652.4	3755.7	

represent a first approach to estimating Cuban national income in dollars and SNA categories.

APPENDIX

The Elaborated PI Method

In this appendix we present our tests of the "elaborated" method (using K_v scale data). We carried out thirteen iterations as suggested by Marer (1985b) and Ehrlich (1985). In the thirteenth iteration our estimate for Cuban GDP per capita fell by less than one dollar from the twelfth iteration. The results of the iterations for Cuba, the reference countries, and the 29 physical indicators are summarized in Tables 5A.1 and 5A.2. Note that Table 5A.1 reports "adjusted" or "corrected" GDP per capita values for different iterations. The "adjusted" GDP per capita for a country at any iteration is the (geometric) average of the 29 predicted (i.e., estimated) GDP per capita values using each physical indicator obtained for that country in that iteration (Marer 1985b: 94). Table 5A.2 shows the highest and lowest predicted values of GDP per capita for the 29 physical indicators in each of the 28 countries. It also reports the standard deviation of the values.

The claims on behalf of the iterations are that they produce successively higher R^2s and they diminish the exchange rate bias from the initial converted dollar GDPs. On a theoretical level, there appears to be no justification for these claims. Regarding the higher R^2s, it is true that with successive iterations the variance of the predicted values of the dependent variable will diminish. This can be proven mathematically.[17] It is theoretically possible, however, for the explained portion of the variance to decrease, as the variance itself gets smaller. In our exercise, the average R^2 over the 29 equations (one for each physical indicator) rose from the first to the second iteration, but it fell steadily thereafter.

Regarding the undoing of the exchange rate bias, no theoretical basis for this claim is offered by either Marer or Ehrlich. In essence, with the iteration procedure, what is being done is regressing a linear combination of all physical indicators from the previous iteration on each physical indicator (with the initial scale being set by the exchange rate converted GDPs). Neither the economics nor the statistics of this procedure appear plausible. It can be demonstrated mathematically that the average of the predicted values of the dependent variable (per capita GDP) will be the same for successive iterations in each of the 29 equations. With this proven, it can then be shown that the beta coefficients will approach zero as the number of iterations gets large. That is, with successive iterations the least squares line flattens out, but always passes through the same mean. This means, of course, that the constant term increases and the variable term (where the difference in physical indicators across countries appears)

Table 5A.1. Predicted GDP Per Capita by Country and Iteration[a] (regression to the mean)

	iter1	iter2	iter3	iter5	iter7	iter9	iter11	iter13
1. Costa Rica	1,960	1,783	1,704	1,647	1,631	1,625	1,624	1,623
2. Dominican Republic	1,304	1,415	1,494	1,576	1,606	1,617	1,621	1,622
3. El Salvador	1,122	1,302	1,425	1,552	1,598	1,614	1,620	1,622
4. Guatemala	1,040	1,239	1,385	1,537	1,593	1,613	1,619	1,622
5. Haiti	505	806	1,076	1,410	1,547	1,596	1,614	1,620
6. Honduras	957	1,201	1,363	1,529	1,590	1,612	1,619	1,622
7. Jamaica	1,634	1,618	1,616	1,619	1,621	1,622	1,623	1,623
8. Mexico	1,814	1,713	1,671	1,637	1,627	1,624	1,623	1,623
9. Nicaragua	1,247	1,389	1,479	1,571	1,605	1,617	1,621	1,622
10. Panama	1,902	1,771	1,703	1,648	1,631	1,625	1,624	1,623
11. Trinidad and Tobago	2,404	2,042	1,864	1,703	1,650	1,632	1,626	1,624
12. Argentina	2,931	2,288	1,982	1,736	1,660	1,635	1,627	1,624
13. Bolivia	1,138	1,308	1,427	1,552	1,598	1,614	1,620	1,622
14. Brazil	1,806	1,706	1,666	1,636	1,627	1,624	1,623	1,623
15. Chile	2,071	1,866	1,759	1,667	1,637	1,628	1,624	1,623
16. Colombia	1,657	1,622	1,615	1,618	1,621	1,622	1,623	1,623
17. Ecuador	1,548	1,561	1,577	1,604	1,616	1,620	1,622	1,623
18. Paraguay	1,270	1,399	1,488	4,575	1,606	1,617	1,621	1,622
19. Peru	1,487	1,528	1,562	1,600	1,615	1,620	1,622	1,623
20. Uruguay	2,378	2,028	1,846	1,695	1,647	1,631	1,626	1,624
21. Venezuela	2,489	2,077	1,871	1,702	1,649	1,632	1,626	1,624
22. Philippines	1,015	1,261	1,405	1,546	1,596	1,614	1,620	1,622
23. Thailand	914	1,184	1,354	1,527	1,590	1,611	1,619	1,622
24. Turkey	1,373	1,455	1,521	1,587	1,610	1,618	1,621	1,622
25. Greece	3,220	2,457	2,066	1,760	1,668	1,638	1,628	1,625
26. Ireland	3,686	2,632	2,145	1,783	1,675	1,640	1,629	1,625
27. Spain	3,218	2,452	2,075	1,766	1,670	1,639	1,628	1,625
28. Portugal	2,393	2,035	1,853	1,697	1,648	1,631	1,626	1,624
Geographic mean[b]	1,803	1,683	1,642	1,624	1,623	1,623	1,623	1,623
Standard deviation[b]	793	443	254	86	29	10	3	1
Cuba[c]	2,325	2,000	1,854	1,643	1,632	1,630	1,625	1,624

[a]Figures rounded to nearest dollar.
[b]Geometric mean and standard deviation of the 28 GDP per capita estimates in each iteration.
[c]Geometric mean. The arithmetic mean for Cuba in the first iteration is $2,418.

gradually vanishes. This leads to a regression to the original mean across all physical indicators and all countries (Joglekar and Zimbalist 1989).[18]

Our results conform to these expectations. By the thirteenth iteration, per capita GDPs, which originally varied from a high of $5,973 to a low of $292, varied from a high of $1,625 to a low of $1,622 across all 28 reference countries plus the one target country. That is, the estimated per capita GDP in Haiti was only $3 below that of Greece, Ireland, or Spain by this procedure! The differential between the high and low predicted values across the 29 indicators within each country also narrows and converges to the mean, as shown in Table 5A.2.

Table 5A.2. High and Low Predicted Values of GDP Per Capita of Physical Indicators within Countries (regression to the mean)

		iter1	iter2	iter3	iter5	iter7	iter9	iter11	iter13
1. Costa Rica	h	8,287[a]	3,197	2,151	1,766	1,670	1,639	1,628	1,625
	l	834	1,096	1,320	1,524	1,590	1,611	1,619	1,622
	sd[b]	1308	408	191	59	20	7	2	1
2. Dominican Republic	h	2,849	2,297	1,987	1,737	1,660	1,635	1,627	1,624
	l	537	811	1,073	1,407	1,546	1,596	1,614	1,620
	sd	476	295	183	67	23	8	3	1
3. El Salvador	h	2,295	2,088	1,870	1,703	1,649	1,632	1,626	1,624
	l	450	793	1,065	1,404	1,545	1,596	1,614	1,620
	sd	472	331	207	76	26	9	3	1
4. Guatemela	h	1,575	1,592	1,634	1,636	1,628	1,625	1,623	1,623
	l	577	820	1,096	1,426	1,554	1,599	1,615	1,620
	sd	301	219	147	57	20	7	2	1
5. Haiti	h	1,292	1,415	1,494	1,576	1,606	1,617	1,621	1,622
	l	163	396	702	1,218	1,471	1,570	1,605	1,617
	sd	280	250	192	87	33	12	4	1
6. Honduras	h	2,358	1,880	1,729	1,645	1,629	1,625	1,623	1,623
	l	394	850	1,111	1,425	1,553	1,599	1,615	1,620
	sd	383	227	144	55	19	7	2	1
7. Jamaica	h	4,141	2,634	2,013	1,738	1,661	1,636	1,627	1,624
	l	768	1,076	1,323	1,522	1,588	1,611	1,619	1,622
	sd	764	393	207	66	22	6	3	1
8. Mexico	h	3,785	2,505	2,075	1,758	1,667	1,637	1,628	1,625
	l	726	951	1,180	1,454	1,563	1,602	1,616	1,621
	sd	705	377	212	71	24	8	3	1
9. Nicaragua	h	2,830	2,155	1,866	1,691	1,644	1,630	1,625	1,624
	l	450	793	1,065	1,404	1,545	1,596	1,614	1,620
	sd	436	267	165	61	22	7	3	1
10. Panama	h	2,853	2,226	1,948	1,724	1,656	1,634	1,627	1,624
	l	1,096	1,261	1,394	1,539	1,593	1,613	1,619	1,622

11. Trinidad and Tobago	sd	558	298	165	54	18	6	2	1
	h	7,466	3,936	2,728	1,936	1,723	1,656	1,634	1,627
	l	753	1,039	1,283	1,513	1,586	1,610	1,619	1,621
12. Argentina	sd	1,522	645	326	97	32	11	4	1
	h	6,605	3,811	2,679	1,923	1,719	1,655	1,634	1,627
	l	774	1,014	1,250	1,491	1,577	1,607	1,617	1,621
13. Bolivia	sd	1,331	581	294	88	29	10	3	1
	h	3,717	2,602	2,058	1,747	1,663	1,636	1,627	1,624
	l	595	864	1,114	1,425	1,552	1,598	1,614	1,620
14. Brazil	sd	595	350	200	71	25	8	3	1
	h	5,695	3,248	2,436	1,864	1,701	1,649	1,632	1,626
	l	801	1,074	1,277	1,494	1,577	1,607	1,617	1,621
15. Chile	sd	960	439	231	73	24	8	3	1
	h	4,112	2,885	2,267	1,815	1,685	1,644	1,630	1,625
	l	1,168	1,389	1,513	1,582	1,609	1,618	1,621	1,622
16. Colombia	sd	617	293	148	44	14	5	2	1
	h	4,924	2,902	2,138	1,760	1,666	1,637	1,628	1,624
	l	1,007	1,195	1,350	1,522	1,588	1,612	1,619	1,622
17. Ecuador	sd	704	308	148	46	16	5	2	1
	h	6,064	2,831	2,101	1,748	1,662	1,636	1,627	1,624
	l	801	1,034	1,239	1,478	1,571	1,605	1,617	1,621
18. Paraguay	sd	940	352	184	62	21	7	2	1
	h	2,539	2,073	1,870	1,702	1,649	1,632	1,626	1,624
	l	578	988	1,209	1,466	1,567	1,604	1,616	1,621
19. Peru	sd	593	361	214	75	26	9	3	1
	h	2,145	1,962	1,804	1,682	1,643	1,629	1,625	1,624
	l	853	1,066	1,259	1,486	1,574	1,606	1,617	1,621
20. Uruguay	sd	346	222	132	47	16	6	2	1
	h	5,061	3,024	2,374	1,861	1,702	1,650	1,632	1,626
	l	1,182	1,351	1,432	1,546	1,595	1,613	1,619	1,622

(continued)

Table 5A.2 (Continued)

		iter1	iter2	iter3	iter5	iter7	iter9	iter11	iter13
	sd	1,107	493	250	76	25	8	3	1
21. Venezuela	h	4,730	2,929	2,311	1,836	1,693	1,646	1,631	1,626
	l	1,078	1,343	1,498	1,583	1,609	1,618	1,621	1,622
	sd	1,027	460	235	71	23	8	3	1
22. Philippines	h	2,736	2,182	1,903	1,711	1,652	1,633	1,626	1,624
	l	110	716	1,076	1,413	1,548	1,597	1,614	1,620
	sd	553	346	207	73	25	9	3	1
23. Thailand	h	3,519	2,567	2,131	1,780	1,675	1,640	1,629	1,625
	l	145	733	1,015	1,381	1,536	1,593	1,612	1,619
	sd	644	394	248	92	32	11	4	1
24. Turkey	h	2,773	2,186	1,230	1,720	1,655	1,634	1,627	1,624
	l	658	868	1,113	1,425	1,552	1,598	1,614	1,620
	sd	600	361	217	77	27	9	3	1
25. Greece	h	10,249	5,453	3,333	2,073	1,763	1,669	1,639	1,628
	l	1,493	1,626	1,592	1,598	1,612	1,619	1,621	1,622
	sd	1,819	797	369	102	32	11	4	1
26. Ireland	h	8,911	3,817	2,682	1,924	1,719	1,655	1,634	1,627
	l	1,307	1,502	1,585	1,620	1,623	1,623	1,623	1,623
	sd	1,767	684	321	91	29	10	3	1
27. Spain	h	5,882	3,586	2,673	1,955	1,733	1,660	1,635	1,627
	l	1,044	1,288	1,457	1,577	1,609	1,618	1,621	1,622
	sd	1,419	622	311	92	30	10	4	1
28. Portugal	h	4,615	2,942	2,294	1,824	1,688	1,645	1,630	1,625
	l	1,143	1,382	1,513	1,596	1,613	1,620	1,622	1,623
	sd	913	426	217	64	21	7	2	1

[a]Figures rounded off to nearest dollar.
[b]Standard deviation of the predicted GDPs per capita for the 29 physical indicators of each iteration.

This result implies that economic development is a uniform, even process wherein different sectors and branches grow at the same rate in all countries. We know reality to be otherwise. Thus, rather than correcting for exchange rate biases, the elaborated PI method produces implausible estimates.

PART II   *Analyzing Sectoral
and Aggregate
Performance*

CHAPTER 6

Capital Goods: Development and Prospects

Capital goods (usually defined as machinery and transport equipment)[1] have played an important role in the capital formation and industrialization process in today's leading industrial nations. This has been true of the nations that started to industrialize in the 19th century as well as of the relative newcomers such as Japan and the Soviet Union (UNCTAD 1985: 2). The capital goods sector has been crucial not only in terms of its linkage effects with the rest of the economy, but also because it has acted as a decisive instrument for the generation and diffusion of technological change throughout the economy. This is so because there is an important theoretical and practical learning process involved in capital goods production (Rosenberg 1976: 144).

The relatively high level of technology—often involving specialized skills—usually required for the production of capital goods has represented an important barrier to the entry into these industries by developing countries, especially those with a weak industrial base and a lack of skilled people. Another obstacle is the economies of scale that are often required for efficient capital goods production. Most developing countries today have only embryonic capital goods industries or none at all. In fact, 74 percent of capital goods production in the developing countries is concentrated in six or seven newly industrializing countries (NICs) (UNIDO 1985: 1). But the developing countries are large importers of capital goods. The developing countries' share in capital goods output in 1980 was only 6 percent of world output, while their share of world imports of capital goods was 29 percent (UNCTAD 1985: 24).

The absence of a domestic capital goods industry is undeniably a serious hindrance to rapid capital accumulation and a sustained rate of economic growth for a developing country. Such a country could, of course, depend for quite some time on the importation of such capital goods, but then it would likely be forced to depend on the traditional exports of primary goods, the price prospects of which are rather gloomy.

Cuba has faced an additional problem. At the outset of the revolution in 1959, Cuba emphasized the meeting of basic needs and the rapid elimination of unemployment as relatively *short-term* goals. At the same time, it was more or less taken for granted that the needs of capital accumulation—a sine qua non for the sustained rate of growth of the economy in the long run—would not be neglected. As the experiences of other countries have demonstrated, however, it is quite difficult to reconcile these two objectives in the short run, and Cuba proved to be no exception, as will be discussed below.

There are both costs and benefits to building up an indigenous capital goods industry. There are immediate benefits of the process, such as saving foreign exchange, making the country less vulnerable to price changes of capital goods on the world market, and assuring secure supplies of spare parts. More long-term benefits may be experienced when skill acquisition and product innovations in the capital goods sector lead to productivity increases in the rest of the economy as well as in the capital goods sector itself.

But there may also be large social costs in building up an indigenous capital goods sector. These costs may be reflected in a lower efficiency of locally produced capital goods, as compared with similar goods on the world market. This might lead to a diversion and waste of resources. The timing of the building up of an indigenous capital goods sector is thus essential in planning. The planning of capital goods production is a long-term operation. The sector's diversity extends from the production of small parts and components to large and sophisticated machinery. Programming and planning, then, embrace not only the production of machinery that is economically viable, but also the evaluation of various alternative production possibilities in terms of socioeconomic costs and benefits.

Machinery and equipment have always been considered important in a "socialist" growth strategy. Such a strategy is often based on two postulates: that industrialization should take place at the fastest rate possible, and that capital goods growth should continuously outpace that of consumer goods. This latter postulate is sometimes referred to as "the law of the preferential expansion of Department I," with a reference to Marx's celebrated model of accumulation. Department I in Marx's analysis is, however, a much wider category since it also includes what we today call intermediate goods (such as steel, paper, cement, and fertilizers) and not only means of production in the sense of machinery and equipment. But even so, it is quite clear that also in Marx's analysis the "law" implies a preferential increase in the production of capital goods (machinery and equipment).

Marx's model was in the forefront of the industrialization debate in the Soviet Union in the 1920s as well as in the discussion of long-term planning in India in the 1950s. Since these experiences have been treated at some length elsewhere (e.g., Brundenius 1984a, 1986), it is sufficient here to stress that for Feldman in the Soviet Union as well as for Mahalanobis in India (and later on, Raj and Sen), the fraction of investment allocated to the investment goods sector itself (and hence machinery and equipment) was the key element in the growth model of the economy.

One major flaw in the Feldman-Mahalanobis model, however, was that it excluded foreign trade and was based—at least implicitly—on the assumption of a closed economy. This is a highly unrealistic assumption today and could at best be valid for large economies with huge potential markets and with large untapped reserves of natural resources. The Raj-Sen model is more realistic since it allows for "stagnant foreign exchange earnings." The model demonstrates how such a rigid exchange constraint—rather typical for most non-oil exporting developing countries today—justifies the building up of a domestic capital goods industry. If limited foreign exchange is used to import consumer goods, then the economy will stagnate, yet if it is used to import capital goods for the production of consumer goods, there will be a steady rate of investment and a steady rate of growth. If, however, foreign exchange is used to import capital goods to expand the capital goods sector itself, then the capital goods sector will increase at an accelerated rate, with a resulting rise in the investment ratio and, consequently, the economy as a whole will tend to grow at an accelerated rate.

THE STRATEGY AND EXPERIENCE OF CUBA

Starting from Scratch

Cuba was basically a sugar economy in 1958, on the eve of the revolution. There had been a slow but clearly noticeable industralization process taking place since the end of World War II, but this proved to be a difficult phase since it met with much resistance from powerful sectors of the Cuban population. It is clear from reading some recently released documents from that period (CEE 1981a) that there were strong vested interests involved (particularly on the part of plantation owners) in adhering to the reciprocal trade treaties with the United States, which gave Cuban sugar preferential treatment in the U.S. market in return for tariff exemption on U.S. industrial exports to the island. The Cuban National Association of Manufacturers was not sufficiently strong to counter the vested interest in perpetuating dependency on the United States, with its retarding effects on the country's industrialization.

It has been estimated that at the end of the 1950s, sugar accounted for about one-fourth of total industrial output, while the whole metallurgical sector (including the mechanical industry) only represented 1.4 percent of industrial output (G. Rodríguez 1980: 145). The production of the engineering goods industries (ISIC 38) in the 1950s was characterized by small artisan workshops, low levels of mechanization, practically no engineers, and insufficient skills of the labor force (Castro and Fernández 1982: 16).

The obsolescence of the Cuban sugar industry was acutely apparent, with the most "modern" plant dating from 1927, and 40 percent of the *centrales* (sugar factories) built during the last century (ibid.). This obsolescence implied that most of the machinery, equipment, and spare parts for this industry were no longer produced on the world market, and it was therefore necessary to produce them nationally to guarantee continuing supplies.

When the revolutionary government took over in January 1959, capital goods production was not on the agenda. The main preoccupation of the government was to take care of the *immediate* social needs of the people by eradicating illiteracy, providing health care, reducing the tremendously high unemployment rates, and initiating redistributive reforms such as rent control and the agrarian reform (Brundenius 1984b: ch.3). It was more or less taken for granted that capital accumulation would occur almost automatically at a later stage.

Industrial production increased during the first years of the revolution, but mainly as a result of utilization of idle capacity. Several well-known economists visited the island in those first years, and they were all very optimistic about the prospects for the rapid industrialization of Cuba. It was in this mood that Michal Kalecki, the well-known Polish economist and planner, in 1960 sketched a five-year plan for the period 1961–65, basing his optimistic projections on demand criteria alone (as a result of income redistribution effects) and seriously neglecting supply conditions (Kalecki 1976). Kalecki projected an *annual* rate of growth of the Cuban economy of 13 percent, spearheaded by a spectacular growth of the capital goods sector of no less than 36 percent per year! It should be pointed out that the capital goods industries only accounted for an estimated 2.9 percent of total industrial output at the beginning of the plan period (see Table 6.1), but even so, Kalecki predicted the construction of a wide range of capital goods industries within such a short span of time.

In spite of mounting pressures against resources that were already being felt in 1961, the four-year plan (1962–65) presented by the government in the fall of 1961 contained much of the flavor of Kalecki's original sketch. At the center of this "first growth strategy" was rapid industrialization through a chain of import-substituting industries including metallurgy, chemical products, machinery, and even an assembly plant for passenger cars. Most of the machinery and equipment for these new plants was to be supplied by the Soviet Union and other socialist countries. Nowhere in the plan was it envisaged that there might be a curtailment of consumption via rationing as a consequence of this high investment rate. This was because of an underlying assumption that was more or less taken for granted: The rapid expansion of nonsugar agriculture would lead to self-sufficiency in food production and eliminate queuing and problems of food supply by the end of 1962 (Brundenius 1984b: 49).

Harsh reality very soon made these plans unworkable. Far from achieving an accelerated growth, the Cuban economy encountered more and more difficulties, especially after the United States announced a full-scale naval blockade against the island following the "missile crisis" in October 1962. The plan was soon abandoned altogether. Already in October 1960, President Eisenhower had imposed an embargo on exports to Cuba, effectively curtailing vital Cuban imports of raw materials and spare parts for its industry. In February 1962, President Kennedy extended the embargo to all imports from Cuba, those

Table 6.1. Gross Value of Production of Engineering Goods Industries and Total Industry in Constant (1981) Enterprise Prices (million pesos)

	Total industrial output[a]		Output of engineering goods industries (ISIC 38)		Engineering goods' share of total industry
	Value	Index	Value	Index	(%)
1961	2,567.8	46.6	73.4	18.6	2.9
1962	2,623.0	47.6	75.7	19.2	2.9
1963	2,584.4	46.9	74.8	19.0	2.9
1964	2,689.1	48.8	76.6	19.5	2.8
1965	2,793.8	50.7	68.2	17.3	2.4
1966	2,744.2	49.8	72.7	18.3	2.6
1967	3,041.7	55.2	76.6	19.5	2.5
1968	2,992.1	54.3	94.3	23.9	3.2
1969	2,959.1	53.7	87.4	22.2	3.0
1970	3,609.3	65.5	131.7	33.4	3.6
1971	3,818.7	69.3	160.0	40.6	4.2
1972	4,055.7	73.6	185.6	47.1	4.6
1973	4,540.6	82.4	249.7	63.4	5.5
1974	4,898.7	88.9	310.4	78.8	6.3
1975	5,585.7	100.0	404.2	100.0	7.2
1976	5,658.5	101.7	431.5	106.8	7.6
1977	5,831.3	104.4	458.3	113.4	7.9
1978	6,359.3	113.8	545.6	135.0	8.6
1979	6,532.0	116.9	630.6	156.0	9.7
1980	6,736.3	120.6	663.8	164.2	9.9
1981	7,729.2	138.4	795.4	196.8	10.3
1982	8,018.4	143.6	887.1	219.5	11.1
1983	8,403.8	150.5	1,042.6	257.9	12.4
1984	9,053.9	162.1	1,225.9	303.3	13.5
1985	9,621.4	172.2	1,361.6	336.9	14.2
1986	9,808.4	175.6	1,382.1	341.9	14.1
1987	9,445.5	169.1	1,162.7	287.7	12.3
1988[b]	9,719.4	174.0	1,218.0	301.3	12.5

Source: Series 1975–86 is constructed from CEE/AEC 1986 (table III.27); 1987 and 1988 preliminary figures from CEE/BEC 1987 (January–December) and 1988 (January–June); series 1961–75 (originally in 1965 prices) constructed from Brundenius (1984b: appendix table 1) and linked to 1975–88 series.
[a]Includes mining and electricity.
[b]Based on trend for January–June 1988.

coming directly from Cuba as well as via a third country, and ships going to Cuba were blacklisted and denied entry into U.S. ports.[2] Surrounded by hostile ex-trade partners, Cuba had to resort to foreign financing of its necessary imports of machinery and equipment (and even basic consumer goods) while, at the same time, measures were taken to guarantee a decent living standard to the majority of the population.

But even if economic growth in Cuba was faltering in the 1960s, this does not mean that there was no increase in capital goods production. On the contrary, the capital goods industry was the most rapidly expanding sector in the Cuban economy during the second half of the 1960s. In those years there was also a drastic restructuring of imports, with priority given to the import of machinery and equipment, especially that needed to increase worker productivity and land yields in agriculture.

In 1964 Ernesto "Che" Guevara, then Minister of Industry, inaugurated a mechanical plant in Santa Clara, the output of which was to supply the industries related to agriculture with spare parts and also, in the longer run, machinery and equipment. This is when Cuba's long, burdensome (but not always impatient) process of "learning by doing" began. The embargo imposed by the United States actually converted such a "learning process" from a virtue into a necessity. Shoemakers and carpenters were retrained to become skilled industrial workers, manufacturing spare parts for the old, obsolescent machine park of Cuban industry. When this process started in 1964, the capital goods industry in Cuba only employed between one and two thousand people. The Santa Clara plant was the largest, with 350 workers.[3]

The 1960s was thus a most difficult period in Cuba. Real GDP grew slowly, scarcely making up for the increase in population. But there were positive trends as well. The massive effort to mobilize resources for education and health and the gradual elimination of the specter of unemployment were important instruments in creating a well-educated, healthy, and motivated work force in Cuba—an important condition for the rapid economic transformation of the country.

Already in the 1960s there had been a modest, but nevertheless important, increase in nonsugar manufacturing activities, with an annual rate of growth of 4.1 percent between 1961 and 1970. Engineering goods broadly defined (ISIC 38) increased at an annual rate of 6.7 percent (see Table 6.1), far from the Kalecki dreams of 36 percent per year, but nevertheless a good start. Engineering goods still accounted for only 3.6 percent of total industrial output as of 1970.

The First Five-Year Plan (1976–1980)

During the first half of the following decade (1971–75), the Cuban economy experienced a boom. Real GDP is estimated to have increased at the rate of 7.8 percent per year. Nonsugar manufacturing grew by 10.8 percent per year and the engineering goods industries by no less than 24.5 percent per year (see Table 6.1). One likely explanation for this boom is that much of the construction work that was started in the late 1960s was completed during this period. The construction sector grew at a rate of 22.6 percent during the first half of the 1970s. Gross investments again started to increase after having stagnated in the 1960s. Gross investments reached the amount of 2.3 billion pesos by 1975, or almost three times the 1970 level (see Table 6.2). Gross investments as a share of the

Table 6.2. Gross Investments and Global Social Product, 1963–87 (million pesos, current prices)

	Gross investments	Global social product	GI/GSP (%)
1963	732.6	6,013.2	12.2
1964	809.5	6,454.5	12.5
1965	841.7	6,770.9	12.4
1966	935.1	6,709.3	13.9
1967	1,031.5	7,211.6	14.3
1968	918.0	7,330.9	12.5
1969	896.4	7,236.1	12.4
1970	800.1	8,356.0	9.6
1971	963.8	8,966.5	10.7
1972	1,094.0	10,417.9	10.5
1973	1,475.0	11,921.8	12.4
1974	1,711.9	13,149.0	13.0
1975	2,304.2	14,063.4	16.4
1976	2,587.4	14,458.2	17.9
1977	2,765.9	14,772.8	18.7
1978	2,623.6	16,457.6	15.9
1979	2,605.8	16,986.8	15.3
1980	2,739.1	17,605.6	15.6
1981	3,386.1	22,172.5	15.3
1982	2,995.2	23,112.8	13.0
1983	3,408.5	24,336.9	14.0
1984	3,989.4	26,052.7	15.3
1985	4,289.3	26,956.7	14.9
1986	4,326.9	26,473.6	16.3
1987	3,751.9	25,795.8	14.5

Sources: DEC/BEC 1968, 1971; CEE/AEC 1974, 1979, 1981, 1982, 1984, 1986; CEE/BEC January–December 1987; CEE, *Cuba en cifras* (1981c).

global social product (GSP) grew from a record low of 9.6 percent in 1970 to 16.4 percent in 1975.

The economic strategy behind the boom in the 1970s had been formulated already in the 1960s. Miguel Figueras, until April 1986 Vice-Minister of the Central Planning Board and in the 1960s a close aide of Che Guevara, gives an interesting account of how the strategy was gradually hammered out (Figueras 1985: 36–37).

It was clear, says Figueras, that one of the objectives of the blockade imposed by the United States was to paralyze the Cuban economy (by preventing the flow of spare parts to U.S.-made machinery, which accounted for some 90 percent of the total machine park). In view of this situation, the revolutionary government drew up the following strategy:

1. To attempt to find equivalent spare parts and components in the socialist countries and, in the cases where such goods were not available, to reach

assistance agreements with those countries for the production of such goods specifically for Cuba.

2. To try to purchase similar spare parts when possible from capitalist countries maintaining relations with Cuba. This proved to be extremely difficult for two reasons: lack of foreign exchange (in convertible currencies) and because of the pressure exercised by the United States on Western countries to not trade with Cuba.

3. To develop a massive national movement for the production of spare parts and to strengthen interplant collaboration in order to find joint solutions. This should be accomplished by:

(i) having the workshops in each plant fabricate (or find out how to fabricate) the greatest number of spare parts and attempt to fabricate spare parts for other plants less skilled in this field;

(ii) creating specialized factories for the production of spare parts, training and upgrading workers on the job, acquiring the necessary machine tools from the socialist countries, and requesting the assistance of technical expertise from these countries in training and, if necessary, supervising production;

(iii) asking the workers and technicians in the few mechanical industries that existed at the time (most of them supplying the sugar industry) to increase production and to try to incorporate new types of components and equipment in their lines of production.

That was the recipe followed and, according to Figueras, it caused the U.S. embargo to fail. In view of the accelerated growth of the economy during the first half of the 1970s, the projections for the first five-year plan (1976–80) were also cautiously optimistic. JUCEPLAN (the central planning agency) prepared three variants of the plan to allow for possible reverses in the price of sugar (which in 1974 had skyrocketed to unprecedented levels). Since prices fell more than expected (much more than even the most pessimistic variant of the plan had foreseen), 22 major investment projects had to be cancelled, most of which were to be financed with credit lines from the West (Brundenius 1984b: 58). Thanks to steadily improving terms of trade with the Soviet Union, the Cuban trade balance with that country was favorable in 1976 for the first time since the early 1960s.

The first five-year plan thus projected continuing accelerated growth and the completion of a number of ambitious industrial projects. Among the industrial projects that were planned and actually executed during this period were two cement plants with an annual capacity of three million tons, two medium-sized sugar mills (the first ones to be built since 1927), four bulk sugar terminals, one modern textile plant, two piping and irrigation spray unit factories, one plant producing wheels for heavy equipment, and the start of the modernization of the nickel refining and petroleum refining plants (CEE 1981b). It should be mentioned that in the case of the sugar factories, all of the technical plans were designed in Cuba and more than 60 percent of the machinery, including the mechanized and automated units, were of Cuban origin (ibid.). The most successful part of the Cuban expansion program for its capital goods sector has no doubt been the development of equipment for the sugar industry.

The growth rate of the economy during the first five-year plan was considerably lower than expected. National income grew at a rate of only 3 percent (compared with the originally planned rate of 6 percent), agriculture by 0.4 percent, and industry by 1.9 percent (see Table 6.3). On the other hand, the investment goods industries grew considerably. The construction sector, for instance, grew at a rate of 4.6 percent, and the gross value of output of the engineering goods industries increased by 10.3 percent per annum.

During the first five-year plan, the share of engineering goods in total industrial output increased from 7.6 percent in 1976 to 9.9 percent in 1980 (Table 6.1). An increasing share of investment also went to the engineering goods industries as well as to industrial activities as a whole (see Table 6.4).

Table 6.3. Growth Rates During the Five-Year Plans

	National income[a]	Agriculture[b]	Construction[b]	Industry[b]	Engineering goods industry[c]	Gross investments
First Plan (1976–80)						
1976	5.1	3.1	5.4	4.4	6.8	12.3
1977	8.3	4.8	10.6	0.7	6.0	6.9
1978	6.9	7.6	4.8	8.6	20.2	−5.1
1979	0.7	−20.0	−11.6	−0.4	15.2	−0.7
1980	−5.2	−10.2	13.8	−3.1	4.1	5.1
Average 1976–80	3.0	0.4	4.2	1.9	10.3	3.5
Second Plan (1981–85)						
1981	20.8	18.7	25.1	29.8	23.9	23.6
1982	5.0	−5.2	1.1	6.2	11.8	11.5
1983	5.5	−8.5	14.2	7.1	18.2	13.8
1984	7.4	2.7	19.2	13.4	16.5	17.0
1985[d]	4.8	4.2	2.7	6.6	7.9	2.4
Average 1981–85	8.6	1.9	12.1	12.3	15.6	8.3

Sources: CEE/AEC 1984, (table III.5) and CEE/BEC (November 1985). Reprinted from Brundenius 1987a.
[a]National income (or net material product) equals gross value of production minus productive consumption in the productive sphere (that is, agriculture, industry, construction, transport, communication, and trade).
[b]Net value of production.
[c]Gross value of production.
[d]Estimate based on first 11 months of 1985.

Table 6.4. Gross Investments in Agriculture and Industry, 1974–87 (million pesos, current prices)

	Total economy		Agriculture		Industry		Engineering industry	
	Value	%	Value	%	Value	%	Value	%
1974	1,711.9	100.0	466.3	27.2	328.2	19.2	n.a.	n.a.
1975	2,304.2	100.0	559.6	24.3	630.1	27.3	63.2	2.7
1976	2,587.4	100.0	553.9	21.4	807.9	31.2	82.9	3.2
1977	2,756.9	100.0	540.1	19.5	966.5	34.9	93.7	3.4
1978	2,634.6	100.0	466.0	17.8	987.1	34.2	97.7	3.7
1979	2,605.8	100.0	435.5	16.7	1,003.7	38.5	148.0	5.7
1980	2,739.1	100.0	584.5	21.3	1,007.1	36.8	145.0	5.3
1981	3,386.1	100.0	895.5	26.4	1,176.6	34.7	142.6	4.2
1982	2,995.2	100.0	737.1	24.6	1,058.5	35.3	143.5	4.8
1983	3,408.5	100.0	760.5	22.3	1,244.0	36.5	125.5	3.7
1984	3,989.4	100.0	875.8	22.0	1,422.5	35.7	135.3	3.4
1985	4,289.3	100.0	933.6	21.8	1,655.9	38.6	156.0	3.6
1986	4,326.9	100.0	975.1	22.5	1,472.9	34.0	129.9	3.0
1987	3,751.9	100.0	862.3	23.0	1,221.8	32.6	n.a.	n.a.

Sources: CEE/AEC 1981, 1982, 1983, 1984, and 1986; CEE/BEC (January–December 1987).

The Second Five-Year Plan (1981–85)

When the guidelines for the second five-year plan (1981–85) were drawn up in 1980, the prospects for its implementation seemed poor. The last year of the first plan (1980) had ended with a considerable slowing down of growth rates on practically all fronts, and targets had not been fulfilled in a number of areas. Accordingly, the growth rates for the second plan were set more realistically, with an overall rate of growth for the economy of 5 percent per annum (PCC 1981). However, it was considered that the capital goods sector should be instrumental in making this growth target realistic. The capital goods industries were, according to the plan, expected to increase at an impressive rate of 12 to 15 percent per year. The detailed plan for these industries spelled out these ambitions in the following terms:

- To start, during the five-year period, the construction of no fewer than 7 new sugar mills; to extend 23 and modernize 18 of the existing ones, to reach a potential daily grinding capacity of about 690,000 tons of cane in 1985.
- To continue the development of engineering production for the sugar industry, in order to meet its growth plans. To reduce the use of imported equipment and components, and to produce these items for export.
- To achieve sustained growth in the production of the nonelectrical machinery and metal products industries to meet demand more fully. To eliminate imports and increase participation in exporting.
- To increase the production of agricultural machinery, equipment, and implements. To develop new lines of machinery and equipment with a

view to guaranteeing to a larger extent the internal demand and the replacement of imports.

- To increase and develop the production of new lines of transport equipment, to work on the production of diesel engines on an experimental scale, and to evaluate the results.
- To increase the production of machinery and equipment for the sugar industry, including substantial parts of sugar mills and refineries with the aim of guaranteeing national needs, and of converting this production into one of the fundamental export lines of the engineering industry.
- To increase and develop the production of steel structures and technological equipment, including complete lines and plants; to increase the national production of equipment; and to develop exports.
- To increase production of those goods that support construction activities, such as moulds for concrete building elements, bronze fittings, and locks and accessories for, *inter alia*, sanitary fixtures.
- To raise the utilization of production capacities for stainless steel equipment, parts, and spares.
- To develop the production of fishing and leisure craft, for both export and for replacement, with the introduction of more productive technologies as well as the improvement of both quality and design, according to end use and destination.
- To encourage the production of technical means for computing, with a view toward contributing to national needs and to creating new export products (Castro and Fernández 1982: 55–56).

As seen from this listing of medium-term goals, during the plan period the Cuban capital goods industry would continue to specialize in the construction of machinery, equipment, and spare parts, including the production of complete plants. At the same time, priority would

continue to be given to the creation of a solid base for the development, design, planning and manufacture of new types and models of equipment for automobile transport (both freight and passenger) and for the railways, including technical and feasibility studies, technical projects, a greater part of the equipment (60% or more), with the construction, erection and commissioning of the said installations with the object of continuing to replace imports of those products which can be manufactured in the country and also to create new and exportable items. (Castro and Fernández 1982: 4)

The plan period could not have gotten off to a better start. In 1981 there was a tremendous boom in the economy, with two-digit growth rates (see Table 6.3). Although growth rates have since tapered off, there seems to be little doubt that most of the overall objectives of the 1981–85 plan were fulfilled. By the end of the plan period, Cuba produced 1.36 billion pesos worth of engineering goods, accounting for 14.2 percent of total industrial output (see Table 6.1), a doubling of the production level of 1980.

The Capital Goods Industries

Let us now take a closer look at the capital goods industries in Cuba. As mentioned before,[4] it is not always easy to separate purely capital goods (machinery and equipment) from engineering goods in general (which also include consumer durables). Cuban statistics, however, allow for the distinction between nonelectrical machinery, electrical machinery, and metal products, groups that more or less correspond to the United Nations International Standard Industrial Classification of All Industrial Activities (ISIC), namely ISIC 381 (fabricated metal products), ISIC 382 (manufacture of nonelectrical machinery), ISIC 383 (manufacture of electrical machinery and appliances), and ISIC 384 (manufacture of transport equipment). Such a breakdown is available for Cuba after 1975, and production figures for these three branches are shown in Table 6.5.

As can be seen from Table 6.5, the most significant increase has taken place in the nonelectrical machinery sector (which in Cuban statistics includes transport equipment) with an almost fourfold production increase between 1975 and 1985. The electrical machinery sector experienced a threefold increase in the same period, while the metal products sector more than doubled its output. All three subsectors accelerated output growth during the second plan (1981–85): nonelectrical machinery went from a growth rate of 11.9 percent during the first plan to a rate of 15.5 percent during the second plan, electrical machinery from 8.3 percent during the first plan to 18.7 percent during the second plan, and metal products from 7.0 percent during the first plan to 13.1 percent during the second.

Table 6.5. Gross Value of Production of Engineering Goods Industries, 1975–86 (million pesos, 1981 enterprise prices)

	Nonelectrical machinery		Electrical machinery		Metal products		Total	
	Value	Index	Value	Index	Value	Index	Value	Index
1975	262.6	100.0	51.5	100.0	90.1	100.0	404.2	100.0
1976	284.5	108.4	53.3	103.5	93.7	104.0	431.5	106.8
1977	303.1	115.5	56.8	110.3	98.4	109.2	458.3	113.4
1978	367.2	139.9	65.0	126.2	113.4	125.9	545.6	135.0
1979	431.2	164.3	79.6	154.6	119.8	133.0	630.6	156.0
1980	460.8	175.5	76.6	148.7	126.4	140.3	663.8	164.2
1981	553.4	210.8	100.6	195.3	141.4	156.9	795.4	196.8
1982	636.9	242.6	92.1	178.8	158.1	175.5	887.1	219.5
1983	738.6	281.4	118.3	229.7	185.7	206.1	1,042.6	257.9
1984	872.5	332.4	147.6	286.6	205.8	228.4	1,225.9	303.3
1985	946.4	360.5	180.8	351.1	234.4	260.2	1,361.6	336.9
1986	922.7	351.5	206.5	401.0	252.9	280.7	1,382.1	341.9

Sources: CEE/AEC 1985, 1986.

A closer look at the three branches reveals that nonelectrical machinery is by far the most important of the engineering goods industries, accounting for 7.2 percent of total industrial output in 1981 and 9.3 percent in 1984 (see Table 6.6). If anything, these shares are probably understated due to the tendency in Cuba (and in other centrally planned economies) to price capital goods low. In terms of employment, the nonelectrical machinery branch is even more significant, with 12.2 percent of total industrial employment in 1981 and 12.4 percent in 1984. The contribution of electrical machinery and metal products is much more modest both in terms of output and employment (between 3 percent and 4 percent together in both 1981 and 1984).

Measured labor productivity is considerably lower in the engineering goods industry than in industry as a whole (perhaps a function of pricing policy more than anything else), although the gap narrowed significantly between 1981 and 1984 (Table 6.6). Productivity is highest in the metal products sector, which is only slightly below the industrial average, with nonelectrical machinery falling far behind in 1981. The nonelectrical machinery sector, however, seems to be the most dynamic, and by 1984 the productivity gap had narrowed considerably. Between 1981 and 1984 labor productivity increased by 35 percent in the nonelectrical machinery sector, by 24 percent in the electrical machinery sector, and by 11 percent in the metal products sector—compared with only 5 percent for the industry as a whole. Average salaries increased in a more uniform pattern between 1981 and 1984, rising by around 10 to 11 percent compared with an industrial average of 9 percent. In spite of much talk in Cuba about the need to link wages to productivity, the data in Table 6.6 question whether such a policy is indeed being implemented. It seems, rather, that wage increases in Cuban industry are annually decided at a uniform rate, irrespective of sector productivity.

In 1981 the capital invested in the engineering goods industries amounted to 481 million pesos, compared with a sector gross value of output of 795 million pesos. This suggests a capital/gross output ratio of .60, lower than the industrial average of .89 in that same year. By 1984 this gap had widened, implying that both the average and incremental productivity of the capital invested in the engineering goods sector is higher than for industry as a whole. Annual gross investments in the sector averaged 10 percent of total industrial investments during the first three years of the first plan, then increased to around 15 percent in 1979 and 1980, but the share then gradually went down again to around 10 percent by the end of the second plan (see Table 6.3).

The rate of investment has been highest in the nonelectrical machinery branch. Capital invested in that subsector increased by 55 percent between 1981 and 1984, compared with an industrial average of 28 percent. The nonelectrical machinery sector is also the most important capital goods–producing sector. According to a special, unpublished survey of the most important enterprises producing capital goods (or *medios de producción*—means of produc-

Table 6.6. Engineering Goods Industries: Basic Indicators, 1981 and 1984

	Nonelectrical machinery (ISIC 382 and 384)	Electrical machinery (ISIC 383)	Metal products (ISIC 381)	Engineering goods industry (ISIC 38)	Total industry
1981					
Gross value of production (MMP)[a]	553.4	100.6	141.4	795.4	7,729.2
Number employed (000)	70.5	12.3	11.2	94.0	576.4
Productivity[b]	7,849.0	8,178.0	12,625.0	8,462.0	13,409.0
Average salary/year	2,220.0	2,040.0	2,184.0	2,196.0	2,136.0
Gross investments (MMP)	112.9	19.7	10.0	142.6	1,176.6
Capital invested (MMP)[c]	350.7	71.0	59.2	480.9	6,889.9
Investment ratio	0.20	0.20	0.07	0.18	0.15
Capital/output ratio	0.63	0.71	0.42	0.60	0.89
1984					
Gross value of production (MMP)[a]	876.2	144.5	203.9	1,224.6	9,377.4
Number of employed (000)	82.8	14.2	14.6	111.6	665.7
Productivity[b]	10,582.0	10,176.0	13,966.0	10,973.0	14,087.0
Average salary/month	2,460.0	2,256.0	2,412.0	2,428.0	2,328.0
Gross investments (MMP)	103.7	12.6	19.0	135.3	1,422.5
Capital invested (MMP)[c]	544.9	79.1	87.9	711.9	8,788.0
Investment ratio	0.12	0.09	0.09	0.11	0.15
Capital/output ratio	0.62	0.55	0.43	0.58	0.94

Source: CEE/AEC 1984 and data supplied to the authors by CEE. Reprinted from Brundenius 1987a.
[a]Million pesos.
[b]Gross value of production per worker (pesos).
[c]At year end.

tion),[5] no less than 84 percent of the capital goods produced in Cuba in 1983 originated in that subsector. The survey comprises 45 of the 175 enterprises producing engineering goods in Cuba. The capital goods production of these 45 enterprises accounted for 37 percent of total engineering goods output in Cuba in 1983. The most important goods produced by the same enterprises in 1983 were: transport equipment (buses, trucks, railway wagons, fishing boats)— 23.8 percent; agricultural machinery and equipment (combine-harvesters, plows, harrows, trailers, towed scrappers, seed drills, and irrigation and planting equipment)—19.7 percent; and machinery and equipment for the sugar industry (including boilers and mill tandems)—8.6 percent. Over half of the output (or 52.1 percent) was thus accounted for by these three types of machinery, all of which are part of the "nonelectrical machinery" branch. Other capital goods covered by the survey included water pumps, industrial tanks, lathes, cranes, and prefabricated steel dies and moulds. The capital goods produced by the electrical machinery sector are mainly found in the nascent computer industry, which as of 1983 only accounted for some 2 percent of the total output of capital goods in Cuba.

One interesting aspect of the development of the capital goods industries in Cuba is that an obvious effort has been made to spread the industries around the island, instead of concentrating most of the production in the largest city, Havana, as is so often the case in developing countries.[6] Thus, according to the survey, no less than 59 percent of the capital goods production occurred outside the city of Havana. In fact, some of the largest capital goods industries are found in the provinces of Villa Clara and Holguín. The largest capital goods-producing plant in Cuba, in terms of employment, is the earlier mentioned Santa Clara mechanical plant, with 2,388 people on the payroll, followed by the combine-harvester plant in the eastern part of the island in Holguín, with 2,301 people employed. Most of the larger capital goods–producing industries in Cuba were either constructed or largely expanded during the latter part of the 1970s or early 1980s.

AGRICULTURAL MACHINERY—THE BASE

It is quite clear that the strategy of building up a capital goods industry in Cuba has been based on the need to supply agriculture with the machinery and equipment requisite for raising productivity and efficiency. This was envisaged already in 1964 by Ernesto "Che" Guevara when, as Minister of Industry, he inaugurated the Santa Clara mechanical plant.[7] According to Guevara, the production of agricultural machinery for the needs of not only the Cuban sugar industry, but also nonsugar agriculture, would be the cornerstone in the Cuban capital goods industry. From the earlier mentioned survey, it is also clear that machinery and equipment production designated for agriculture accounts for the lion's share of capital goods output in Cuba. Machinery and equipment for the sugar industry and other agricultural machinery account for almost 30 percent of capital goods production. This, however, is certainly an underestimate of agriculture-related capital goods production, as several other types of machinery and equipment (such as tracks, railway equipment, water pumps, etc.) are also used in agricultural activities.

The role of agricultural machinery as a point of entry into capital goods production is also stressed by the United Nations Industrial Development Organization, (UNIDO 1985). In a worldwide study on the agricultural machinery industry in 1979, UNIDO classified agricultural machinery into four categories in accordance with the technical complexities involved (UNIDO 1979).

Category A: Hand tools, very simple equipment, and animal-drawn implements
Category B: Simple equipment and tractor-drawn implements
Category C: Machines and items of equipment, tractor-drawn machinery
Category D: Self-propelled power machines and stationary equipment of a high technological level

Although this categorization is useful as a guide to the complexities involved in the production of various types of agricultural machinery and equipment, it no doubt oversimplifies the difficulties entailed in moving from one category to the other. As Hans Gustafsson has pointed out in an interesting essay criticizing the UNIDO approach (Gustafsson 1986), it is not obvious that a country that produces category A and B goods automatically will move up to category C and D levels, which are much more technologically complex, requiring different and much more advanced technical skills. A true indigenous capability to manufacture capital goods, such as pumps, valves, turbines, gearboxes, speed-reducers, and engines does not exist unless a country has the technical capabilities to manufacture a significant proportion of the relevant components and subassemblies that together constitute the final products. Consequently, according to Gustafsson,

> in order to serve as a point of entry into the production of capital goods, agricultural mechanization must generate technical capabilities and form an industrial base that is conducive to the manufacture of parts and components which are similar or near similar to the essential constituent parts of other capital goods. It is a necessary condition that various standard technologies are mastered and that a certain degree of specialization is attained in some activities. This would include, among other things: gear-making, heat treatment, steel foundry, special and precision machining, press forging just to name a few key technologies. (Ibid.)

The experience of Cuba is a case in point. Cuba had no doubt already mastered the techniques of producing A and B goods before the revolution. Then, when the U.S. embargo of the island in the early 1960s made the production of spare parts for existing machinery—especially in the sugar industry—necessary for survival, Cuba "moved up" to the production of C goods. Although it is no doubt true that much of the success in this field can be attributed to "learning by doing," the success would have remained quite limited if Cuba had not at the same time launched a massive educational campaign to upgrade the skills of the labor force, among other things sending thousands of workers and engineers abroad for training.

The real breakthrough came in the 1970s when Cuba started producing advanced machinery and equipment, all of it Cuban designed, for the sugar industry. Already in 1965 a program had been set up in cooperation with several socialist countries for the modernization of the sugar factories. As a result, most of the sugar mills were modernized or their capacity expanded during the 1970s. By 1980 obsolete equipment had been reduced to 50 percent, and by 1985 this figure was expected to have decreased to 36 percent (MINAZ n.d.: 20). The year 1976 also marked the initiation of construction of completely new sugar mills, entirely designed by Cuban engineers and with 60 percent of the equipment produced in Cuba (most of it at the expanded Santa Clara mechanical plant).

Cuba "moved up" to the production of category D goods (self-propelled power machines) in 1977, when a plant was set up in Holguín for the mass production of sugar combine-harvesters. But this step had been in no way easy. The story behind this success is briefly as follows.

In the early 1960s, just after the revolution, sugar cane was cut entirely by manual labor (*braceros*) in Cuba. To increase efficiency—but also to eliminate the arduous work of *braceros*—the revolutionary government soon made a commitment to rapidly introduce and diffuse mechanization in the sugar fields of the island. The whole decade of the 1960s was, however, filled with disappointments. Much effort went into the design of a Cuban-made harvester. The first model, named "Henderson" after a Cuban engineer, was a simple machine that would be easy to construct in Cuba by adapting a heavy tractor.[8] A total of 148 units were produced for the 1969/70 *zafra* (sugar harvest) at the Santa Clara mechanical plant. But even with the introduction of these Henderson harvesters, mechanization was as low as 1 percent during the 1970 *zafra*. The Henderson machine, however, was not very successful (especially since it could not clean extraneous matter from the cane), and it was decided to discontinue production in 1972.

While working on the Henderson model, however, the same group of Cuban engineers had been working on the design of a new machine that would be able to cut and clean as well as load efficiently. The test results were so positive that in 1968 Castro symbolically named the machine *Libertadora*, since it would now liberate field labor from the burden of cutting cane by hand. The model was gradually modified, and 24 units were produced at the Santa Clara plant for the 1969 *zafra*. The *Libertadora* was built on the chassis of a Soviet-made sugar harvester that had been taken out of operation in 1968. In 1970 more powerful Libertadora models were produced, and the upgraded 1400 model turned out to be quite successful. At about that time negotiations had started with the West German company Claas Maschinenfabrik for collaboration on the large-scale manufacture of a modified *Libertadora*. The patent rights were handed over to the Germans in exchange for an agreement allowing the Cubans to import the machine at a subsidized price (Edquist 1985: 48–49).

Claas Maschinenfabrik was evidently not interested in exploiting the patent rights for the home market, since there is no cane production in Germany. Thus this transfer of technology from the developing country, Cuba, to West Germany meant that Claas Maschinenfabrik could begin mass production of a cane combine-harvester intended for export. Since 1972 Claas has reportedly exported the Libertadora 1400 model to 44 countries, including the United States (which paradoxically—at least officially—still prohibits products of Cuban origin!). Claas has sold 169 units to Cuba, 121 to Argentina, 99 to the United States, and 82 to Mexico, just to mention a few markets (ibid.: 129).

An interesting and controversial question then arises. Why did the Cubans give a West German firm the patent rights for a machine they had designed? Presumably there was no other viable alternative open to the Cubans at the time. The Cubans were simply incapable of anything beyond the basic design stage; they were not then able to carry out detailed design, nor were they able to manufacture complicated pieces of equipment on a large scale. The mechanical industry was not developed enough to handle all the sophisticated stages involved. For example, Cuba did not possess an adequate technical capability in the field of hydraulic components, which the production of the Libertadora 1400 required. One commentator concluded that "an important lesson of the Libertadora story is that it is easier for a developing country to design a machine indigenously than to produce it on a large scale" (ibid.: 130).

But the story does not end here. In 1969 Cuban engineers had constructed another prototype intended to cut green cane in the field and provide high yields. After some trial runs the prototype was sent to the Soviet Union, within the framework of a collaboration agreement. There two identical prototypes were constructed, and after several modifications and further testing in Cuba serial production of this Cuban-Soviet designed machine, named KTP-1,[9] was begun in the Soviet Union in 1973. In that same year, 50 KTP-1 units were sold to Cuba, and by the mid-1970s there was a yearly import of some 200–300 units.

The KTP-1 model is a self-propelled machine that can efficiently cut cane at the ground level, chop it into pieces, clean it, and subsequently deposit it on a cart that follows the combine. The KTP-1 is similar in principle to the Massey-Ferguson 201, also introduced on a mass scale into Cuba (imported from Australia) in the 1970s (Edquist 1985: 52).

In 1977 a huge plant was inaugurated by Fidel Castro in Holguín. The plant, named "60th Anniversary of the October Revolution," exclusively produces sugar combine-harvesters—at first only the KTP-1 model, but recently also a

Table 6.7. Mechanization of Sugar Harvest by Type of Harvester, 1972–83 (percentages)

| | Type of harvester | | | Total cut by harvester |
	MF-201	Libertadora 1400	KTP-1	
1972	4	1	—	7[a]
1973	1	3	1	11[a]
1974	10	4	4	18
1975	12	4	9	25
1976	13	5	14	32
1977	13	4	19	36
1978	10	4	24	38
1979	10	4	28	42
1980	9	4	32	45
1981	8	3	36	47
1982	6	3	41	50
1983	5	2	45	52

Source: Information supplied by Ing. Jorge Abreu. Deputy Director of Research of CICMA. Reprinted from Brundenius 1987a.
[a]Including other types of harvesters (mainly Henderson).

more sophisticated version, the KTP-2. This plant today produces some 650 units per year, making it by far the largest cane combine-harvester plant in the world.

As of 1983, 52 percent of the cane cutting in Cuba was carried out by combine-harvesters (today the figure is over 63 percent); in 1970 the level of mechanization had been only 1 percent. Most (about 86 percent) of the mechanical harvesting is carried out by the KTP-1, the remainder by the MF-201 and the Libertadora 1400 (see Table 6.7). The total number of cane harvesters operating in Cuba increased from 172 units in 1971 to 1,007 to 1975 (of which there were 422 KTP-1, 418 MF-201, and 167 Libertadora 1400), 2,432 in 1980 (of which there were 1,901 KTP-1, 365 MF-201, and 157 Libertadora 1400), and to no less than 3,727 units in 1983 (of which there were 3,453 KTP-1, 160 MF-201, and 114 Libertadora 1400).[10]

FROM IMPORT SUBSTITUTION TO EXPORT PROMOTION?

Cuba has undoubtedly made significant progress in building a domestic capital goods industry since the revolution. It is estimated that the domestic procurement ratio (DPR)—that is, the ratio of apparent consumption produced by domestic industry—for capital goods today is about 28 percent (see Table 6.8). Compared with the ratio in 1970 (15.1 percent), the increase in the DPR has been remarkable indeed. It should also be mentioned that there is a slight bias in the estimates since production is recorded in constant (1981) prices, while import figures are given in current prices, underestimating apparent consump-

Table 6.8. Production, Imports, and Apparent Consumption of Machinery and Equipment[a] 1958–86 (million pesos)

	Production[b] (1)	Imports (2)	Apparent consumption (3)	Domestic procurement ratio (4) = (1)/(3)
1958	48.2[c]	239.3	287.5	16.8[c]
1970	84.9	477.4	562.3	15.1
1975	307.1	969.5	1,276.6	24.1
1980	528.0	1,638.7	2,166.7	24.4
1981	553.4	1,719.7	2,273.1	24.3
1982	642.7	1,712.3	2,355.0	27.3
1983	746.0	1,903.0	2,649.0	28.3
1984	876.2	2,201.1	3,077.3	28.5
1985	958.8	2,419.3	3,378.1	28.4
1986	890.3	2,329.3	3,219.6	27.7

Source: Table 6.1 and DEC/BEC 1968 and 1971; CEE/AEC 1974, 1979, 1982, 1983, 1984, 1986.
[a]Nonelectrical machinery only (including transport equipment).
[b]Constant prices.
[c]Estimate.

tion (and hence overestimating the DPR) for earlier years.

The domestic procurement ratio is, however, still considerably lower in Cuba than in NICs such as Brazil, Mexico, and South Korea (UNCTAD 1985: table III.2). Cuba will no doubt increase its DPR in the coming years, but there is obviously a limit to the possible success of import substitution industrialization in a country with a market of only 10.3 million inhabitants. A small or medium-sized country industrializing through import substitution must sooner or later begin to export, and capital goods are no exception. There are important economies of scale in capital goods production, and a strategy of self-reliance aimed at production for the home market alone might easily prove both costly and counterproductive in the long run.[11]

But there then arises the problem of how to succeed on the international market, where sharp competition prevails. On top of everything else, the international market for agricultural machinery, Cuba's relative strength, is dominated by large transnational corporations. Cuba will benefit from its integration with the CMEA countries[12] and thereby find an important outlet for exports of some capital goods (Figueras 1985: 53–54; also see Bulnes and Figueras 1987). At a recent conference for Cuban exporters of engineering goods (organized by SIME, the Steel and Mechanical Industry Ministry), it was announced that the Cuban-made truck Taino was being tested in the German Democratic Republic for possible future sale to that country (*Bohemia*, May 9, 1986).

The most interesting future export market for Cuban capital goods is probably other developing countries, especially the poorer and less developed ones, where Cuba might offer cheaper goods (although not necessarily with better quality) and better terms than the large transnational corporations. As a case in point, Cuba is already selling the KTP-1 harvester to Nicaragua. But would the KTP-1 stand a chance in open competition with, let us say, the Claas Libertadora? At least price-wise it would, since the cost of production of the KTP-1 (38,000 pesos, or $38,000 at the current official exchange rate) is reportedly less than half the cost of production of the Claas Libertadora.[13]

EXPANSION OF THE ELECTRONICS AND INFORMATICS INDUSTRY

Although nonelectrical machinery still accounts for the lion's share of capital goods output in Cuba, the electronics industry is the fastest expanding branch (see Table 6.5). The electronics industry is still relatively small, accounting for about 13 percent of total capital goods output in 1986. Before 1959, there was practically no production at all of electronics goods in Cuba or even of electrical machinery, and the automated processing of information was still in an embryonic state. It is only after 1959 that one could really talk about the first stage of development of an electronics and electrical machinery industry in the country (Vega et al. 1987).

From an organizational point of view, important steps were taken with the creation of EMPRODA (Empresa de Procesamiento de Datos) in 1963, with the foundation of CAI (Centro de Automatización Industrial) within the Sugar Ministry in 1964, and with the introduction of the so-called Plan Cálculo within the framework of JUCEPLAN in 1968.

With respect to electronics production, a first step was taken in 1960 with the installation of a Polish radio assembly plant, which produced some 250,000 units between 1962 and 1968. In 1964, the Ministry of Communications set up a central laboratory of telecommunications (LACETEL) that started research in this field. It was also during the first years of the 1960s that the first electronic components were being produced at the University of Havana, and a technology was developed for the production of the first MOS circuits—although with quite a low integration level (share of total value of the product produced in the country).

During this time a center on digital research (CID), also affiliated with the University of Havana, was created to study the feasibility of designing and manufacturing a Cuban minicomputer to resolve the railway traffic problems in the sugar industry. In 1970 this center produced the first Cuban-designed minicomputer, the CID 201 model, an achievement that marked the beginning of a new era in computer development in the country (Carnota 1972).

During the period 1971–75, as industrial growth gained momentum, conditions were gradually created for the application of computer technology in the country, and national production of minicomputers started—although on a limited scale. During the first five-year plan (1976–80), the policy of computer development concentrated on the preparation of technical skills to match the demand of the nascent electronics industry and on increasing the production of components, while gradually incorporating more advanced technologies and developing the production of minicomputers. In 1976 the National Institute of Automated Systems and Computer Techniques (INSAC) was created as the agency in charge of orienting, managing, and controlling the application of state policy to activities related to automated management systems and computer techniques (Santana 1987).

The electrical and electronics branch grew at average annual rate of 8.3 percent during the first plan, and its share of industrial value added increased from 0.9 percent in 1975 to 2.0 percent in 1980. Productivity gains were slow, however, increasing at a rate of only 1.3 percent per year.

During the second plan (1981–85), and especially during the second part of it, measures were taken to ensure an accelerated production of data processing equipment, striving for higher local integration as well as higher integration with the CMEA countries. Production of software also started during this period.

In 1983 a plant was set up in Pinar del Rio for the production of electronic components, with a capacity to produce 42.2 million components a year (CEE 1986). In 1984 COPEXTEL (Combinado para la Producción y Exportación de Tecnología Electrónica), an enterprise specifically aimed at developing new exports, was set up in the outskirts of Havana. COPEXTEL has two subsidiaries: LTEL, which produces and commercializes hardware, and SOFTEL, which manufactures and commercializes software.

During this period several other plants also initiated production of electronic equipment, including the Combinado de Medios Técnicos de Computación and a plant for printed circuit boards, both in Havana. In 1982 EICISOFT, a research center at SIME (the metallurgy and machinery ministry), was established for the study of data processing and design of software. Finally, a research institute (Instituto de Materiales y Reactivos para la Electrónica— IMRE) was set up at the University of Havana.

Skill preparation continued at an accelerated rate during the second plan. There were 3,061 engineers specializing in electronics or related fields who graduated from universities during 1980–86, plus an additional 7,114 electronics specialists who graduated from secondary technical schools. At the same time, data processing was introduced in secondary education and was expanded in higher education.

The overall growth rate of the electrical and electronics industry was 18.0 percent per year between 1980 and 1985, and its share of industrial value added jumped from 2.0 percent to 4.8 percent in the period. The number employed in the sector expanded by 67 percent, with a productivity growth of 6.2 percent per year—a substantial improvement over the first plan period.

The structure of the sector became more unified in 1985 with the creation of the Frente de la Electrónica (Electronic Front). The Electronic Front is directly under the Council of Ministers and is in charge of coordinating the efforts of the different agencies and institutions related to this industry. It is also reported that the current reorganization of the sector will lead to the creation of an electronics ministry within a year or so (*Cuba Business*, April 1988).

The future development of the sector was outlined in the documents of the Third Congress of the Communist Party in 1986, when the third five-year plan (1986–90) was launched. According to the guidelines for the plan, the development of computer equipment in collaboration with the CMEA was emphasized, as were exports to the CMEA market. It stressed the urgency of achieving a higher national integration, especially in the production of monitors, semiconductors, and keyboards. The importance of strengthening the production of mini- and microcomputers was also mentioned, as was the need to elaborate a general program for the development and introduction of computer technology and its applications throughout the economy (PCC 1986).

In the perspective plan for the year 2000, it is emphasized that the process of import substitution must proceed at an accelerated pace and that production for export must increase, especially through cooperation with the CMEA countries. (According to the 1987 plan, there would already in that year be an export of some 2,600 display CID-7205 microcomputers to the U.S.S.R.) Another objective is to gradually reach self-financing in terms of hard currency by limiting imports from hard currency areas (Vega et al. 1987). In order to achieve these goals, a series of development programs have been developed within the context of of PIPPCT (the Integral Program for Scientific and Technical Progress toward the Year 2000), approved by CMEA at the end of 1985.

It might, of course, be questioned whether such a high, and apparently increasing, integration with and dependency on the CMEA is wise considering the relatively backward electronics technology level in the Soviet bloc (a fact openly recognized by the Cubans). However, given the existing embargo situation and the hard currency constraints, the immediate options for Cuba are limited.

Despite its limitations, the Cuban policy in the electronics field appears to be working. As Stelio Venseslai, director general of the Rome-based International Bureau of Informatics (IBI), recently expressed in an interview: "Cuba is transforming itself into one of the few countries in the world with a national integrated data transmission network" (*Cuba Business*, April 1988: 1).

THE PROSPECTS OF CAPITAL GOODS PRODUCTION IN CUBA

As mentioned earlier, capital goods production in Cuba accelerated under the last five-year plan. Between 1980 and 1985, engineering goods output (ISIC 38) expanded at a rate of 15.4 percent per year, of which nonelectrical machinery grew at a rate of 15.5 percent, electrical machinery at a rate of 18.7 percent, and metal products at a rate of 13.1 percent (see Table 6.5). There is, of course, no guarantee that such a high rate of growth will be sustained in the future, although many NICs such as South Korea, Hong Kong, and Taiwan have experienced such high growth rates for 15 years or more. But even if we consider a longer period, 1975–85, the growth rates would still be vigorous, with total engineering goods output expanding at a rate of 12.9 percent. If we extrapolate this trend for the coming 15 years (and assuming simultaneously that total industrial output would also follow the growth pattern of 1975–85) such a projection would indicate that the share of engineering goods in total industrial output would grow to 38.6 percent by the year 2000, which would place Cuba at the same level as the industrialized countries today. Such a projection is, however, of limited interest and can only give a rough idea of the direction of the industrialization process *ceteris paribus*.[14] Further, the hard currency crunch and the economic slump of 1986–87 have already brought a temporary halt to expansion in the engineering branches.[15]

Many other factors, such as demand and cost/benefit criteria, will determine the actual rate of growth of the capital goods industries. As mentioned above, there are important economies of scale in capital goods production, and it simply might not be worthwhile to produce all necessary capital goods even if the resource base is available.

Another aspect of capital goods production is that it could turn out to be a very costly experience if such goods are mainly produced by assembly plants, adding little value added to the products. This is, of course, the case when most of the raw materials and intermediate inputs are imported. Until recently, it has been difficult to determine to what extent there has been import substitution within the capital goods branch itself. In 1986, however, the State Statistical Committee for the first time released data on value added by industrial branch for the period 1975–85, which allows us to get an idea of such a trend. The shares of net value added in gross value of output of the engineering goods industries in constant 1981 prices is shown in Table 6.9.

As seen, the value added share in the gross value of output increased substantially between 1975 and 1985, from 37.3 percent to 48.9 percent. The most dramatic increase has taken place in the electrical and electronics industry, with the value added share increasing from 18.6 percent to 50.2 percent during the same period. The value added share of gross value of output is, however, just an approximation of the trend of import substitution, since it is not possible to determine how much of the increase is attributable to substitution of imports and how much is attributable to the use of local inputs. A more correct indicator of import substitution is the local *integration* level, that is, how much of the total value of the product is produced in the country. Such data is not always readily available. A tour of a recent exhibition of industrial products in Havana, organized by SIME (the Cuban metallurgy and machinery ministry), offered some insights, however. At this exhibition (in January 1987), SIME displayed

Table 6.9. Net Value Added as Shares of Gross Value of Output, 1975–85 (constant 1981 prices)

	Nonelectrical machinery (ISIC 382 and 384)	Electrical machinery (ISIC 383)	Metal products (ISIC 381)	Total engineering goods branches (ISIC 38)
1975	42.2	18.6	33.7	37.3
1976	42.0	18.6	33.5	37.3
1977	42.2	19.7	33.2	37.5
1978	42.3	21.1	34.0	38.1
1979	49.9	37.8	30.9	44.8
1980	46.1	38.0	40.0	44.0
1981	47.5	40.7	39.6	45.2
1982	47.5	46.6	43.8	46.8
1983	51.0	46.6	45.1	49.4
1984	51.2	39.8	44.8	48.8
1985	48.6	50.2	49.1	48.9

Source: CEE/AEC 1985: 118, 144.

several hundred capital goods produced in Cuba, ranging from computers to diesel engines, buses, lorries, and railway equipment to, and above all, a series of agricultural machinery, ranging from simple trailers to sophisticated sugar combine-harvesters. Information given at the exhibition shed some light on the level of local integration of some of the capital goods produced in Cuba.

Buses have been assembled in Cuba since 1970, and the present level of production is about 2,500 buses per year. The Cuban trademark is Giron, but the technology is mainly imported, from either Hungary (Ikarus) or Spain (Pegaso). There are different bus models, from buses used in town traffic to sophisticated, luxurious tourist buses. The more sophisticated the bus, the higher is the level of integration. The integration level of the standard type is at present 36 percent, but will rapidly increase within the next few years when the motor will also be produced in Cuba. A new truck, based on Pegaso technology, is also being produced in Cuba. The present level of integration for the truck is only 9.6 percent, but is planned to increase to about 80 percent by the year 1992. Levels of integration are highest in railway equipment, ranging from 80 percent to 95 percent.

An interesting case is sugar cane combine-harvesters, the KTPs. The first generation of KTP (the KTP-1) has an integration level of 87 percent and is expected to reach 100 percent within the near future. The motor is still imported from the U.S.S.R., but will within the next two years be produced at a new plant outside Havana. Only some 60 units of the new model, the KTP-2, have been produced so far, with an integration level of 87 percent. A prototype of the most modern version, the KTP-3, has already been successfully tested and will be 100 percent produced in Cuba when serial production starts in 1989.

Integration seems to be considerably lower in the electrical machinery and

Table 6.10. Educational Level of the Labor Force, 1982

	With primary education only (6 years)		With lower secondary education (9 years)	
	Thousands	%	Thousands	%
Total labor force	1,046.9	36.4	1,260.5	43.8
Industrial labor force	253.6	40.0	296.8	46.8
Labor force in engineering goods industries	26.9	25.4	58.6	55.3
Nonelectrical machinery	20.8	25.7	45.0	55.5
Electrical machinery	2.2	19.1	6.5	57.3
Metal products	3.9	28.6	7.1	52.6

Sources: Data for total labor force and industrial labor force in CEE/AEC 1983. Data for the engineering goods industries: unpublished data supplied by CEE. Reprinted from Brundenius 1987a.

electronics branch. The level of integration is only 20 percent in the production of television sets and 30 percent in the case of standard diesel motors (4–6 cylinders). In some telecommunications equipment, such as PBX telephone switches (with Hungarian crossbar technology), the integration level is as high as 70 percent, however.

There are several important types of machinery and equipment that Cuba does not produce and that are currently imported on a mass scale every year. For instance, Cuba does not produce tractors, bulldozers, or excavators—in spite of the fact that such equipment is in high demand in Cuba. Between 1963 and 1984, Cuba imported 150,195 tractors worth 667 million pesos,[16] 9,785 bulldozers worth 296 million pesos, and 8,416 excavators worth 323 million pesos. If Cuba had been able to produce all these machines, it would obviously have saved foreign currency. Yet it is quite possible that the cost of production would have been prohibitive even if the skills and industrial base had existed. An important aspect of reducing costs is not only taking advantage of economies of scale, but also making maximum use of economies of scope—that is, using one component in several lines of production. A case in point is the production of diesel engines. The production of diesel engines has begun, although for the time being only on an experimental basis. When full-scale production starts, these diesel engines may be used not only for the cane combine-harvesters, buses, trucks, and fishing boats that are already produced or assembled in Cuba, but might also make possible the production of tractors, bulldozers, and excavators in the future (Figueras 1985: 102–3).

An important line of production in the future might be machine tools. Cuba does not at the moment produce many sophisticated machine tools, although demand for them is quite high, especially in the capital goods industries. Today Cuba has a machine park of some 50,000 machine tools, of which an estimated

With higher secondary education (11–12 years)		With university education		Total labor force	
Thousands	%	Thousands	%	Thousands	%
339.4	13.9	168.4	5.9	2,875.2	100
66.6	10.5	17.7	2.8	634.7	100
16.1	15.2	4.4	4.1	105.9	100
12.1	14.9	3.1	3.8	81.0	100
1.8	16.3	0.8	7.4	11.4	100
2.1	15.5	0.4	3.3	13.6	100

30,000 have been imported since 1963, and almost 20,000 since 1974.[17] Although it is an industry that requires complex technologies, Cuba is considering manufacturing special machine tools used in the sugar industry—machine tools that might also later be exported (Figueras 1985: 104). Most of Cuba's machine tools currently are imported from the CMEA (CEE/AEC 1986: 472–99).

Another factor determining the future output of capital goods in Cuba is the availability of a skilled labor force for the production of such goods. As mentioned earlier, there is no automatic point of entry into the production of capital goods, although a long and sustained "learning by doing" stage is quite helpful. For a sustained rate of growth of capital goods production, a skilled and adequately trained labor force is essential. And it is in this respect that the Cuban prospects seem most promising. As seen in Table 6.10, the level of education of the Cuban labor force is quite advanced for a developing country. In 1982, 60 percent of the industrial labor force had nine years of education or more, and in the engineering goods industries this percentage was as high as 75 percent. Fifteen percent of the labor in the engineering goods industries had completed senior high school (or equivalent technical education), and 4 percent had a university degree.

The future supply of skilled workers and engineers to the engineering goods industries also looks promising, considering the rapid increase in enrollment in relevant subjects at secondary technical schools and at polytechnic universities (see Table 6.11). Enrollments have not only increased overall, but also in directly capital goods-related areas, such as machinery construction and electronics (including automation and communications)—subject areas unheard of before the revolution. Between 1977 and 1984 alone, 72,028 students in the field of machinery construction and 14,136 in electronics graduated from secondary technical schools. In the same period, 3,924 engineers specializing in

Table 6.11. Enrollment at Secondary Technical Schools and at Universities, 1970/71–1984/85

School year	Secondary technical schools			Universities		
	Total	Machinery construction	Electronics, automation, and communications	Total	Machinery construction	Electronics, automation, and communciations
1970/71	27,566	NA	NA	35,137	NA	NA
1971/72	30,429	NA	NA	36,877	NA	NA
1972/73	41,940	NA	NA	48,735	NA	NA
1973/74	56,959	NA	NA	55,635	NA	NA
1974/75	94,634	NA	NA	68,451	NA	NA
1975/76	114,653	NA	NA	84,750	NA	NA
1976/77	159,440	7,207	3,059	107,091	2,945	2,710
1977/78	194,034	27,243	5,757	122,597	3,376	3,000
1978/79	198,261	25,259	5,464	133,014	3,643	3,164
1979/80	214,615	27,099	4,577	146,240	4,469	3,331
1980/81	228,487	25,466	4,986	151,733	4,821	3,293
1981/82	263,981	29,964	6,131	165,496	4,817	3,372
1982/83	285,765	32,177	6,057	173,403	5,188	3,396
1983/84	312,867	36,106	7,718	192,958	5,588	3,837
1984/85	305,556	34,116	9,330	212,155	6,147	4,186

Source: CEE/AEC 1977, 1982, 1983, and 1984. Reprinted from Brundenius 1987a.

machinery construction and 3,466 in electronics graduated from the universities (Brundenius 1986: appendix table 5). So if the future of capital goods production in Cuba were to be determined by the future supply of skills alone, the prospects would seem to be bright indeed.

CHAPTER 7   *Agriculture: Organization and Performance*

In the last chapter we discussed how Cuban agriculture provided a fulcrum for the development of capital goods production. In this chapter we describe more broadly agriculture's contribution to Cuban industrialization. Although lack of information and questions regarding relative prices make it difficult to determine if the agricultural sector has contributed directly to surplus formation, agriculture has released labor for industry through productivity increases and has supplied a growing share of an improving Cuban diet. Through byproduct development, demand for inputs, and mechanization, the agricultural sector has stimulated a plethora of backward and forward linkages. Also, growing rural incomes have enlarged the domestic market for manufactured consumer goods. Finally, gradual diversification of food production has begun to contribute to an expanding export base.

PRE-1959 AGRICULTURE

Prior to 1959, Cuba's agricultural sector contributed little to the country's economic and social development. Land tenure was sharply unequal, land use was extensive and wasteful, and water conservation and irrigation systems were practically nonexistent. The availability of cheap and abundant labor induced little mechanization or application of modern techniques,[1] the transportation infrastructure was poor, working conditions were difficult, social services were underdeveloped, and illiteracy and malnutrition were widespread.[2]

Prior to the May 1959 agrarian reform, while the 8.5 percent of the country's farms with over 403 hectares controlled 73.3 percent of agricultural land, the 68.3 percent with less than 67 hectares accounted for only 7.4 percent of land. Land use, of course, was dominated by sugar, where three-quarters of the land was controlled by 13 North American and 9 Cuban latifundio concerns.[3] These companies planted only 54 percent of their land, and yields per hectare were ranked seventeenth out of eighteen sugar-producing countries worldwide.[4] Regarding the whole agricultural sector, a 1961 United Nations study estimated that only one-third of the cultivable land in Cuba was actually cultivated.[5] Between 1946 and 1958, per capita production of sugar agriculture grew at an annual rate of 1.0 percent, and nonsugar agriculture production fell at an annual rate of 1.2 percent.[6]

"A 1934 memorandum by U.S. Secretary of State Cordell Hull argued that U.S. policy should actively discourage Cuba's agricultural diversification in order to maintain it as a favorable market for U.S. foods and raw materials" (Benjamin et al. 1986). In 1954, Cuba spent some $140 million on imported foodstuffs, more than one-quarter of total imports, including many foods Cuba could easily produce in abundance, such as rice, lard, vegetable oils, beans, fish, pork, poultry, dairy products, eggs, etc.[7]

Approximately 40 percent of Cuba's labor force worked in agriculture. A large share of the agricultural labor force—over 60 percent according to some estimates—was composed of wage laborers (see, for instance, Ghai et al. 1988: 5). A significant proportion of wage laborers, however, also worked small plots of land as tenants, sharecroppers, or proprietors. The high incidence of "proletarian" labor is often held to be an explanation for the relatively peaceful transition to state farming in Cuba after the revolution.

Agricultural labor, though, was frequently underemployed or seasonally employed. According to the 1946 census, roughly half of the agricultural labor force was employed on a temporary basis, and 52 percent of all temporary laborers worked no more than four months of the year (Bianchi 1964: 81). Living standards were abysmal. According to a 1956 survey from the Catholic University, 60.3 percent of agricultural workers' dwellings had wooden walls, thatched roofs, and dirt floors; 82.6 percent had no bath or shower; and 92.7 percent had no electricity. Only 11.2 percent of the rural population drank milk, 4.0 percent ate meat, 2.1 percent ate eggs, and less than 1 percent ate fish.[8] The daily diet, which was deficient by 1,000 calories, was a major cause of disease: 14 percent of the population suffered or had suffered from tuberculosis, 13 percent from typhoid fever, and 36 percent from intestinal parasites. According to a 1951 World Bank report, 80–90 percent of children in rural areas suffered from intestinal parasites.[9] There was only one rural hospital in the entire country.

POST-1959 AGRICULTURE

Structural Changes in Cuban Agriculture

Important structural changes have taken place in Cuban agriculture since the revolution. Although agriculture still plays an important role in the Cuban economy, with a focus on sugar, the characteristics of the sector have changed considerably since the revolution.

Agricultural performance was generally poor during the 1960s. Initial problems with reorganization, mismanagement, bad planning, distorted prices and incentives,[10] insufficient infrastructure, erratic weather, and the effects of the U.S. blockade, among others, have been described at some length by various authors.[11] Gross agricultural output, after expanding a bit during 1959–61, stagnated between 1962 and 1969.[12] It was only the massive transfer of resources to the sugar harvest in 1970 and the near doubling of raw sugar output in that year that salvaged agricultural production figures for the decade. This resource transfer, however, exacerbated already serious problems elsewhere in the economy.

Along with the rest of the economy, agricultural performance in Cuba has improved significantly since 1970. Contrary to a still commonly held belief, however, the sugar subsector has not been leading the way; rather, growth has been concentrated in agricultural production for domestic consumption, including livestock products and nontraditional exports (see Table 7.1).[13]

Thus nonsugar agricultural output grew at an annual rate of 7.6 percent between 1970 and 1975, while sugar experienced a negative growth rate of 1.7 percent. Livestock production had a sluggish growth up until the early 1970s, but has since grown at about the sectoral average. The relative decline of sugar since 1970 is shown in Table 7.2, which gives the percentage shares of the subsectors over time. Sugar's share fell steadily after 1970.

The overall share of sugar (raw plus processed—milled and refined—sugar) has also declined in relation to national output. It had been estimated that the total sugar share declined from 12.6 percent of GDP in 1961 to 7.9 percent in 1981 (Brundenius 1984b: 77). Our estimates show that processed sugar accounted for about 10 percent of industrial value added in 1981. Since manufacturing industry represented an estimated 30.9 percent of GDP (see chapter 4), processed or industrial sugar output accounted for 3.1 percent of GDP in 1981. Sugar cane accounted for 31.1 percent of the agricultural sector output in 1981 (CEE/AEC 1986: 114) and the latter sector accounted for 14.0 percent of GDP in that year (see chapter 4). Sugar cane, in other words, represented around 4.4 percent of GDP in 1981. Adding sugar cane and processed sugar together, we get an estimate of 7.5 percent of GDP in 1981, a slightly lower figure than the earlier estimate.

Sugar's falling share in the economy is also reflected in the falling share of sugar in total investments. Whereas total (agriculture plus industry) sugar

Table 7.1.   Rate of Growth of Gross Agricultural Output (constant 1981 prices)

	1962/70[a]	1970/75[a]	1975/80[b]	1980/86[b]
Sugar	9.7	−1.7	3.3	0.7
Nonsugar	−2.0	7.6	5.1	5.1
Livestock	1.3	3.3	4.0	2.7
Total	3.1	2.2	4.0	2.7

Sources: DEC/BEC 1968: 18, 20; CEE/AEC 1974: 35, 1976: 45, 1986: 122.
[a] 1965 prices. Unless otherwise noted, in this chapter agricultural production data is measured in domestic wholesale prices.
[b] 1981 prices.

Table 7.2. Structural Changes in Agricultural Output

	1962[a]	1970[a]	1975[b]	1980[b]	1986[b]
Sugar	29.3	48.0	32.9	31.7	28.2
Nonsugar	34.7	22.4	23.1	24.3	27.7
Livestock	34.0	29.6	43.2	43.2	43.0
Services	2.0	na[c]	0.7	0.8	1.1
Total	100.0	100.0	100.0	100.0	100.0

Sources: DEC/BEC 1968: 18, 20; CEE/AEC 1974: 35, 1976: 45, 1986: 122.
[a]1965 prices.
[b]1981 prices.
[c]Not available separately, included in total.

investments amounted to 15.9 percent of total investment in the economy in 1975, this share fell to 12.2 percent in 1980 and 12.1 percent in 1986. Over the same period, the share of industrial sugar investment in total sugar investment was increasing from 35.4 percent in 1975 to 41.4 percent in 1980 and 43.8 percent in 1986 (CEE/AEC 1986: 215). This circumstance is, of course, linked to the development of sugar byproducts.

Development of Sugar Byproducts

A significant potential for diversification lies in the development of sugar derivatives. According to Cuban estimates, less than 15 percent of the potential for developing sugar byproducts has been attained. Cuba, however, is the only producer country with an institution Instituto Cubano de Investigaciones de los Derivados de la Caña de Azúcar, ICIDCA) dedicated to the development of sugar derivatives (*Cuba Business*, June 1988: 1).

A recent study for the World Bank found that sugar cane has the highest btu yield per hectare of any crop (Fry 1985: ch. 4). For every 100 tons of sugar cane harvested from the field, it is possible to obtain 55.6 tons of "first generation" subproducts: 9.0 tons of milled sugar, 19.5 tons of bagasse, 2.6 tons of final molasses, 2.5 tons of *cachaza* (filtered cake), 8.0 tons of green leaves, 7.0 tons of dry leaves, and 7.0 tons of shoots (ibid.).

Several derivatives were produced in Cuba before the revolution, but the large majority of the 40-odd byproducts being commercially produced today in Cuba were developed after 1959 (see Table 7.3). There are about 100 additional byproducts that are being researched currently for possible commercialization. Most of the byproducts are derived from bagasse (51 percent) and molasses (24 percent), but an increasing number is also being extracted from *cachaza* (e.g., oil, wax, animal feed, resins) and from plant residue, leaves, and tops (e.g., biogas, animal feed).

The oldest byproduct is, of course, alcohol, especially as alcoholic beverage. *Aguardiente* was produced in Cuba as early as the 18th century, and in

Table 7.3. Sugar Cane Byproducts in Cuba, Partial List

Product	Production before 1959	Production between 1959 and 1987	Production by 1990
From bagasse			
Textile yarn		x	
Textile cord		x	
Cellulose		x	
Cellophane		x	
Textile fibers		x	
Writing paper		x	
Newsprint	x	x	
Cardboard		x	
Carton liner	x	x	
Wrapping paper		x	
Special paper		x	
Cartoncill		x	
Fiberboard	x	x	
Particle board	x	x	
From molasses			
Citric acid			x
Lysine			x
Enzymes		x	
Fertilizers		x	
Animal feed		x	
Urea	x	x	
Soil conditioners	x	x	
Predigested bagasse		x	
Furfural		x	
Pharmaceuticals		x	
Cosmetics		x	
Yeast		x	
Flavorings		x	
Fuel oil		x	
Proteic molasses		x	
From sugar			
Dextrane		x	
Sweets		x	
From cachaza			
Animal feed		x	
Oil		x	
Crude wax	x	x	
Refined wax		x	
Resins		x	
From leaves and tops			
Biogas		x	
Animal feed		x	

Source: Data obtained by the authors from ICIDCA.

1862 the well-known rum factory, "Ron Caney," started production in Santiago. By 1917 there were eight distilleries producing alcohol from molasses. During World War II there was an increasing demand for gasohol (alcohol mixed with gasoline), and the number of distilleries increased to 26.[14]

But prerevolutionary exploitation of byproducts was not limited to alcohol. Already in 1915 there was trial production of wrapping paper made from bagasse, although production was discontinued after a short while for economic reasons. In the 1920s much research went into dissolving pulp from bagasse, and in 1928 a small plant for the production of fiberboards was set up in Marianao, outside Havana.

In 1958 in Las Tunas, two plants began trial production of crude wax which was then exported to the United States for refining. In the same year, just on the eve of the revolution, trial production of newsprint started, and plants for the manufacture of particle board and fiberboard were also set up in the vicinity of Havana. These experimental technologies, however, did not prove viable and were discontinued. Most of the efforts to develop sugar derivatives prior to the revolution occurred through individual initiative, although some projects were undertaken in coordination with the Sugar Research Foundation in the United States (ICIDCA 1986).

The real breakthrough, however, came after the revolution with the foundation of ICIDCA in 1963. The institute had at the outset a modest endowment of approximately 150 people, of whom 36 had graduate and 22 had undergraduate school training, 18 were semiskilled workers, and 26 were foreign experts (mostly from the Soviet Union and Czechoslovakia). Initially, there were 27 specialized laboratories and 3 pilot plants (Cuban Delegation 1967).

The institute was divided into three basic sectors: cellulose, fermentations, and sugar. Working groups were organized in chemical analysis, microscopic and physico-chemical instruments, design, economic evaluation, documentation, and specialized information. These working groups served as teams that cooperated in the execution of research projects from their beginning through their culmination in a preliminary industrial design or pilot plant.

The research capacity of ICIDCA has expanded appreciably. It employs over 1,000 people, of whom 45 have doctoral degrees, an additional 200 have university degrees, and 225 are secondary-level technicians. The institute has 50 laboratories and 5 pilot plants (Silva 1986).

When Ernesto "Che" Guevara inaugurated ICIDCA in 1963, he foresaw that in the not-so-distant future "byproducts from sugar would play as big a role as sugar in the national economy." In hindsight, Guevara's projection was characteristically optimistic. Yet it is a fact that today the value of sugar byproducts is significant and growing at a rapid rate. Production of crude sugar is now energy self-sufficient through the burning of bagasse, and during 1987 bagasse burning provided an additional 10 percent of energy generated by the national grid. Production of the main sugar derivatives equaled or exceeded 1987 output targets, with 1.38 million hectoliters of alcohol, 52,699 tons of torula yeast, and 86.8 thousand cubic meters of particle board being produced in that year. In addition, several byproducts are being exported, including pharmaceuticals, cosmetics, bagasse boards for furniture and construction, and torula yeast. Among significant new projects, a factory "to produce 1,000 tons per year of furfural (an organic compound used in the manufacture of resins and adhesives) from bagasse is scheduled for completion in Las Tunas in the first half of 1988, and doubled yields have been reported from an experimental project using detoxified waste water from the [sugar] refineries for irrigation and fertilising" (EIU 1988 No. 2: 12). Today, the value of sugar derivative production exceeds 150 million pesos (Fiandor 1988: 19).

Import Substitution

The increase in agricultural production for domestic consumption has resulted in a decreasing dependence on imports of a series of basic food commodities. One of the staple food products in Cuba is rice. Before the revolution, Cuba imported 43.2 percent of the rice consumed (see Table 7.4). In the early 1960s domestic output decreased drastically, and large amounts of rice had to be imported, mainly from China. Since then, however, serious efforts have been made to increase yields (through large investments in irrigation, fertilizers, and pesticides and adding new land for rice production). By 1970 rice production per capita had increased by 16 percent over the 1958 level (and by almost 600 percent above the lowest level of 1965).

During the 1970s imports continued to grow in absolute terms, however, and it was not until the beginning of the 1980s that rice imports started to decrease in volume. The level of imports in 1986 was about one-quarter of apparent consumption, compared with 34.7 percent in 1970 and 43.2 percent in 1958. Rice production per capita in 1986 was 50.3 percent above the 1958 level.

Table 7.4. Output, Imports, and Apparent Consumption of Rice

	Output (000t)	Import (000t)	Consumption (000t)	Import/ consumption (%)	Output per capita (Kg)	Consumption per capita (Kg)
1958	253.0	192.4	445.4	43.2	37.4	65.9
1962	206.9	na	na	na	28.3	na
1965	49.9	281.8	331.7	85.0	6.3	42.0
1970	374.5	199.0	573.6	34.7	43.5	66.7
1975	455.8	199.8	646.5	30.9	48.7	69.0
1980	477.8	229.6	707.4	32.5	49.3	73.0
1983	517.6	207.0	724.3	28.5	52.0	72.8
1986	575.8	188.8	764.5	24.7	56.2	74.6

Sources: DEC/BEC 1968; CEE/AEC 1972, 1986; Mesa-Lago 1978.

The pattern for rice production is typical for most domestic food staples. Food imports as a percent of total imports fell from 20.5 percent in 1958 to 9.3 percent in 1986 (CEE/AEC 1986: 425). Viewed differently, the amount of food consumption that was imported fell from around 33 percent in the late 1950s to below 20 percent in the mid-1980s (Benjamin et al. 1986: 8; Figueras 1985: 47). Over the same period the Cuban diet has improved, and the per capita intake of calories and proteins has increased.[15]

Export Diversification of Food Products

After a slow beginning, diversification of food exports began to pick up in the early 1970s and to accelerate in the late 1970s and early 1980s. In 1958, nonsugar food exports came to only 9.1 million pesos, or 1.5 percent of sugar exports. By 1970, the value of nonsugar food exports had grown modestly to 27.8 million pesos, but still represented only 3.4 percent of sugar exports. Thereafter, the value of nonsugar exports began to reach appreciable levels and to sustain a healthy dynamic of growth (see Table 7.5).

Naturally, many of the high individual product growth rates are a function of the low starting points.[16] Although nonsugar food export growth is clearly concentrated in two product groups (fish—mostly shellfish—and citrus fruit), there is nonetheless substantial growth in these items and new food export products are being introduced. Despite their still modest absolute magnitude, the high average annual growth rates for total nonsugar food exports during 1975–80 and 1980–85 suggest a new and promising export dynamic. We shall return to the matter of export diversification in chapter 9.

Table 7.5. Nonsugar Food Exports (thousands of pesos)

Product	1975	1980	1985	Annual Rates of Growth (%)	
				1975–80	1980–85
Live animals	—	243	673	—	22.6
Meat	—	460	628	—	6.4
Milk and eggs	—	273	1,269	—	40.0
Fish	51,346	89,251	118,008	11.7	5.7
Grains	—	206	273	—	5.8
Potatoes	—	3,264	7,754	—	18.9
Peppers	686	3,567	4,596	39.1	5.2
Citrus fruits	11,920	41,315	143,973	28.4	28.4
Conserved fruits and vegetables	2,481	7,551	16,632	24.9	17.1
Total	79,490	223,246	344,809	22.9	9.1

Source: Calculated from CEE/AEC 1986: 426–27.

Investment

The improvement in agricultural performance, especially after 1970, is mainly the result of impressive investments in the sector (see Table 7.6), especially in irrigation and mechanization. Further, as discussed in the previous chapter, agricultural machinery is to an increasing extent being supplied by Cuban plants.

The investment rate in the agricultural sector was high already in the 1960s, although the absolute levels were quite modest in comparison with expenditures in the 1970s and, above all, in the 1980s. Agricultural investment accounted for between 30 and 40 percent of total investments in the country in the 1960s. This percentage then dropped to around 25 percent in the 1970s and has since then stayed between 22 and 24 percent. As a share of gross agricultural output, however, investments have increased since the late 1960s and early 1970s. In the early 1970s the investment rate was around 23 percent (itself quite a high figure), and by the mid-1980s the ratio was over one-fourth of gross output.

The rising ratio of agricultural investment to gross output, of course, denotes a falling incremental output-capital ratio, or decreasing capital productivity. While such a trend is to be expected, it appears to have progressed at an accelerated pace in Cuba.[17] There are several explanations. First, large infrastructural investments with low short-run payoffs, such as in irrigation, roads, and electrification, have been necessary. Second, most imported equipment has come from the CMEA and has not been top quality. Downtime is often very high. Between 1981 and 1985, for instance, downtime on tractors averaged 50.3 percent and even higher on sugar cane combines (A. González 1986: 54). Third, the Cuban agricultural machinery industry is still young and its

Table 7.6.   Gross Investments in Agriculture (constant prices[a])

	Total investment (million pesos)	Agricultural investment (million pesos)	Agricultural/ total (%)	Agricultural production (million pesos)	Agricultural investment/agricultural production (%)
1962	626	184	29.4	941	19.6
1966	935	378	40.4	1,042	36.3
1970	800	254	31.8	1,165	21.8
1975	2,394	581	24.3	2,516	23.1
1980	2,821	602	21.3	3,065	19.6
1981	3,386	896	26.4	3,468	25.8
1982	2,996	737	24.6	3,350	22.0
1983	3,409	761	22.3	3,284	23.2
1984	3,989	876	22.0	3,474	25.2
1985	4,289	934	21.8	3,499	26.7
1986	4,396	991	22.5	3,607	27.5

Sources: DEC/BEC 1968: 18; CEE/AEC 1974: 35, 1976: 45, 1986: 100, 122, 214; Brundenius 1984b: 78.
[a] 1962–70: 1965 prices; 1975–86: 1981 prices.

products frequently exhibit quality defects. Fourth, since the late 1970s Cuban agriculture has suffered from unusual pest infestations, a severe, prolonged drought, and a devastating hurricane. Among other things, the drought, occasioned the transport of over half a million head of cattle across several provinces. Fifth, new planting programs accelerated in the late 1970s and early 1980s, and yields for many new crops are low during the initial years . Sixth, planning inefficiencies, institutional changes, and pricing patterns have retarded productivity growth (see ch. 8; Staff of Radio Martí 1988–3/4: 58–72).

These high investments and related costs help to account for the low growth in measured net value added in agriculture since 1975, as reported in chapter 4. The discrepancies in gross and net output growth are also explained in part by the method of value added accounting used for estimating the statistical yearbook series[18] and the not-infrequent irrationalities in Cuban relative prices.

Nevertheless, these investments have resulted in the substantial development of Cuba's agricultural infrastructure. Since 1959 there has been: a 16.5 percent increase in cultivated area; a 125-fold increase in water storage capacity; a sevenfold increase in irrigated land; an eightfold increase in the stock of tractors; a tenfold increase in the application of fertilizers; a fourfold increase in the use of pesticides; and the construction of around 3,000 new agricultural and industrial facilities in rural areas (J.L. Rodríguez 1987: 31). Finally, as in other sectors of the economy, investment in human capital has been appreciable as well as necessary in order to operate the modernized production process.

Labor Productivity and Income Equalization

The massive investments in the agricultural sector have led to rapid increases in labor productivity during the 1970s and 1980s, after stagnation or even decline during the difficult 1960s. In fact, since 1975 labor productivity[19] increases in agriculture have outstripped those of most other sectors belonging to the so-called productive sphere, especially manufacturing industry (see Table 7.7). Labor productivity in agriculture increased at a rate of 4.95 percent during the first five-year plan (1976–80) and accelerated to 6.1 percent per year during the second five-year plan (1981–85).

These productivity gains, along with generalized labor shortages in agriculture, have facilitated the rapid leveling of wages between agriculture and other sectors (Table 7.8). To be sure, it is possible that the causality worked in both directions. That is, higher agricultural wages may have served both to boost morale and to attract more qualified workers. In 1962, the average agricultural wage was only 49.1 percent of the average wage in industry. In 1966, this wage differential was still 51.3 percent. By 1975, however, the agricultural wage was already 88.9 percent of the industrial wage, and today it is practically the same as the industrial average.

It should be added that the specter of widespread seasonal unemployment

Table 7.7. Productivity Changes in the State Sector[a] (constant 1981 enterprise prices)

	1975	1980 (pesos)	1985	Annual rate of change (%) 1976/80	1981/85
Industry	10,635	12,401	13,565	3.15	1.80
Construction	4,562	5,423	7,443	3.50	6.55
Agriculture	3,039	3,865	5,185	4.95	6.10
Forestry	2,470	3,408	4,154	6.65	4.05
Transport	5,156	6,869	9,124	5.90	5.95
Communication	4,658	6,734	8,817	7.65	5.55
All productive spheres	5,923	7,273	9,316	4.20	5.10

Source: CEE/AEC 1986: 194.
[a]Gross value of output divided by average number of workers per year.

Table 7.8. Wage Differentials between Agriculture and Industry (average yearly wage, pesos)

	1962	1966	1975	1980	1986
Agriculture	954	1,059	1,562	1,706	2,180
Industry	1,941	2,063	1,758	1,883	2,280
Agriculture/industry (percent)	49.1	51.3	88.9	90.6	95.6

Sources: DEC/BEC 1968; CEE/AEC 1981, 1986.

has been eliminated in the countryside. Along with job security, educational, medical, and pension benefits have been extended to all agricultural workers.[20]

Finally, along with falling capital and increasing labor productivity, it remains to note that land productivity or yield per hectare has increased at approximately the same rate as agricultural output since 1970. This is because the amount of agricultural land in use, after rising appreciably between 1959 and 1970, stablized between 1970 and 1986 (CEE/AEC 1973: 46; 1986: 302).

Transformation of Ownership and Employment

Cuba's post-1958 agrarian reforms have been described and analyzed at length by several authors.[21] The first national reform began in May 1959. The principal aims of the reform were to expropriate the holdings of large landlords (those holding over 30 *caballerías* or 403 hectares, exempting those on highly efficient farms) and to give property rights to smallholders who had been farming the land under various contractual arrangements.

Following implementation of this reform, the state controlled approximately 41 percent of the land and the private sector controlled 59 percent. Significantly, however, there were still over 10,000 private landowners with between

67 and 403 hectares. This private sector not only made it more difficult for the state to coordinate production for export but also served as the basis for counter-revolutionary activity and economic sabotage, particularly in the provinces of Camaguey and Las Villas.[22]

As a consequence, a second agrarian reform was promulgated in October 1963 that called for the expropriation (with compensation) of all land over 67 hectares. With implementation of this reform, the state came to own some 70 percent of the land "but only 57 percent of the arable land and only 40 percent of the high yield acreage" (J. Domínguez 1979: 452). No further land reforms have been passed, but the private sector has gradually diminished from 43 percent of the arable land in 1965 to 21 percent in 1977 and to approximately 16 percent in 1987.[23]

This diminution of the private sector has transpired through voluntary land sales to the state.[24] The state has also gained increased control over the farms remaining in the private sector through affiliation of individual farms with a nearby state farm or through the formation of private producer cooperatives in recent years. Unlike the agrarian reform process in other socialist countries, the Cuban transformation has occurred with a minimum of popular resistance; presumably this is attributable to the widespread existence of wage labor prior to the revolution as well as to the flexible policies of the leadership that allowed, first, the expansion in the number of private holders and, then, the continued existence of the private sector. Even severe critics of Cuban agriculture have remarked on the voluntary and peaceful nature of change.[25]

The state farm is the main institution in Cuban agriculture today. In 1986 there were 417 state farms, each with an average of 14,260 hectares and 1,372 workers. State farms in 1986 accounted for 79.1 percent of gross agricultural output and approximately 75 percent of the agricultural labor force. The private sector produced the remaining 20.9 percent of output on around 16 percent of the arable land using 25 percent of the agricultural labor force. In mid-1987, 72 percent of private land was organized in 1,397 production cooperatives, each averaging 728 hectares and 50 members.[26]

As a share of total employment, agriculture has decreased from 41.5 percent in 1953 to 35.0 percent in 1962, 30.0 percent in 1970, 21.8 percent in 1981, and to 18.6 percent in 1986. Unusual in Latin America, the absolute number of

Table 7.9. Employment by Type of Ownership (percentage shares)

	1962	1970	1981	1982	1983	1984	1985
State	35.3	66.5	76.0	73.6	73.2	74.7	75.4
Cooperative	—	—	4.9	7.6	10.2	9.6	9.6
Individual	64.7	33.5	19.1	18.8	16.6	15.7	15.0

Sources: DEC/BEC 1968; CEE/AEC 1986; and unpublished data supplied to the authors by the CEE. The figures for individual plots in 1962 and 1970 include a small percentage of farmers working on cooperatives.

agricultural workers has also declined from 841,000 in 1962 to 731,000 in 1986.

The Transformation of Management

There have been major changes in the management of the agricultural sector since the First Party Congress of 1975 and the decision to adopt the new system of planning and management, the SDPE. Although other changes have occurred, such as the creation of the Ministry of Agriculture in 1976 and its 1980 division into the Sugar and Nonsugar Ministries, the formation of agro-industrial complexes, the coming and going of free farmers' markets (analyzed in chapter 8), and the introduction of self-provisioning,[27] we shall concentrate on the emergence of two new and important institutions: production brigades on the state farms and producer cooperatives in the private sector.

Brigades

Since the early 1970s, there has been a process of amalgamation of state farms that has reduced the number by two-thirds. The greatly enlarged units average over 14,000 hectares and, according to Cuban officials, offer significant economies of scale in organization.[28] These economies are achieved in terms of specialization, mechanization, irrigation, aerial pesticide spraying, social and cultural development, and so on. There are, however, some diseconomies of scale related to remoteness of decision-making and work incentives as well as to bureaucratic tendencies. In 1981, in an effort to combat the latter, the Cubans began to introduce production brigades.

Production brigades are conceived as self-managing subunits of state farms[29] and eventually are to become self-financing. As smaller administrative units, the brigades are expected to promote worker participation in decision-making and to enhance work incentives through a more direct, immediate link between effort and reward.

According to Cristobal Kay: "The introduction of the brigades reflects a certain stage in Cuban development as they require a level of qualified administrative and technical manpower which only became available in recent years" (Kay 1987: 19). While Kay certainly identifies an important factor, it must be stressed that the development of skilled managerial and technical labor in Cuban agriculture is still insufficient, and this has been an impediment to the more effective operation and dissemination of the brigades. To be sure, this limitation is clearly recognized by Cuban agricultural officials, who cite this shortage as the reason for the slow extension of the brigades since 1984.

As can be seen in Table 7.10, 599 of 913 brigade chiefs (65.6 percent) and 502 of 837 brigade planning officers (60.0 percent) have 10 years of schooling or less. Furthermore, training and skill levels on the state farms constituted in brigades tend to be higher than on those farms where brigades have yet to be formed. This skill shortage has surely not facilitated the devolution of management functions to the brigade level. The Cubans have, however, opened special management training schools for brigade personnel, and they report significant progress since 1984.

The first brigades were established by the Ministry of Agriculture (MINAG) in 1981. (The Ministry of Sugar did not begin experimenting with brigades on the agro-industrial complexes until 1985.) Nineteen brigades were created in this year, scattered among various state farms. It was not until 1983 that some state farms were entirely organized into brigades. The gradual extension of the brigade system is depicted in Table 7.11.

Internal documents of the Ministry of Agriculture have given the brigades a positive evaluation overall.[30] Worker involvement in management has increased and economic results appear to have been good. Increasingly unfavorable weather conditions between 1983 and 1986 and the preselection of the most efficient state farms for the brigade experiment, however, make the economic impact of the brigade system difficult to sort out.

Table 7.10. Level of Education and Skill of Managerial and Technical Personnel on 57 of the 65 State Farms Constituted in Brigades in 1984

	Total	University level	Technical school	From 10th to 12th grade	From 7th to 9th grade	Up to 6th grade
Directors	57	18	20	14	5	—
Subdirectors	100	33	52	19	6	—
Chief accountants	41	12	20	5	4	—
Brigade chiefs	913	55	169	90	530	69
Planning and control technicians	837	6	191	133	488	14

Source: MINAG 1985: appendix, table 7.3.

Table 7.11. The Evolution of Brigades under MINAG

Year	Number of state farms entirely under brigade system	Percent of all state farms under MINAG with brigade system	Number of brigades	Number of workers	Average number of workers per brigade
1981	0	0	19	3,021	159
1983	13	3.6	—	—	—
1984	65	18.0	1,051	80,562	77
1985	73	20.3a	1,199	89,456	75
1986	77	21.4	1,469	99,231	68

Source: MINAG 1985 and 1986.
aThese farms produced 22 percent of the gross output under MINAG in 1985.

On state farms organized in brigades, worker productivity in 1984 was 20 percent above its average during 1981–83. In 1985 worker productivity rose 2.6 percent, and in 1986 it rose only 0.2 percent.[31] Similarly, cost per peso of output of these farms fell during 1981–84, stayed level during 1985, and rose during 1986. It might appear from these and other trends that the positive impact of the brigades began to wear off. It could be reasoned, for instance, that this trend was statistically inevitable as more farms joined the experiment (since the best farms where selected first), and that it was also the natural result of the waning of initial enthusiasm and priority attention. Whereas such an explanation might tell part of the story, other evidence suggests that most of the explanation lies elsewhere.

First, all of Cuban agriculture performed poorly during 1985 and 1986. This was principally attributable to two factors: One, there was an intensifying drought from 1983 through 1986 (by 1986 rainfall was 35 percent below the historical average); two, in November 1985 Cuba experienced its most devastating hurricane since the revolution.[32] It should be added that large capital investments, the decision to transport cattle due to the drought, and new accounting rules for depreciation and cattle valuation also contributed to poorer performance in efficiency-related indicators during 1985 and 1986.

Second, state farms organized in brigades significantly outperformed those not organized in brigades. Although there was probably always a differential performance between these two groups of farms, no data is available to confirm the extent of this differential prior to 1984. Table 7.12 shows that farms with brigades outperformed farms without brigades by significant margins according to two efficiency-related criteria. This data, however, along with all efficiency-related data for the Cuban economy, must be interpreted with caution since it is directly affected by government-fixed relative prices.

Third, various indicators of worker discipline show superior performance on farms with brigades. On state farms with brigades, work days lost declined by 25.4 percent in 1984, and there were 396 fewer work-related accidents than in 1983 (MINAG 1985: 14). Compared to farms without brigades, the rate of

Table 7.12. Differential Economic Performance on State Farms with and without Brigades (centavos)

	Material consumption[a] per peso of gross output		Labor costs per peso of gross output	
	1985	1986	1985	1986
Farms with brigades	65.4	66.8	22.4	22.0
Farms without brigades	74.1	74.1	29.7	28.5

Source: MINAG 1986: 3–4.
[a]Includes all nonlabor costs, including amortization of capital.

disciplinary sanctions was 24 percent lower, infractions of work hours were 50 percent lower, unjustified absences were 27.7 percent lower, and health and safety violations were 40 percent lower (MINAG 1985: 14; appendix, table 26).

Although not conclusive, this evidence is consistent with the positive evaluations of the Ministry of Agriculture. It should also be noted, however, that the process of brigade formation has continued at a slower pace in recent years. This slowdown suggests not only that the Cubans are bumping up against their constraint of skilled managerial and technical labor, but also that several problem areas in the central planning of the agricultural sector need to be addressed before the experience with brigades can be successfully generalized. The 1986 MINAG document mentions the following weak points: Planning and control at the brigade level multiplies the demands on information processing; technical norms and input-output coefficients often lack a scientific basis; the arrival and quality of inputs is not always reliable; the breakdown of the plan into trimesters is not carried out rigorously; plan figures frequently arrive months late, and related targets do not always arrive at the same time; and so on. These problems, of course, are common to central planning (see discussion in chapter 8) and tend to be more intractable in agriculture, where production units are more numerous and scattered and nature's unpredictability can thwart the best-laid plans. Enumeration of problem areas is interesting, but it tells us little about the seriousness of the problems or the prospects for their amelioration. It is clear, however, that until these and other difficulties are dealt with, the realization of the brigade model as self-financing, flexible production units will remain elusive.

Production Cooperatives

Since the early 1960s, private farmers have been required to deliver a certain share of their output to the state. Although the output quotas have generally been set low (Ghai et al. 1988: 90) and have not always been enforced, they do represent the effort of the central government to coordinate and plan the activities of tens of thousands of individual farmers. This formidable task has become somewhat easier over the years as more individual farmers have affiliated with state farms and as increasing numbers of private farmers have joined together in production cooperatives.

Private production cooperatives (called agricultural societies at the time) actually began to form in the early 1960s. By 1962 there were 358 agricultural societies, but discouragement of this form by the state led to their gradual diminution—by 1975 only 43 survived (J. Domínguez 1979: 449). Attitudes toward collective farming, however, began to change in the mid-1970s. At the Fifth Congress of the National Association of Small Farmers, held in early 1977, the policy promoting the formation of producer cooperatives was formally adopted. Although joining producer cooperatives was and is entirely voluntary, the state provided a host of inducements, including: improved infrastructure; improved social services; access to more land, equipment, and technical support; cheaper credit; and favorable tax treatment and social security coverage.[33] Accordingly, the cooperative movement grew rapidly, from 44 cooperatives in May 1977 to 725 in December 1979 and to 1,416 in December 1982 (Ramírez 1984: 6). The number of cooperatives stabilized around 1,400, but the hectarage and membership continued to grow from an average size of 487 hectares and 44 members in 1982 to 728 hectares and 50 members in mid-1987.[34]

Production cooperatives are formed initially by private farmers pooling their individual land.[35] All land and productive assets transferred to the cooperative by its members are carefully valued. The cooperative sets aside between 25 and 30 percent of its annual net income to compensate members for their contributed assets.

The cooperative is run by a general assembly (which meets monthly) and a management board (which meets biweekly). The management board has eleven to fifteen members who are elected by direct, secret ballot for two year terms. All the main targets, plans, and policies are approved by the assembly.[36]

The majority of cooperatives have been profitable: The average cost per peso of output for all cooperatives for which data was available was 68 centavos in 1982, 70 centavos in 1983, and 77 centavos in 1984 (Kay 1987: 29).[37] Here again, it is difficult to decipher what these figures imply about efficiency. While they suggest high profit-sales ratios, they are skewed by nonscarcity pricing, subsidies, and shifting accounting practices. The cooperatives also suffer from a lack of experience with practical accounting, making much of the microperformance data suspect, particularly for financial indicators. This issue is further complicated by the fact that much female labor worked the land without pay as family farmers prior to cooperativization and now do the same work with remuneration (Stubbs 1987). Nevertheless, as with the production brigades, the cooperatives appear to represent a positive development in Cuban agriculture from both a social and economic point of view. They bring more resources and more control over decision-making to local production units and enable increased mechanization of production and far greater provision of social services.

Several organizational hurdles have thwarted the effective development of the cooperative sector. First, to a greater extent than the state farms, the co-ops suffer from a shortage of skilled technical and managerial personnel. The co-ops tend to be geographically isolated with less developed productive and social infrastructures. A large share of wages comes as a residual from the cooperatives' net income. These conditions do not generally attract skilled labor. Second, the co-ops still need to be better integrated into the planning apparatus. Many co-ops have experienced an unusually difficult time in obtaining needed inputs. Apart from systemic factors, the problem here was aggravated by the general procedure of co-ops receiving their inputs through nearby state farms rather than through the relevant ministries and their branches. This meant less systematic attention, lower priority in input procurement, and, frequently, lower state price subsidies. Many of these institutional encumbrances are being attended to, but they will take time to resolve.

CONCLUSION

The organization and management of Cuban agriculture has been in flux practically since 1959, although greater institutional stability has been characteristic of the period since 1976. The strategic conception of the role of agriculture in the country's economic development has also shifted over time, but the general strategy has been in place since 1963. Increasingly, the agricultural sector has diversified and mechanized, although the extent of diversification has been limited by an ongoing commitment to expand sugar output. This commitment has been underwritten by the heavy price subsidy for sugar paid by the Soviet Union (see chapter 9).

Production performance has been creditable since 1970, although many obstacles to greater efficiency remain. Finally, agricultural labor productivity increases, rural income growth, and backward and forward linkages to industry have made an important contribution to Cuba's overall economic development.

CHAPTER 8   *Incentives and*
                   Planning

During 1986–87 Cuba found itself once again debating the relative merits of material and moral incentives. Analysts outside Cuba have rushed to their word processors to pronounce judgment on the Cuban economy's alleged uncertain footing. Erroneously, some writers have declared Cuba to have abolished their post-1973 system of tying pay to productivity, and some have interpreted changes in the Cuban economic system to mark the failure and demise of the SDPE (Cuba's post-1976 system of economic management and planning). This chapter endeavors not to uncover the errant interpretations of Western observers but to explore the underlying problematic and dynamic that Cuba confronts in attempting to balance moral and material incentives within the framework of central planning.

The ideological imperative for limiting the importance of material incentives in a socialist economy is clear enough. Too much reliance on material incentives will eventually produce excessive inequality, unemployment, materialism, and selfishness—outcomes antagonistic to socialist goals.

There is a powerful economic imperative as well to circumscribe the operation of material incentives in socialist societies. The prevalence of shortages and the dominance of physical indicators in centrally planned economies (CPEs) where the price mechanism is suppressed greatly reduce the effectiveness of material incentives. The alternatives for CPEs become 1) to release central controls, allowing some scope for the price mechanism to operate and some private activities (the path of Hungary, China, and Gorbachev's U.S.S.R.), 2) to develop new, nonmaterial incentives, decentralized planning structures, and motivating forces (a largely unchartered territory, though experiments are under way in a number of CPEs), 3) to accept the status quo with its extensive allocational inefficiences and waste (an increasingly untenable option as the CPE industrializes), or 4) some combination of the above. We shall trace the development of Cuba's incentive system to elucidate the dynamic of central planning and to throw some light on the prospects for economic reform.

Incentives may be divided into two basic types: material and nonmaterial. Material incentives may take the form of wage and salary differentiation, piece-rate payments, bonuses for meeting certain goals, and profit sharing. They may apply to individuals as well as to groups of workers. In market-type economies these material stimuli are generally complemented by the threat of unemployment, which provides a strong stimulus to a large share of the workforce. Viewed dynamically, the possibilities of promotion or demotion with attendant income effects can also be considered material incentives.

Nonmaterial incentives can take several forms: coercion, moral incentives, or internal incentives. Coercion might take the form of introducing military officers and/or discipline into factories, such as the labor conscription drive during the 1918–21 civil war in the Soviet Union or, to a lesser degree, Cuba in the late 1960s; or, it might be indirect, such as the threat of transferring deviant workers or managers to undesirable areas. Moral incentives connote workers being motivated by a concept of goodness or the commonweal. The vast majority of workers, experience has demonstrated, cannot be sustained by such abstractions for extended periods of time. The possible exception here is during periods of war or perceived external threat. The state often encourages moral incentives with a panoply of banners, awards, blandishments, exhortations, perquisites, and other forms of public recognition. It would be an overstatement to say that moral incentives accomplish nothing. They do motivate some workers, sometimes. During normal periods, however, they do not function effectively alone no matter how frequent or forceful the hortatory calls of the leadership.

Another form of nonmaterial stimulus is internal incentive. We use this term to denote the workers' internalization of the goals of their work center or the economy (see Koont and Zimbalist 1984). The best way to stimulate this internalization is to involve the workers in the setting of their work center's or the economy's goals. To the extent that the workers participate in setting the goals, they are more likely to consider those goals their own. Further, the more the workers control the conditions of their work (the work process, the division of labor, health and safety conditions, etc.), the stronger the resulting effect. This relationship should be readily grasped by scholars who control their work environment (e.g., the classes they teach, the subjects and methods of their research) and receive pittances of monetary reward. Their control over their work has engendered internalization of the goals of academe and intellectual inquiry.

An important and, we believe, unresolved question is to what degree can production workers internalize norms and goals of their work place. There is certainly abundant evidence that points to the potential salutary effects on productivity of worker participation,[1] but it is unclear how long these effects can be sustained and how effective they can be in a planned economy. How extensive and meaningful can worker participation be in a CPE where enterprise autonomy typically is tightly circumscribed and where the perceived imperative of central coordination limits input from the base in setting national priorities?

Post-1958 Cuba has experimented with different emphases and combinations of incentives. It is reasonable to say that Cuba has grown more sophisticated over time in applying both material and nonmaterial incentives. It is not clear, however, whether this sophistication has yielded much in the way of increased output.

THE 1960S

The unequal development of the Cuban economy prior to the revolution left a markedly skewed distribution of wages. In 1958, whereas average monthly wages in sugar and nickel manufacturing were 120 pesos, in beer they were 273 pesos and in cigarettes, 359 (Acosta 1982: 305). At the time, straight time wages were paid in 76.5 percent of Cuba's work centers, straight piece wages were paid in 10.5 percent, time and piece wages were used together in 10.1 percent, and time and (nonpiece) bonuses were combined in 2.9 percent (Acosta 1982: 302; Codina 1987: 127).

The need to apply a uniform wage scale, based on consistent wage-forming principles, was immediately apparent. In 1961 a wage freeze was declared and training begun of specialists in work organization. By 1963 a new wage scale had been experimentally introduced in 283 work centers. It was gradually extended to the whole economy by 1966, and there was a significant compression of wage inequality. Agricultural wages rose by an average 74 percent, while industrial wages rose 24 percent. The ratio of the top to the bottom wage (including all workers, technicians, managers, planning bureaucrats, etc.) on this scale was 4.33 to 1. It must be mentioned, though, in order to curtail the flight of skilled workers and not alienate others, a decision was taken to allow workers who received a wage above what the new scale stipulated to continue to earn the higher wage. This higher wage is referred to in Cuba as the historical wage and the difference between the two wages is referred to as *el plus*.[2] In 1965, some 70 percent of nonagricultural workers continued to receive a historical wage; this proportion was lowered to 25 percent by 1973 and to an estimated 11 percent by 1981 (Codina 1987: 311).

Accompanying the new wage scale was a new system of piece payments and, in agriculture and foreign trade where enterprise self-financing[3] was theoretically introduced, profit sharing. For every 1 percent of output in excess of a worker's norm, his or her wage would rise by 0.5 percent (up to the next step on the wage scale). The inaccuracy and outdated character of most of the applied norms, however, impeded the effective operation of this intended incentive. There was also a profit-sharing scheme in the self-financing sectors. Bonus payments were restricted to 5 percent of the enterprise wage fund. Prices, however, had been frozen and profitability bore only a tenuous relationship to effort and efficiency. One Cuban expert writing about the new piece payment and bonus policy noted that, "in practice, this policy did not stimulate an increase in production or in labor productivity (Codina 1987: 130)."[4]

Between 1963 and 1965, a debate over incentives and planning took place in

Cuba. Two basic positions were propounded.[5] Che Guevara argued for central planning, budgetary financing (all enterprise profits go to the state budget, all losses are covered by the budget), and moral incentives. Moral incentives, Guevara maintained, were necessary to create a new socialist consciousness, although he recognized that material incentives could not be abandoned all at once. He urged, therefore, that material incentives be collective (applied to groups of workers, not individual workers) and limited in scope. According to Guevara, Cuba's low level of material development at the time meant than an extensive use of material incentives, and the corresponding income differentiation, would begin to recreate the extensive inequality of prerevolutionary Cuba.[6]

The other side of the debate was presented most cogently by Carlos Rafael Rodríguez. He argued for central planning, enterprise self-financing, and material incentives. Rodríguez argued that budgetary financing encouraged the wasteful use of resources by enterprises. Material incentives, he averred, were needed to motivate workers who were not ideologically ready for the communist principle of distribution: "from each according to his ability, to each according to his need." The issue of worker participation in enterprise decision-making and popular participation in plan formulation was scarcely broached by either side (Bengelsdorf 1985: ch. 7).

At the time of this debate economic management consisted of a rudimentary, almost ad hoc system of central planning, a mixture of budgetary and enterprise financing and the incentive system already described. In 1966 things began to change. Guevara's policy prescriptions had won out (although Guevara himself had been out of office since 1965) and were implemented in extreme fashion. Piece payments and bonuses were ended. Budgetary finance was applied universally. Enterprises ceased to exist as separate economic entities and became part of larger consolidated enterprises. The powers of JUCEPLAN (the central planning board) were reduced and formal one-year planning was abandoned. In its place were substituted Castro-inspired miniplans that prioritized certain sectors (such as sugar), assuring them adequate resources. Nonprioritized sectors, however, fared poorly and bottlenecks spread throughout the economy. The combination of bottlenecks and the high investment ratios of the late 1960s created serious shortages of consumer goods. Thus, even if the leadership had wanted to, it would have been impossible to meaningfully implement a policy of material incentives. Workers could be paid more for producing more, but there was little to buy.

The late 1960s was a difficult time economically. A minority of workers responded to the exhortations of sacrifice, but overall absenteeism rose and productivity lagged. According to one estimate, unit labor costs rose by 12.65 percent between 1966 and 1970 (Codina 1987: 131). In a sense, then, Cuba had tried both material and moral incentives in the 1960s and, in the absence of effective internal incentives,[7] both had failed.

THE 1970s

This decade began with the leadership's recognition of the importance of 1) its failure to develop worker involvement in decision-making and 2) its neglect of material incentives. Since 1970, with varying intensity at different times, the leadership has sought to nurture worker participation and, up to April 1986, to promote the extension of material incentives.

One of the first and most important measures taken was to revitalize unions, which had become passive instruments of state policy in the 1960s. Over 26,000 new union locals were established and new elections were called. Eighty-seven percent of the nearly 118,000 elected officials had not previously served. The unions became active in implementing the new policies of worker participation and the setting of work norms.

Although new elementary work norms began to be set in 1970, the process proceeded very slowly. While some analysts have attributed the early 1970s' rapid growth in worker productivity to the use of material incentives, the relationship between the two is tenuous.[8] The new norms were not tied to pay until 1974. Moreover, in the first years of the decade there was still considerable excess liquidity held by Cuban households. It is difficult, then, to see a significant connection between the 1971–74 jump in labor productivity and material incentives. Although other factors were certainly involved, it seems likely that the shift in enterprise social relations (invigoration of unions, labor representation on management boards, revitalization of worker assemblies and work councils, etc.) aided in the development of internal incentives as well as the elicitation of useful ideas for improving productivity.

One other factor that might have contributed to increased worker productivity in the early 1970s was the promulgation of the 1971 compulsory work law. The law specified that workers guilty of absenteeism were to be deprived of vacations, excluded from certain social benefits and, in severe cases, transferred to labor camps. The law, however, affected productivity in contradictory ways. On the one hand, one would expect output per unit of labor input to drop as thousands of reluctant and often poorly trained individuals reentered the workforce. On the other hand, in reducing absenteeism, productivity per employed person (rather than per hour worked) undoubtedly improved. There is no a priori basis for suspecting the net effect of these two forces to be positive.

In the course of the 1970s worker participation in enterprise and economywide affairs continued to develop, although the range of activity in which workers had input, and their ability to impose changes opposed by management, the Party, or the government, remained limited. Labor, for example, acquired the right to allocate scarce but coveted consumer durables and housing. The central government began to allot work centers, in some instances in accordance with work performance, consumer durables and building materials for housing. The workers then decided how the items would be distributed among themselves—reportedly on the basis of merit (attendance and work record) and need (family size and living conditions).

Workers were increasingly consulted about national plans as well as their implementation at the enterprise level. According to official reports, the number of workers participating in the discussion and amendment of annual economic plans at the enterprise level increased from 1.26 million in 1975 to 1.45 million in 1980.[9] There is also some evidence suggesting that workers felt their participation to be effective and not merely formal. A 1975 study found that 85 percent of surveyed workers believed workers must be consulted in enterprise affairs, and 58 percent felt worker input to be influential (Pérez-Stable 1976: 331–34).[10] Eighty percent of the 355 workers interviewed in conjunction with another survey conducted the following year reported, in turn, that they "always or nearly always" made a meaningful personal intervention at production assemblies (Herrera and Rosenkranz 1979: 48). In a 1977 survey conducted by two Cuban researchers of 1,000 randomly selected workers in large Havana enterprises, the conclusions regarding worker participation in enterprise management were yet more sanguine: There was broad agreement among workers of six different strata that production meetings were held monthly, that there was active worker participation at these meetings, that management was receptive to worker suggestions, and that the deficiencies discussed at these meetings were "always or almost always" addressed and alleviated (Hernández and Rios 1977: 159–79).

These surveys hardly constitute conclusive evidence, and they must be interpreted with the usual cautions surrounding survey work. Nonetheless, they do suggest that a certain degree of worker participation had been established, that a positive momentum had been created, and that the expectation of greater participation had become a part of worker consciousness. The actual impact of workers on economic decision-making still must have been quite minimal, however. Whatever salutary effects opening the channels of participation might have had in the 1970s would not be maintained in the 1980s without deepening participation.

Material incentives also developed during this period, but slowly, unevenly, and inadequately. By the end of 1973, counting the norms borrowed from the early 1960s and those created or revised since 1970, almost two million workers—or over 80 percent of the labor force—were in normed jobs. When the idea of linking pay to norm fulfillment was put into effect in 1974, however, it was quickly realized that most norms were hopelessly out-of-date. Thus, by the end of 1975, after many norms were invalidated, fewer than one million workers had their pay tied to norms. Even then, most norms were unrealistically low (affected workers participated in their setting) and were surpassed by significant margins with worker remuneration increasing one percent for every one percent of norm overfulfillment. More norms were invalidated, so that by the end of 1976 there were only 630,000 workers with pay linked to norms. The decertification of norms continued in 1977. At the end of this year, only 570,000 workers had pay tied to norms. By this time a sufficient number of time and motion specialists had been trained to reverse the trend. The number of workers with pay tied to norms rose gradually to 719,140 (or 35.8 percent of all workers in the productive sphere) by September 1979; yet, only 59.3 percent of normed workers' working time was connected to normed work (Acosta 1982: 317–18).[11]

It is important to stress that the great majority of these norms were elementary, as opposed to semitechnical or technical. Basically, an elementary norm is one that is generated jointly by a technical normer and a worker (without a motion study), or one that is carried over from an earlier period. Even by 1987, 75.5 percent of all norms were elementary, 24.2 percent were semitechnical, and 0.3 percent were technical.[12] As such, there was still a significant subjective component to the norms in the Cuban view and, in practice, the norms were still too low. During the last quarter of 1979, for instance, 95.5 percent of workers operating with norms either met or exceeded their quotas (JUCEPLAN, 1980: 297). In part, they were too low because of the worker and union involvement in their fixing and, in part, because they were not revised frequently enough. As we shall see, the ongoing difficulties with perfecting the norming system encouraged the Cubans to introduce new material incentive mechanisms in the 1980s.

The biggest change in economic management in Cuba during the 1970s was the introduction of their new planning system, the SDPE, beginning in 1977.[13] The SDPE basically was modeled after the 1965 Soviet reforms. It attempts to 1) put enterprises on a self-financing basis, 2) introduce a profitability criterion with its corresponding incentives, and 3) promote decentralization, organizational coherence, and efficiency. As with the earlier Soviet reform, it has met with the obstacles, *inter alia*, of bureaucratic resistance, pervasive shortages, and an irrational price structure. Possibilities for decentralized decision-making in Cuba have been constrained by the inadequate supply of skilled managerial and technical labor. Moreover, Cuba confronted additional difficulties in adapting the Soviet-styled reform to Cuban political culture. The Cubans have been tinkering with and evaluating the system since the outset. Critical judgments have been increasingly aired in public since the onset of severe foreign exchange problems in 1985, the formation of the *Grupo Central*,[14] and the 1986–88 rectification campaign.[15] Nevertheless, given the underdeveloped state of Cuba's planning institutions in 1976 and the lack of economic consciousness engendered by budgetary financing, the SDPE has brought progress and some improved efficiency to the Cuban economy.

Our concern, however, is not with the SDPE itself, but with how it has interacted with Cuba's incentive system. From this perspective, the SDPE represented the first organized attempt in Cuba to implement mature central planning, with stable institutions and defined functions. As such, when problems did appear, their source was more identifiable and their systemic nature was more apparent. At the same time, it is important to keep in mind that the SDPE only began to be implemented in 1977, in an environment in which many essential planning institutions did not yet exist. The introduction of SDPE coincided with Cuba's first five-year plan, indicating the inchoateness of Cuba's planning system at the time. Cuba still lacked an adequate statistical network, a legal system for enforcing contracts, a management training program, proper financial institutions, and so on. Many of the SDPE's core elements were not introduced until 1979 and 1980, and even then on an experimental basis. It is to the 1980s, then, that we must turn to consider the recent evolution of planning and incentives in Cuba.

THE 1980s

A major theme of the SDPE was decentralization. Having been put on a self-financing scheme that included profit sharing, enterprises were supposed to exercise increasing autonomy from the center. This, in turn, was to promote efficiency. Without some degree of independence, moreover, the possibilities for worker participation are limited to matters of work organization internal to the enterprise and to possible modification of the economic plan's control figures.

Nominal self-financing and profit sharing by themselves did little, if anything, to enhance the scope of enterprise decision-making. Among other things, in the context of centrally fixed prices, centrally determined investments, and extensive input shortages, these mechanisms do not alter the basic mode of operation of CPEs. If prices are centrally set every five years, they cannot reliably be a rational guide to production or allocation choices; nor can they systematically identify through a profitability index enterprises that are well managed. If shortages are commonplace, then otherwise efficient enterprises are often thwarted in their production efforts because of nondelivery or untimely delivery of inputs, or delivery of improperly specified, poor quality inputs. Bottlenecks and planning imperfections, in turn, necessitate amendments to the plan after the beginning of the year—often raising an enterprise's output target without increasing its supply of raw materials. Enterprises behaving rationally in this environment, will hoard inputs, thereby aggravating the shortage problem. If the behavior of profits is fickle because of these and other factors, the planning authorities must limit, on equity grounds alone, the extent of profit retention and distribution, thus weakening the incentive effect. And if profits thrive in certain enterprises despite the absence of properly specified, high-quality production, then the center must devise new administrative regulations to control this behavior. In the end, the profitability algorithm becomes hopelessly complicated and the incentive mechanism debilitated. If the center decides which investment projects are to be undertaken, then the fact that enterprises pay for increasing shares of investment costs out of their bank funds rather than state budget funds (the share of enterprise- financed investments in total investment financing in Cuba rose from 1 percent in 1981 to 30 percent in 1985) (BNC, March 1986a: 6) does not imply a substantive decentralization of capital allocation.

The SDPE, then, like the 1965 Soviet economic reforms, did not bring about a significant change in underlying centralization of decision-making in the economic mechanism. There were, however, peripheral changes that accompanied the SDPE, many introduced in an effort to adapt the Soviet centralized model to Cuban conditions, that did increase the flexibility of the system and allow for some decentralization of decision-making. Among these new policies was the post-1976 system of popular power that controlled the management of locally oriented service and production enterprises. In the mid-1980s, such enterprises accounted for 34 percent of all Cuban enterprises. The local budgets of popular power grew from 21 percent of the total state budget in 1978 to 26 percent in 1980, 30 percent in 1982, and 33 percent in 1984. The local budget share in the Soviet Union in 1980 was 17.1 percent (Mata 1986: 56).

Another policy allowed for enterprises to make their own contracts for products that were not in the *nomenklatura* and were not centrally balanced. As of 1983, approximately 600 products or product groups, covering between 70 and 80 percent of gross social product, were centrally balanced (Palacios et al. 1986: 9–36). There has also been encouragement for the development of "secondary" (nonplan) production, once the plan is fulfilled. Further, the realization of growing stocks of unused inputs within enterprises led to the practice of "resource fairs" where enterprises traded freely and directly with each other, first organized by the State Technical and Material Supply Committee in 1979. The fairs of 1979 and 1980 witnessed the sale of 40 million pesos' worth of inputs. Inventory sales of production inputs by enterprises have continued to grow. In October 1982 the President of JUCEPLAN reported that some 500 million pesos of such resources had already been identified (*Granma*, October 5, 1982: 2).[16] In May 1985, at the conclusion of the Fourth Plenary of the SDPE, the judgment was reached that the State Technical and Material Supply Committee was still allocating too many products and the number should be significantly reduced, allowing enterprises to contract directly with each other for these products (JUCEPLAN 1985: 25).[17]

Other measures of decentralization included the strengthening of the Cuban Institute of Internal Demand, the introduction of free labor contracting in 1980,[18] and an increasing acceptance of private productive and service activity—most notably housing construction cooperatives and free farmers' markets. The farmers' markets were opened in 1980. Sales of fresh vegetables and fruits grew rapidly until the government crackdown on "abuses" (exhorbitant prices, excessive middleperson profits, resource diversion from the state sector, etc.) in February 1982. Sales began to grow again after the promulgation of new regulations (20 percent sales tax, progressive income tax on private farmer income of 5 to 20 percent, and the expansion of the state-controlled parallel market to compete with the farmers' markets) in May 1983. However, new abuses, more serious diversion of resources from state uses, and reported incomes above 50,000 pesos for truckers, wholesalers, and some farmers led to the indefinite closing of these markets in May 1986. Although such free market sales of produce are permitted elsewhere in the Soviet bloc, private plots (except for Poland) tend to be no larger than one-quarter or one-half hectare. In Cuba, such plots typically range from 20 to over 60 hectares; hence the potential for economic and political disruption emerging from the private agricultural sector in Cuba prima facie is greater.

Nevertheless, these decentralizing measures taken together did not alter the key dynamic of Cuban planning. Prior to the beginning of the rectification campaign in April 1986,[19] it was apparent from various government documents and speeches that the need for further decentralization and greater worker participation was clearly perceived. In particular, the documents of the Fourth Plenary evaluating the SDPE, held in May 1985, outlined a series of decentralizing measures that the Cubans intended to carry out (JUCEPLAN 1985).[20] With the severe difficulties concerning foreign exchange earnings that Cuba began to experience around that time, along with the growing excess of uncompleted investment projects, however, resources became too scarce to sustain the momentum toward decentralization, and the state tightened its grip on the economy in order to economize on the use of foreign exchange as well as to bring existing investment projects to successful completion.[21]

Unintended or profligate use of resources in both the private and public spheres came under increasing scrutiny, as did the lack of coordination among sectoral ministries of the economy and among state planning institutions (e.g., the State Committee on Finances, the State Price Committee, the National Bank, JUCEPLAN). Together with the difficulties of increasingly lax labor discipline and enterprise overstaffing, these problems brought on the rectification campaign. Market-oriented decentralization was put on hold,[22] although some efforts at administrative decentralization (e.g., production brigades, reducing the staff and the power of the ministries) have continued.[23] A central theme of the rectification campaign has been the deficient functioning of Cuba's material incentives and it is to this matter we now turn.

Wage and Salary Scale

The first change in material incentives during the 1980s was the wage and salary reform of 1981. The basic thrust of the reform was to increase relative salaries of highly skilled labor. Accordingly, the ratio of the highest to lowest wage in the new structure rose from 4.67 : 1 to 5.29 : 1. Whereas the lowest wage rose from 75 to 85 pesos per month, the highest salary increased from 350 to 450 pesos. Of course, those at the top of the scale are also likely to be recipients of various perquisites. (More recently, the austerity measures of January 1987 provoked concern for lower income earners, and the minimum wage was raised to 100 pesos as of February 1, 1987.[24]) As part of the wage reform process, the average monthly wage continued to climb, from 148 pesos in 1980 to 195 pesos in 1986. The 1987 wage and salary schedule is shown in Table 8.1.

In any case, the changes in the basic wage and salary scale were very modest. It is difficult to believe that they stimulated an increased supply of skilled labor. This is especially so since managerial and technical personnel generally were not eligible for piece-rate increases or *primas* (the new, 1980 system of work-related bonuses).

Table 8.1.   The Cuban Basic Monthly Wage Schedule (in 1987 pesos)

Group	Production workers	Administrative and service workers	Technical workers			Directors
			I	II	III	
1	107[a]	100[a]				
2	118[b]	100[a]				
3	122	111				111
4	141	128	128	138	148	128
5	162	148	148	160	171	148
6	187	171	171	185	198	171
7	217	198	198	205	211	198
8			211	221	231	211
9	254	231	234	250	265	231
10			250	265	280	250
11			265	280	295	265
12			280	295	310	280
13			295	310	325	295
14			310	325	340	310
15			325	340	355	325
16			340			340
17			355			355
18			370			370
19			385			385
20			400			400
21			425			425
22			450			450

Source: Information supplied to the authors by the State Statistical Committee.
[a]These rates were raised to these levels on February 1, 1987, from 93 pesos for group 1 production workers, from 85 for group 1 administrative and service workers, and from 97 for group 2 administrative and service workers. Altogether this increase benefited 186,000 workers.
[b]This rate was raised on June 1, 1987, from 107 pesos. It affected 208,343 workers.

Payment According to Output

Norm or piece payments at first continued to be extended to a growing number of Cuban workers.[25] With the aid of some 20,000 normers, by 1981 1.23 million Cuban workers had their pay tied to their output.[26] This number stabilized, so that by the end of 1985 1.2 million workers (or 37.2 percent of the labor force) had their pay linked to output. The value of payments for norm overfulfillment is shown in Table 8.2.

Even though payments linked to output grew rapidly (by 150 percent) between 1980 and 1985, they still constituted only 6.0 percent of the average worker's basic wage in 1985. By early 1986, then, the average worker had not grown to depend on the extra payments related to norm fulfillment for a significant part of his or her income. The timing was perhaps right for the regime to launch its rectification campaign attacking abuses in the system of material rewards.

To be sure, there were sectors of the workforce such as construction and forestry where these payments were more important. And there were individual workers who succeeded in grossly abusing the system. At the *Reuniones de Empresas* (enterprise meetings) held throughout the country during June and July of 1986 and extensively covered in *Granma* of that period, there was ample identification and discussion of such abuses: maintainence workers who were paid five times for repairing the same machine; radio announcers paid according to a piece rate; construction workers with ridiculously low norms;[27] sugar mill workers who received triple extra pay for the same work (exceeding their

Table 8.2. Payments for Overfulfillment of Norms (millions of pesos)

	1980	1981	1982	1983	1984	1985
Total economy	121.7	183.0	204.8	218.1	261.8	274.5
	(3.9)[a]	(4.7)	(4.7)	(5.1)	(5.8)	(6.0)
Industry	35.8	49.3	56.6	70.9	93.1	97.1
	(3.7)	(4.3)	(4.6)	(5.4)	(6.5)	(6.8)
Construction	26.6	38.9	42.8	51.1	64.6	70.8
	(5.2)	(7.0)	(7.9)	(8.4)	(9.4)	(10.3)
Agriculture	23.8	32.5	31.1	26.5	19.7	20.4
	(2.6)	(2.9)	(2.6)	(2.3)	(1.7)	(1.8)
Forestry	2.9	3.5	4.1	5.3	5.9	5.8
	(9.2)	(9.6)	(11.1)	(11.5)	(12.1)	(10.6)
Transport	13.6	17.0	19.6	16.7	21.6	21.3
	(3.9)	(4.2)	(4.8)	(3.8)	(4.8)	(4.8)
Communication	0.4	0.5	0.4	0.6	0.5	0.6
	(1.1)	(1.2)	(0.9)	(1.2)	(1.0)	(1.1)
Commerce	12.8	30.0	34.8	22.7	30.8	32.1
	(2.7)	(5.7)	(6.1)	(3.5)	(4.4)	(4.6)

Source: Calculated by the authors from data provided by the State Statistical Committee.
[a]Percentage of basic wage.

norm, working overtime, and increasing exports), and so on. Not only were these abuses of the system generating unjustified wage inequality, but they were causing considerable resentment among conscientious workers who did not bend the rules. Further, the severe hard currency difficulties of 1986–87 (hard currency availability in 1987 was estimated to be one-third of its 1984 level) implied even greater consumer goods shortages, raising questions about the efficacy of attempting to motivate greater work effort with pesos during this period.

There is an abundant literature in the West about the difficulties in effectively implementing piece-rate systems.[28] U.S. managers have increasingly abandoned the old-style, Tayloristic piece-rate methods, while the Soviets have moved away from Stakhanovism (Kirsch 1972). Human relations and group work approaches from Japan and Scandinavia have gained ascendancy in personnel management in the West. Part of this shift is attributable to the ways in which technology has transformed the work process, part to the higher levels of workforce educational attainment, and part to the unrealistic expectations of "scientific management." Yet ever since Lenin extolled the virtues of scientific management in 1918 (Lenin 1918), the socialist bloc has clung to the notion of technical work norms. The theoretical underpinning of such norms, as laid out by F. W. Taylor (1947), is highly dubious. Can a worker's motions really be treated as those of a machine part? Can all mental processes really be removed from the shop floor to the engineer's drawing boards? Will not the subjective and social elements of work always play a major role?[29]

In this regard, it should be observed that in 1987 more than 75 percent of Cuba's work norms were still elementary. Even if norms could somehow be technically and accurately set at some point in time, it is important to note that there are over 3 million work norms in Cuba. With 20,000 trained normers, it takes a long time before a technical norm can be revised. One enterprise, a metal parts workshop under the Sugar Ministry, reported that a new traveling crane had been introduced that tripled productivity, but the norm had not been altered (*Granma Resumen Semanal*, December 14, 1986: 4). According to Castro's remarks at the closing session of the Third Party Congress in December 1986, many sectors of the economy went from January 1983 through 1986 without norm revision.

Judging from the Cubans' own figures, elementary norms in particular continue to be set at unrealistically low levels. In 1986, over one-third of all workers with norms produced over 130 percent of their output norms (*Granma*, January 14, 1987: 5). The figure would doubtless have been higher but for the workings of the ratchet effect. There is always the likelihood that if a worker significantly exceeds the set norm, the norm will be raised during the next period. This stands as a powerful deterrent to most workers in countries with piece payments, who fear that they will have to work harder and harder just to maintain their income. Policymakers in some countries have endeavored to skirt the problem by promising workers (or factories with output quotas) that their norms would not be adjusted throughout the five-year plan. Trust in policymakers can postpone the ratchet effect for the early years of a five-year plan in the case of workers with a short time horizon. The Cubans, however, have tended to adjust norms upward on a yearly basis when they are surpassed, and they have made clear their intention to continue to do so in order to avoid excessive piece-rate payments (L. R. González 1987: 49–57). Further, at times the norm, intended to stimulate more effort, can have precisely the reverse effect. That is, if a worker has a set output norm and he or she is mindful of the ratchet effect, then once the worker has reached the norm he or she may simply stop work, or, for appearances sake, continue to work at a slower pace as the norm is approached. For example, during the discussions of rectification at the closing sessions of the Third Party Congress in December 1986, Manuel Valladares, first secretary of the Party in Vertientes, Camaguey, reported that many sugar cane workers in his municipality completed their norms after four hours and then left work (*Granma Resumen Semanal*, December 14, 1986: 3). There is also the danger that quality will be sacrificed in order to meet quantity norms. This is particularly troublesome in an economy of synthetic success indicators evaluated by hierarchical superiors, rather than by the consumer of the product.

With the rectification campaign, many abuses have been curtailed and norms have been raised for many jobs (and suspended for a few). Thus, in 1987 (through October) only 29.6 percent of all industrial workers with norms exceeded their norms by more than 20 percent, and the payment for overfulfilling norms for all workers fell to 4.4 percent of the basic wage in 1986 and to 3.2 percent of the basic wage in 1987 (CEE/BEC 1988: 112, 116).[30] Naturally, some of the decrease in bonuses is attributable to the difficult macroeconomic conditions of 1986–87 rather than to the rectification campaign itself.

Although most of the deficiencies with work norms apply equally to market and planned economies, it would seem that the workings of piece payments would be even more problematic in a shortage-ridden economy where collectivist goals are being pursued. To be sure, Cuba has increasingly developed collective piece payments (*destajo colectivo*); by October 1986, while 356,200 workers were on individual work norms, the number of workers on collective norms had risen to 224,700.

There is little evidence that Cuba's experimentation with individual piece payments, despite the enormous investment in training work specialists and implanting the system, has augmented worker productivity. It is perhaps in part for these reasons that Cuba began to develop two new types of material rewards in 1979, and why today material rewards are being deemphasized and "political solutions" are being sought.

Bonuses

A second type of material reward, the *prima* or bonus, was introduced experimentally in 1979 and then gradually applied economywide in 1980.[31] One function of the bonus is to plug up the loopholes left by the rest of the system of material incentives. With vertical rather than horizontal responsiveness in CPEs, there is an endemic problem with quality and properly specified output. The overriding logic of the central plan requires the center to attempt to balance the economy, to coordinate its parts, and this can only be done if enterprises produce what they are planned to produce. This logic, then, places a premium on the physical output target, no matter how many other success indicators (such as profitability) are assigned to an enterprise. Profitability may have value, but given the often distorting effect on relative prices of centrally set prices, input shortages, lack of competition, etc., central planners have long realized that profitability or other synthetic financial indicators cannot take precedence over physical output. But if the enterprise is told by its superior ministry to make sure it meets its output target above all else, the enterprise will often respond by reducing quality, choosing a simpler product mix, hoarding inputs or using them inefficiently, not introducing new methods or products, and so on. This is where the *prima* comes in.

Varieties of *primas* abound in Cuba, but most involve a bonus to a group of production workers for increasing exports, saving raw materials or energy, overfulfilling quality and quantity[32] targets, or developing new products. These bonuses are generally paid every one to three months when merited, and they are statutorily set at a limit of 30 percent of a worker's basic wage. The total value of *primas* paid out in 1980 equalled 14.0 million pesos. This value rose steadily from 43.4 million pesos in 1981 to 54.4 million in 1982, 58.3 million in 1983, 81.4 million in 1984, and 90.7 million pesos in 1985. In 1985, *primas* were paid to approximately one million workers, but, despite their rapid growth, they still represented only 1.9 percent of the basic wage on average.[33]

It seems that the main problem with the *prima* was that it overlapped with other material incentives, so that a worker was getting paid many times over for the same work. In a number of cases it was clear that the system had been designed and implemented carelessly.[34] In other cases, the criteria for earning *primas* were too complex for the affected workers to understand. The rectification campaign, then, brought not a repudiation of the *primas* but a decision to streamline and clarify them. The number of *primas* was cut by one-third in agriculture and by similar proportions elsewhere in the economy. Overall, the share of *primas* in the basic wage fell from 1.9 percent in 1985 to 1.5 percent in 1986, and to 0.9 percent in 1987 (CEE/BEC 1988: 112).

Stimulation Funds and Profit Sharing

The concept behind stimulation funds (*fondos de estimulación*) is that if enterprises can retain a certain share of their profits for their own use, this incentive will stimulate productivity. Originally it was intended that the stimulation fund would be divided into three parts: the prize fund (*fondo de premios*) for distribution to the workforce as profit sharing; the socio-cultural fund for collective use by the enterprise in social projects, for example, building beach cabins, recreational facilities, and buses; and the investment fund for small investments at the enterprise's initiative. However, due to the lack of resources, the strong investment drive typical of CPEs (Kornai 1980b), and the plethora of unfinished investment projects nationwide, the investment fund was put on indefinite hold. The sociocultural fund, again due to the shortage primarily of construction materials, is generally limited to be no greater than 30 to 40 percent of the prize fund.

The stimulation funds were first introduced on an experimental basis in 191 enterprises in 1979. On the basis of actual enterprise performance, however, only 65 enterprises were able to form their planned funds. By 1985, after the major price reform of 1981, yearly price modifications, and many adjustments to the regulations governing the funds, 1,167 enterprises were able to form funds, benefiting some one million workers (or 53 percent of the workers in the self-financing sphere of the economy).[35] The total value of *premios* or profit sharing paid out to workers rose steadily from 4.2 million pesos in 1980 to 71.1 million pesos in 1985. Although this represented a 935.5 percent growth during the quinquennium, by 1985 total *premios* were still only 78.4 percent of the total *primas* paid to workers, and only 25.9 percent of the total for norm overfulfillment. Viewed differently, in 1985 *premios* averaged only 1.6 percent of the basic wage in the productive sphere of the economy.[36] From the standpoint of the *premio* as a stimulus to work effort and creativity, there are several additional problems apart from their still diminutive size as of 1985.

One of the more straightforward problems with the *premios* is that they are paid out once a year if at all, whereas the *primas* and norm payments are paid out either quarterly or monthly. This payment schedule renders the *premios* more remote than they would be otherwise.[37] The problem, of course, is that the state wants to encourage sustained profitability, not just profitability during a particular fiscal quarter. Another problem the Cubans have had with the stimulation funds is that efficient enterprises instructed in the economic plan to make major investments out of their own profits have not had sufficient monies left over to form the funds.

A more important and troublesome problem with the stimulation funds has to do with the basic operation of CPEs. As discussed above, with prices set centrally and infrequently; with shortages, delays, and poor quality of inputs; with shortages of available consumer goods; with little if any competition or choice of supplier, the allocational or incentive meaning of profits is highly dubious.[38] Some very efficient enterprises may earn no profit, while other inefficient enterprises may earn large profits. The state attempts to compensate for these haphazard outcomes by creating regulations, rules, contingencies, etc. to make the system more equitable. In doing this, however, it also makes the system of stimulation funds largely inscrutable and unpredictable to workers as well as enterprise directors.[39] If there is no clear link between the size of the *premios* and the workers' effort or the enterprise's choices, then the incentive function of the *premio* has broken down.

In discussing the system of stimulation funds in the Soviet Union, Alec Nove once warned: "The payments into the incentive funds are calculated in a manner so bewilderingly complex that both author and reader would be reduced to paralytic boredom if the rules were here reproduced" (Nove 1977: 88). We shall heed Nove's admonition only partially, because it is instructive to grasp the nature of the problem. The actual system for forming stimulation funds has been changed a number of times since 1979 and its precise application is different for different enterprises. For instance, enterprises with unavoidable losses (because of relative prices or other factors) are allowed to form stimulation funds out of reductions in losses from one year to the next. The actual funds come from the relevant ministry, which collects a "tax" from profitable enterprises in its branch in order to finance the fund for enterprises in the red. We describe below the system of stimulation funds that was in operation in mid-1985. Since then one important change has been made. The normative adjustment coefficient was at first a function of planned and actual increases in success indicators from one year to the next. This system penalized enterprises with already taut (near capacity) plans. The coefficient is now principally a function of the enterprise's performance relative to the average performance in the enterprise's branch, rather than the performance of the enterprise itself in the previous year.[40]

Stimulation funds are formed in three stages. The first is the planning stage. Each enterprise is limited to three indicators in generating the fund. The three most common are: increases in worker net productivity, decreases in cost per unit of output, and increases in output or exports. For each peso of planned value in each indicator there is a normative that determines the peso value to be contributed to the fund. This normative is then multiplied by an adjustment coefficient—which before 1986 was the ratio of the planned value of the indicator in the current year to that of the previous year—to arrive at the planned *premio* for each indicator. The total *premio* is arrived at by summing the *premios* for each indicator. The adjustment coefficient is part of the attempt to induce enterprises to reveal their true production capacity. The higher the plan they set for themselves, the higher the coefficient and the greater potential size of the stimulation fund.

The second step is referred to as the formation stage. In this stage the planned *premio* is multiplied, first, by the ratio of the actual value of the indicator achieved relative to its planned value, and second, by a "reduction coefficient" that varies between 0.2 and 0.8—being lower for overfulfillment than underfulfillment and lower for larger deviations (above or below) from planned values. After this double multiplication is performed, the resulting value is the "formed" *premio* for each indicator. Again, this is summed over the three indicators to arrive at the total *premio*, with the additional constraint that the *premio* cannot exceed enterprise profits. The reduction coefficient, together with the adjustment coefficient, is intended to produce larger *premios* for the fulfillment of higher targets than the overfulfillment of lower targets (for any given level of actual output). This is the so-called taut planning algorithm.

In the third stage, the "formed" *premio* is adjusted downward if the enterprise has not met a series of additional conditions. For instance, for every 1 percent of the value of the enterprise's supply contracts it doesn't meet, its *premio* is reduced by 1 percent; likewise for every 1 percent deterioration in the relationship between productivity and the average wage, or the share of output in the top quality category as well as other indicators. If underfulfillment for some indicators goes below a certain level, then the enterprise is prohibited from forming *premios* at all.[41] Although there has been discussion of lifting the limit, the stimulation funds have been restricted to a maximum of 8.5 percent of the enterprise's previous year wage bill.

Given the complexity of the determinants of the stimulation fund and the fact that many of the elements affecting its formation are out of the enterprise's control, it is little wonder that enterprises continue to place priority on meeting the physical indicators of the plan. Former JUCEPLAN chief Humberto Pérez stated the problem clearly at the Fourth Plenary (authors' translation): "In this sense our system has functioned in great measure in a formal sense only, superimposing a veil of monetary and financial relations when, just as in the past, production for production's sake still prevails and material indicators still dominate, and profit and profitability play a derivative and passive role" (H. Pérez 1985: 25). Financial indicators such as profitability will continue to play a distant secondary role without major structural reforms, probably including scarcity pricing for most goods.

Taken together, payments for norm overfulfillment, *primas*, *premios*, and overtime work (or what the Cubans call the *parte móvil*, mobile part, of the wage) came to only 10.6 percent of the basic wage on average in 1985. In the mid-1970s in the other CMEA countries, the mobile part of the wage varied between 15.2 percent in Hungary and 55.2 percent in the GDR, with Bulgaria at 39.8 percent, Poland at 31.7 percent, the U.S.S.R. at 36.4 percent, and Czechoslovakia at 43.8 percent (Acosta 1982: 291).

Although conditioned by a country's political culture and economic structures, material incentives have functioned most effectively in CPEs when the state has relaxed controls over parts of the economy, usually implying an expansion of private sector activities. This relaxation is necessary so that there are available resources and goods not accounted for by the plan. Without a material counterpart, the extra pesos of income offered by incentives cannot be translated into higher worker utility and quickly will lose their motivational impact. (It is also possible for the state to plan for surplus production to be made available for unplanned purchases. Cuba does, in fact, attempt to plan surplus production and to a certain degree is successful. The real problem, however, is that when the center attempts to take unplanned, decentralized purchases into account, the spirit of flexibility and enterprise autonomy is undermined. This effort is also constrained by the center's instinct for taut planning.) The conflict arises, however, as the private sector grows and takes on a dynamic of its own, challenging the hegemony of the state sector. As opportunities for private gain expand, material and labor resources intended for the state sector are often diverted for private uses. Thus, the free farmers' markets in Cuba prompted the use of state trucks for delivering private produce; and with the trucks went their drivers, who frequently left their state jobs early to carry out their new, handsomely remunerated tasks. According to Castro, some truck drivers were earning over 50,000 pesos a year, while Cuba's top surgeons earned 5,000 pesos. Many private farmers were moving away from sugar production to produce vegetables and condiments for sale on the free markets, increasing their own incomes but reducing the economy's foreign exchange earnings.[42] Wealthy farmers were known to offer 20,000 pesos and up for Soviet Ladas on the free market, while model workers had to queue for years to be able to purchase a car. Other free marketeers bought state-subsidized toothbrushes, melted the plastic and resold it as jewelry on artisan markets. None of this behavior runs against the ethical norms of market economies, but it does create or aggravate conflicts within a socialist, planned economy. These conflicts (with both their economic and ideological dimensions), above all, provoked the rectification campaign and the decision to place more emphasis on political consciousness and moral incentives.

Conciencia and Worker Participation

The insufficient stimulation and growing disruptiveness of material incentives led the leadership to look once again to political consciousness or *conciencia* to motivate Cuban workers. In speech after speech and meeting after meeting the leadership emphasized the importance of political work, socialist values, and discipline.[43] To be sure, according to accounts in the Cuban press, there is evidence that the new emphasis on combining *conciencia* with streamlined material incentives has yielded some short term gains in productivity and work organization.[44] Exhortations without substantive structural reform, however, sooner or later wear thin. During normal periods, political consciousness is insufficient to stimulate production in the absence of meaningful worker involvement in enterprise and economywide decision-making.[45]

There is some evidence of renewed commitment to worker participation, and there have been some favorable developments. The rhetoric, if not the substance, of Soviet bloc policies calling for greater worker democracy seem to improve the prospects for growth in this area. On the one hand, publicly issued figures suggest that growing numbers of workers are discussing the plan and making modifications in the plan's control figures. Some leadership pronouncements have also been sanguine. Humberto Pérez, for instance, claimed before the National Assembly in December 1983 that worker participation in the 1984 annual plan was the most extensive to date (*Granma*, January 1, 1987). Three years later, before the National Assembly, the new JUCEPLAN head, José López Moreno, referred to radical changes in the methodology for drafting the 1987 plan and a significant deepening in worker participation (*Granma Weekly Review*, January 11, 1987).[46] Unfortunately, no details were provided.

On the other hand, other leadership assessments have been more pessimistic. Humberto Pérez, in an interview published in *Bohemia* (May 29, 1985) stated that one of the greatest weaknesses of the SDPE was its failure to further develop worker participation and that most improvements were only in form, not substance. In June 1986, Roberto Veiga, the general secretary of the Cuban Trade Union Federation (CTC), warned that worker dissatisfaction with the inadequate solutions and explanations offered at worker assemblies could undermine the positive role of worker participation in promoting economic efficiency.[47] An article in the CTC newspaper *Trabajadores* of September 9, 1986 reported on a discussion at the Fourth Congress of the National Union of State Agricultural Workers to the effect that continuing problems with worker participation were resulting in the workers feeling insufficiently identified with the economic plans.[48] Overall, it seems that progress with regard to worker participation has been partial and uneven to date, leaving much to be desired.

There appear to be at least three aspects to deepening worker participation. The first involves a significant shift in power relations at work centers toward the workers. The weakening of work councils' control over worker discipline at the beginning of this decade may have been necessary, but symbolically at least it represented a move to strengthen the hand of the enterprise director (Fuller 1987: 139–52). The pendulum must swing back to give the workers greater control over the internal labor process and work conditions. According to a broad body of evidence, without worker involvement in basic production decisions at the shop floor level, effective participation in extra-enterprise issues is unlikely.[49] That is, if workers do not develop participatory habits in their daily work experience, they are unlikely to be participatory in more remote and intractable areas.

The second aspect involves stretching out the parameters of enterprise decision-making. This can be done by the state restricting the purview of the economic plan, allowing more production decisions to be made at decentralized levels. This, in fact, appears to be one of the major thrusts of the present Gorbachev reform, as it was earlier in the Hungarian and Chinese reforms. The idea is that the state will plan more effectively if it plans less. Castro has seemed to resonate to this theme at times. At a meeting of the Party's leadership in July 1986 (after the beginning of the rectification campaign), Castro was reflecting on the excess of paperwork and administrators and on the state attempting to do too much. He was quoted as saying: "Por exceso de controles, no tenemos control" (Because we have too many control devices, we don't have control) (*Bohemia*, July 4, 1987). Even though decentralization through extension of the market mechanism or the sphere of private activities has been on hold since April 1986, administrative decentralization in Cuban planning has proceeded cautiously forward. The March 1988 report of the national commission set up to study the SDPE calls for ongoing efforts in this direction, including, among others: extension of direct contracting between enterprises, reduction in the number of enterprise success indicators, moving the execution of material balances away from the center and toward production units (mostly *uniones*), and the development of new mechanisms to stimulate worker participation and experimentation with direct importing by some enterprises. In our view, an eventual return to experimentation with market-type decentralization is also likely.[50]

Another potential way to increase enterprise flexibility is through amalgamation. Since 1977, Cuban enterprises have been joined together with other horizontally or vertically related enterprises to form *uniones de empresas*.[51] By bringing units at the base together, it is hoped that the new larger units will be able to carry out more functions (e.g., research and development, materials supply, maintenance and repair) and become less dependent on the center. As of December 31, 1985, there were 42 *uniones* in industry (involving some 390 of the 800 industrial enterprises) and 61 economywide (involving almost 500 of the 2,240 enterprises on the island). There is not enough evidence at this time to assert that the *uniones* have facilitated the intended decentralization, but several planning administrators have expressed this judgment to the authors.[52]

Another organizational change that holds significant promise for enhancing worker participation is the post-1981 system of production brigades. Production bridgades are subunits of an enterprise that perform a distinct productive task. While they remain part of the enterprise, in theory they also begin to function as a separate accounting unit. Enterprises contract out a production plan to the brigade and the brigade receives bonuses according to its performance. It is expected that eventually brigades will also be self-financing and will form their own stimulation funds. Brigades are allowed to organize their own work as well as hire (after suggestion from above) and fire their own brigade chief.[53] By making the productive unit smaller and the incentive more immediate, it is hoped that this organizational change will promote greater worker participation and productivity.

The brigades began experimentally in agriculture in 1981 and in industry in 1983. By 1986 there were 2,500 brigades in some 300 enterprises—120 state farms and 180 enterprises outside agriculture. Agricultural brigades average approximately 75 workers each. Early indications are that the brigades are stimulating both increased worker involvement in decision-making and increased productivity.[54]

The brigades might appear to work in the opposite direction of the *union*—one enlarges the administrative unit and the other diminishes it. This is true, but the purposes are different and their effects on participation operate in distinct, and potentially complementary, ways. The *union*, which can be (but usually is not) an accounting unit, allows more activities to take place at local initiative, free of central tutelage. The brigade reduces the size of the decision-making and incentive unit related to direct production matters.

The third aspect of increasing worker participation is identifying a more effective avenue for popular input in setting the basic priorities of the economic plan. One cannot speak meaningfully about democracy with regard to material balances, technical supply allocations, financing arrangements, or other details of the plan, but democratic procedures for defining the central goals of one- or five-year plans seem to be practicable. The present methods of representation through commissions of the National Assembly, the CTC, and the Institute of Internal Demand are not entirely hollow, but they are too tenuous and indirect. Referenda and extensive educational campaigns on such issues as the development of nuclear power, the economy's investment ratio, relative priority to residential construction, etc. are also desirable, albeit costly in resources.

In short, the 1980s have witnessed some movement toward broader and more meaningful worker participation, but the progress has been uneven and incremental. More fundamental reforms are required in our view if the desired effects on *conciencia* and productivity are to be attained.

CONCLUSION

Central planning politicizes the economy. It constrains the dissemination of market signals (namely, prices) and seeks to keep producers from being driven solely by self-interest. In theory, economic coordination is administered and purposeful.

In the absence of universal altruism, CPEs must find a method to motivate producers. This is particularly problematic given the tendency of CPEs to maintain full employment. Limited use of material incentives and simulated market signals have had some success, but the logic of central planning and the ethical values of socialism preclude excessive reliance on these motivational and allocational instruments. The effective operation of a planned economy, then, requires the development of nonmaterial incentives. To date, however, the extreme economic and political centralization of CPEs has also precluded the full development of internal incentives via greater worker democracy.

The present political-economic climate in CPEs favors greater pragmatism, eclecticism, and openness. There is widespread experimentation with both market and administrative decentralization as well as forms of enhanced worker participation.

Cuba fits this pattern. After a decade of decentralizing reforms, a moratorium on further market and private sector liberalization was declared in April 1986. Similar moratoria were called in Hungary and China after periods of rapid liberalization. In more deliberate fashion, both Hungary and China have resumed their course of reform. Ideological and political forces are, of course, different in Cuba and the eventual character and celerity of the reform process will be distinctly Cuban. As Cuba continues to struggle with the best balance of material and nonmaterial incentives, market forces and official plans, private and public spheres, the success of its economic system, this chapter has argued, will be directly correlated with the introduction of decentralizing and democratizing reforms.

CHAPTER 9

Foreign Sector: Dependence, Aid and Debt

It is commonplace to assert that foreign trade plays a central role in the economic development of small, developing countries. In fact, revolutions in communications and information technology as well as vast improvements in transportation technology have created conditions of strong interdependence for all the world's economies. Even the United States, the world's largest and most developed economy, with a rich endowment of natural resources, is intimately involved in and dependent upon the international trading and financial networks.

There is certainly no country in Latin America whose economic fortunes are not intricately bound up with developments in the world economy. Generally, this observation applies with greater force to the smaller economies of the region.

Cuba is no exception. In 1985, average Cuban exports and imports as a share of net material product came to 50.1 percent, and as a share of gross social product, to 26.0 percent.[1] Cuban growth has slowed dramatically in recent years as the prices of its exports have fallen more rapidly than the prices of its imports, foreign markets have closed, export production has been hampered by unfavorable climatic conditions, and the debt burden has become more imposing.

Through 1985 the Cuban economy was more resilient to world market shocks than other Latin economies. It is generally held that the magnitude and character of Cuba's economic relations with the Soviet Union and other CMEA countries made Cuba's differential performance possible. At the same time, most analysts have concluded that Cuba is at least as dependent on sugar exports today as it was in 1958 and that Cuba has generally failed in its project of export diversification.[2]

Each of these arguments about the Cuban economy is misleading. First, claims of Cuba's sugar dependence and lack of export diversification have been greatly exaggerated. Second, while it is uncontestable that Cuba has benefited prodigiously from Soviet economic aid and favorable terms of trade within the CMEA, the size of this aid has been significantly overstated by improper methodology. In this chapter, each of these propositions is reexamined and, then, the current situation of Cuba's external economy is analyzed.

SUGAR DEPENDENCE

Sugar has been dubbed "the albatross" of the pre-1959 Cuban economy. During the 1948–58 period, sugar exports averaged 84.1 percent of total Cuban exports. Despite the beginnings of some sugar byproduct production prior to 1959 (see chapter 7), forward and backward linkages to sugar production went largely undeveloped. Employment was seasonal, land use was wasteful, large profits were repatriated, and prices were volatile. Under these circumstances, sugar's ability to stimulate a broader economic development was nonexistent. Lack of diversification and dependency went hand in hand with underdevelopment and stagnation.

In a quantitative sense, Cuba is certainly as dependent on the Soviet Union in the 1980s as it was on the United States in the 1950s. Dependency theory, however—whatever its limitations—is an effort at analytical explanation, not just empirical description, of the development process. It is impossible to conclude that the qualitative relationship of dependence on the Soviet Union is commensurate with that of the earlier dependence on the United States.

Cuban dependence on the Soviet Union is not altogether benign, but its effects on Cuban development have been, on the whole, salutary. Terms of trade have been generally stable and favorable, technological transfer and training have been readily forthcoming, capital goods and heavy industry production has been encouraged (see chapters 3 and 6), the nature of the sugar industry and its market has been transformed (see chapter 7), spin-off industries have been promoted, profit repatriation has ceased, and so on. These issues are too complex for an extended treatment here. The main point is that a simple number like the share of sugar in total exports does not have the same implications for Cuban development today as it did thirty years ago. Depending on world market conditions, Cuba still sells between 10 and 40 percent of its sugar on the volatile world market, but the CMEA market provides a soft and reliable cushion. Sugar has also been the basis for significant forward and backward linkages since 1959, and harvest mechanization, production integration, and labor force reorganization have eliminated the noxious social and economic effects of seasonal *zafra* labor. Despite this and despite the positive prospects for the further development of sugar cane byproducts, the argument could be persuasively made in our opinion that, given conditions of world sugar demand, Cuba is putting too many eggs in the cane basket.

Although Cuba continues to invest in expanding sugar production and milling capacity, investments in other, nontraditional export products have allowed for a significant diversification of Cuba's exports in recent years. Table 9.1 shows the share of sugar in total Cuban exports since 1979. There is a clear downward trend. As Pérez-López points out (Pérez-López 1986b: 22; 1986c), several percentage points of this decreasing share is attributable to Cuban reexports of Soviet oil. These reexports are made possible by an agreement with

Table 9.1. Share of Sugar and Its Byproducts in Total Exports, 1979–86 (percentages)

1979	1980	1981	1982	1983	1984	1985	1986	1987
85.9	83.7	79.1	77.2	74.0	75.5	74.5	77.0	74.3

Source: Calculated from data presented in CEE/AEC 1985: 396–97; 1986: 422; CEE 1988d: 20.

the Soviet Union stipulating that Cuba may export any petroleum shipments specified in the five-year trade protocol agreement that it does not consume due to energy conservation measures. Cuba reduced its energy consumption per peso of gross social product by 25 percent between 1980 and 1985 (BNC, *Informe Económico*, March 1986a: 5). A large share of this saving is attributable to replacement of oil by bagasse as the sole source of energy in Cuba's sugar mills. Bagasse provides an additional 10 percent of energy to the national electricity grid. Further supporting these exports has been a very rapid expansion in Cuban domestic petroleum output, which more than tripled between 1981 and 1985, from 258.9 thousand tons of crude oil extraction to 867.6 thousand tons. In 1988, crude oil extraction is expected to surpass 1.2 million tons, and by 1990 production is projected at two million tons (CEE/AEC 1985: 237; CEE/BEC 1988: 19; S. Rodríguez 1987; Pérez-López 1988). Pérez-López, (1986b, 1986c) however, overstates the importance of oil reexports (and hence understates the decrease in the sugar share) by assuming that naphta, a petroleum byproduct exported by Cuba, is from the Soviet Union when in fact it is produced in Cuba.

More important, if one is going to make qualifications to the above sugar shares to gauge the true extent of production diversification, it is necessary to express the value of sugar and other exports in constant prices. That is, one would have to adjust for the manifold increase in sugar prices paid by the Soviet Union after the mid-1970s. If this were done, the diversification of the productive base for exports would be much more extensive than suggested in the nominal sugar share, as can be seen in Table 9.3.

Constant-price raw sugar exports are straightforward to compute. Volume for each year is multiplied by the average 1965 raw sugar price received by Cuba. Constant-price total exports are considerably more complicated to compute. The latter entails developing an export price index without complete price information. Although some shortcuts are necessary, the Cuban statistical yearbook does have sufficient price data for Cuba's principal exports to allow for a reasonable estimation. The 1985 yearbook divides Cuban exports into six categories: sugar and its derivatives, mining, tobacco and beverages, fish, agricultural products, and other. Within each category, several principal export products are included with volume and sales data for 1965, 1970, 1975, 1980, and 1985; hence, average export prices are calculable for each year and price indexes can be computed for each category. The issue then becomes how to aggregate the category indexes into one overall export price index. We aggregated using both 1965 and 1985 value shares (in current prices) of each category in total exports. Since sugar prices rise more rapidly over the 1965–85 period than the prices of other exports, and since raw sugar's (current price) share in exports was greater in 1965 (85.8 percent) than in 1985 (74.4 percent), using 1965 value shares (weights) causes the export price deflator to rise more rapidly. Thus, using the 1985 weights causes constant price total exports to increase more than using 1965 weights and produces a lower estimate for sugar's share in total exports in 1985.

In Table 9.2 we show the two estimated price indexes of Cuban exports, with 1965 and 1985 weights, respectively. The estimated index with 1965 weights is similar to an earlier export price index for the period 1962–79 developed by Olga Torres of the United Nations Economic Commission for Latin America (Torres 1981: 291).

In Table 9.3, we present our estimates of constant 1965 price raw sugar exports and total exports and the constant-price sugar export share. In the last column, the constant-price sugar export share is recalculated assuming no petroleum reexports.[3] Further, for each year an alternative weighting method is used to estimate the export price deflator, constant price exports, and raw sugar export shares. These results are reported below each year and are marked with an asterisk.

Table 9.2.   Price Index of Cuban Exports

	1965	1970	1975	1980	1985
Using 1965 export shares	100	120	385	510	519
Using 1985 export shares	100	116	357	428	447

Source: CEE/AEC 1985: 371–470.

Table 9.3.   Constant Price Sugar Export Shares

	Total exports (1965 prices, million pesos)	Raw sugar exports (1965 prices, million pesos)	Sugar share (1965 prices, %)	
1965	690.6	583.3	84.5[a]	84.5[b]
1970	874.6	757.9	86.7	86.7
1970[c]	904.7	757.9	83.8	83.8
1975	766.9	630.3	82.2	82.2
1975[c]	827.0	630.3	76.2	76.2
1980	777.8	677.1	87.1	89.1
1980[c]	926.8	677.1	73.1	74.8
1985	1,152.8	790.8	68.6	74.6
1985[c]	1,338.5	790.8	59.1	64.3

Source: CEE/AEC 1985: 371–470.
[a]Figures in this column include all exports.
[b]Figures in this column include all exports except petroleum reexports.
[c]Calculations in this row use 1985 export value shares (weights) to estimate the export price deflator. See explanation in text.

The constant-price sugar share in exports falls dramatically after 1980 when the 1965 weighted price deflator is used, and it falls steadily over the entire 1965–85 period when the 1985 weighted price deflator is used. Unfortunately, neither deflator is theoretically more correct than the other. One frequently used technique in similar cases is to average the results from the two methods. If this is done, the constant-price sugar share in exports goes from 84.5 percent in 1965, to 85.3 percent in 1970, 79.2 percent in 1975, 80.1 percent in 1980, and to 63.9 percent in 1985. That is, there is a mild and gradual decrease in the sugar share from 1965 to 1980 and, once again, a dramatic decrease after 1980. Even when one removes the influence of petroleum reexports (see the last column of Table 9.3), the same basic pattern obtains. Whether the change was more gradual over the entire period or more sudden after 1980, the basic conclusion is that there has been an appreciable decline in the (constant-price) sugar share in exports; or, stated differently, an appreciable diversification in the productive base of exports. Further, it seems that the pace of this diversification accelerated in the early 1980s. This is not to say that Cuba could not or should not have done better. It is only to recognize that more has been done than is generally claimed.

One very revealing indication of Cuba's success at diversification can be seen by comparing Cuba's efforts at increasing nontraditional exports with other nations in the Caribbean Basin—nations that have benefited from specialized tariff treatment and preferences by the United States under the Generalized System of Preferences and the Caribbean Basin Initiative.

The Cuban growth of nontraditional exports from 258.4 million pesos in 1980 to 611.6 million pesos in 1985 constituted an average annual growth rate of 18.8 percent, 8.2 percentage points above the growth rate of the Dominican Republic, the next best performer in the group. The growth rates alone can be deceptive if Cuba begins from a much lower base. In fact, the Cuban base level in 1980 of 258.4 million pesos (or, $360.4 million converted at the official 1980 rate of exchange) is considerably above that in Panama ($90.3 million), the Dominican Republic ($105.3 million), and Jamaica ($106.5 million), about the same as that in Honduras ($291.9 million), and below that only in Costa Rica ($441.9 million) and Guatemala ($707.7 million).

Table 9.4. Annual Growth Rate of Nontraditional Exports, 1980–85

Cuba	18.8%
Costa Rica	−4.7
Guatemala	−5.1[a]
Honduras	−2.7[a]
Panama	2.3
Dominican Republic	10.6
Jamaica	7.4

Sources: CEE/AEC 1986: 426–35; BNC, *Informe Económico*, March 1986; 10; SRI International 1987.

Between 1980 and 1985, Cuba introduced 111 new export products and experienced significant growth in exports of citrus fruits, fish products, steel products, recycled raw materials, scrap metals, gas stoves, paper products, soldering irons and electrodes, nonelectrical machinery, transportation materials and machinery, fiberboard, radios, sulphuric acid, batteries, and teletransmission and processing equipment, among others. A major new copper discovery near Matahambre and the expected 150 percent increase in nickel production capacity by 1990 offer significant promise for export expansion in the medium term. Cuba is also exporting several manufactured items that hold interesting potential for the future, including: agriculture machinery and implements, boats, computer keyboards and terminals, digital integrated circuits, pharmaceutical products, and refrigerators. In 1985 Cuba's nonsugar exports, excluding petroleum reexports, were 1,023.1 million pesos; of this, 448.9 million pesos or 43.9 percent were for convertible currency. Thus, more than half of Cuba's nonsugar exports benefit from the CMEA's protected market, but over two-fifths were exported to competitive world market countries (mostly LDCs).[4] Further, considering only industrial nontraditional exports, out of a total 147.7 million in 1986, 90.8 million (61.5 percent) went to market economies (*Cuba Business*, December 1987: 6).

Cuba, moreover, has succeeded in breaking into these markets without the benefit of direct foreign investment. The 1982 foreign investment code, allowing 49 percent foreign ownership, did not attract any foreign investment in manufacturing through 1986.[5] Although Cuba initiated negotiations with a number of West European and Canadian firms, strong negative pressure from the Reagan administration, among other factors, put prospective projects on indefinite hold. Cuba's hard currency trading possibilities have, however, been

Table 9.5. Selected Nontraditional Exports, 1980–85 (million pesos)

Product	1980	1983	1985
Fish and shellfish	86.1	102.7	115.1
Ethyl alcohol	1.3	6.3	6.7
Citrus fruits	41.3	119.5	143.9
Other fruits and vegetables	14.4	15.6	40.2
Coffee, tea, and cocoa	23.3	47.2	39.0
Copper concentrate	5.3	5.1	6.2
Refractory chrome	1.6	1.3	3.2
Medicines	1.2	6.4	9.9
Chemical elements	2.1	7.2	7.3
Manufactured articles	29.0	55.6	59.9
Cement	11.5	5.8	2.2
Marble	1.3	1.9	2.2
Iron and steel products	2.6	19.2	21.9
Nonelectrical machinery	2.8	29.3	18.6

Source: CEE/AEC 1986: 394–405.

facilitated by capitalist trading companies. The Italian trading company, SOCOMET, for instance, represents several Italian exporters to Cuba and is committed to marketing a return flow of Cuban products to Italy. In 1986, SOCOMET marketed Cuban nickel, canned fruit juices, textiles, marble, tractor tires, electronic components and customized software in Italy.

The development of Cuban manufactured nontraditional exports benefits from a well-developed infrastructure, state support, and a stable, skilled labor force. It is hindered, *inter alia*, by supply shortages, insufficient quality control, inadequate packaging and port facilities, lack of marketing ties, and foreign exchange difficulties.

The trade data presented above, of course, does not reflect the rapid growth in tourism and tourist services in recent years. Tourism revenues in 1985, for instance, grew by 33 percent. The total number of tourists visiting Cuba grew from 96.6 thousand in 1978 to 240.5 thousand in 1985; of the latter number only 48.3 thousand were from socialist countries. Put differently, out of 100.4 million pesos of total tourism revenues in 1985, only 19.4 million (or 19.3 percent) came from visitors from socialist countries. If air and ground transportation, communications, and other tourist services were included, tourist revenue in 1985 would rise to 118 million pesos.[6] In 1986, the number of tourists increased to 281.9 thousand and tourism revenues increased by 7.2 percent, placing tourism ahead of tobacco as fourth on the list of hard currency earners, behind sugar, oil reexports, and fish products. In 1987, the number of tourists grew to 298.3 million and tourism revenues expanded by 11.4 percent (BNC, *Informe Económico* 1987: 19; 1988: 9).[7] Nor does Table 9.4 register the sizeable service exports in the form of construction and educational and medical personnel to other Third World countries.[8]

Finally, along with Cuba's modest success in export diversification, it should be emphasized that Cuba has made considerable strides in its import substitution program. Rapid growth in capital goods (12.8 percent average annual growth from 1961 to 1985), in construction materials (7.8 percent average annual growth from 1965 to 1985), metal products (14.4 percent annual growth rate), electrical energy (7.9 percent annual growth rate), and chemicals (7.5 percent), among other branches, has denoted a profound transformation in Cuba's industrial base.[9] As a consequence of this transformation, the share of manufactured goods in Cuban imports fell from 58.9 percent in 1970 to 44.7 percent in 1983 (UNIDO 1986.)

Additionally, Cuba is making important strides in import substituting for its energy supplies (S. Rodríguez, 1987). Domestic crude oil extraction has increased from 258 thousand tons in 1981 to over one million tons in 1988. With the opening of new onshore and offshore fields, production is scheduled to reach 2 million tons by 1990. The main difficulty with Cuban crude is its high sulfur content, but new refineries are being built to adjust for this "density" and some existing industrial plants are being retrofitted to be able to consume the heavier crude. Four nuclear reactors in Cienfuegos will come on stream in the early 1990s, and additional reactors are planned to provide 75 percent of Cuba's electricity requirements. It has been estimated that every kilowatt-hour of energy saved or produced in Cuba saves 4.73 cents in foreign exchange. Since Cuba still imports nearly 70 percent of its energy, these savings can amount to significant sums (*Cuba Business*, December 1987: 4).[10]

Cuba has also diversified its agricultural base and become less dependent on food imports. Substantial improvements in Cuban nutrition have been accompanied by a steady decline in the share of food products in total imports, from 20.5 percent in 1958 to 9.3 percent in 1986 (CEE/AEC 1986: 425).

It should also be mentioned that one significant impediment to further diversification since 1980 has been the tightening of the U.S. blockade under Reagan, to be discussed below. The Third World debt crisis and growing protectionism have also limited Cuban markets. To be sure, Cuba has continued to run overall trade deficits, and in 1986 Cuba experienced a hard currency trade deficit for the first time in this decade.[10] We shall return to Cuba's balance of trade and payments predicament in the last section of this chapter.

SOVIET AID

Cuba's membership in the CMEA has, among other things, provided a stable market (with subsidized prices and guaranteed sales) for its primary exports. This stability has not only facilitated economic planning, but it has made the quest for developing new export products less pressing than it would otherwise have been.

Cuban social or economic accomplishments, when acknowledged, are often attributed to massive doses of Soviet aid (see, for one, Theriot 1982). Implicit in this attribution is that Cuba's economic dependence on the Soviet Union is different and more benign in its economic impact than Cuba's previous dependence on the United States, although this is rarely made explicit. In fact, Soviet economic aid is enormous and the Cuban economy would scarcely be what it is without it. Yet several caveats must be made. First, as we shall demonstrate below, the magnitude of this aid has been greatly overstated by faulty methodology. Second, even if the exaggerated aid figures were accepted, on a per capita basis Cuba would still be receiving less CMEA aid than many other Latin America economies receive in Western aid. Third, if one is attempting to disentangle the sources of Cuban growth and isolate its domestic and foreign components, it is hardly sufficient to consider only the beneficial effects of Soviet aid. One must also consider the monumental and ongoing costs to Cuba of the U.S. blockade. In 1982, the Cubans estimated these cumulative costs to be approaching $10 billion (BNC, *Informe Económico* 1982).[11]

Most Cuba scholars have relied upon the Soviet aid estimates provided by the U.S. Central Intelligence Agency. The CIA estimates include not only direct balance of payments and project aid, but also price subsidies for sugar, nickel, petroleum, and other products. The sugar price subsidy is by far the largest component of Soviet aid in the CIA reckoning (e.g., 68.3 percent of total aid in 1983) (CIA 1984: 40). To estimate this subsidy the CIA 1) uses the official peso/dollar exchange rate, 2) ignores the tied nature of the aid, that is, payments are overwhelmingly in ruble credits usable only for inferior Soviet goods, and 3) assumes the aid to be the difference between the converted dollar price paid by the Soviets and the free market price. Steps 1 and 2 have no economic justification and engender a significant upward bias. Step 3 is arbitrary and betrays either a political bias or a miscomprehension of world sugar trade.

Roughly only 14 percent of world sugar is sold at free market prices; the rest is sold under preferential agreements at above world market prices (Fry 1985: 20). The "free" market price is thus not a true scarcity price, because the subsidized prices of preferential trade cause the quantity of sugar supply to be higher and the quantity of sugar demand to be lower than would prevail under true free market conditions. The world market price is, therefore, lower than the true scarcity price of sugar and cannot be employed properly as the opportunity cost (the price at which Cuba would have to sell its sugar if it did not have a preferential agreement with the Soviet Union) to calculate Soviet subsidies.

Some have suggested that an appropriate alternative price might be the preferential U.S. market price, at which Cuba used to sell the vast bulk of its sugar exports prior to the U.S. embargo (Zimbalist 1982; Radell 1983). In mid-March 1988 the world market price was approximately 8 cents, per pound, in contrast to the U.S. preferential price of around 22 cents, the EEC preferential price of near 20 cents and the Soviet price of approximately 36 centavos a pound for raw sugar.[12]

If the Soviet price is converted at the official commercial exchange rate of 1 peso equals $1, then it equals 36 cents, and when compared to the world price it constitutes a subsidy per pound, as computed by the CIA, of 28 cents. If the opportunity cost were taken to be the U.S. market, the subsidy would fall by half, to 14 cents per pound using the official exchange rate. However, given Cuba's chronic current account deficit, it seems that the Cuban peso is significantly overvalued at the official fixed rate, so even 14 cents a pound would be too high an estimate.[13]

To be sure, in all but three years between 1960 and 1974 the U.S. preferential price was above the Soviet price, implying a reverse subsidy until the mid-1970s. One author has estimated that Cuban sugar revenue would have been $800 million higher over this period had Cuba been trading with the United States instead of the Soviet Union (Smith 1984: 337–74).

Also part of the CIA estimate are price subsidies of oil and other products. The oil price subsidy was substantial in 1983, the last year for which the CIA published an estimate for Soviet aid to Cuba. Since 1984, however, Cuba has paid above the world market price for Soviet crude, denoting a reverse subsidy. The 1976 trade agreement between Cuba and the U.S.S.R. stipulated that Cuba buy crude oil from the U.S.S.R. at the average price of the previous five years on the world market. When oil prices were rising, this meant that Cuba was purchasing Soviet oil at subsidized prices. However, as oil prices first leveled off in the early 1980s, they began to fall during 1981–82 and entered a precipitous decline in 1986, this pricing formula meant that Cuba was paying above world market prices for its crude. One Cuban official stated that Cuba was paying the U.S.S.R. $26 a barrel in early 1987, implying a reverse subsidy of some $8.[14] Of course, since Cuba pays for the oil in convertible rubles and then sells much of it for hard currency, the market value of this reverse subsidy would be less than $8.

Between 1980 and 1985 the Soviet purchase price for Cuban raw sugar rose by 32.7 percent, while the price Cuba paid for Soviet crude oil rose by 155.6 percent. Overall, between 1980 and 1985 the (weighted) average price of Cuban imports from the Soviet Union rose by 82.49 percent, while the average price of Cuba's exports to the Soviet Union rose by only 32.15 percent.[15] The direction of the price subsidies during the first half of the 1980s, then, moved against the Cubans. That is, the 1980–85 period of rapid growth in Cuba was accompanied by worsening terms of trade with the Soviet Union. From the partial information available, it appears that this tendency has continued since 1985.

It is also essential to note that Soviet payments for Cuban exports are in ruble credits. Thus Cuba is tied to buying lower quality and often overpriced Soviet goods, lessening the real value of the subsidy further. The very fact that the Soviet Union cannot compete on world markets with its manufactured goods is ample evidence of either lower quality or higher prices, or both. There are also many specific examples. Examples from earlier periods have been discussed elsewhere (Zimbalist 1982); some evidence for the mid-1980s is provided in Table 9.6.[16]

The prices in Table 9.6 show that for several products Cuba pays the Soviet Union a price higher than the world market price. Many of the products listed are not homogeneous and the quoted price is not adjusted for quality. The price comparison, then, is not precise and may either understate or overstate the actual differential between Soviet and world market prices.

There is also new evidence of deficient quality of Soviet goods and services. For instance, there have been repeated structural problems with the new, Soviet-designed and -built Celia Sanchez textile factory in Santiago, Cuba that have forced drastic production cutbacks. The factory cost Cuba several million rubles. The two new, Soviet designed nickel plants have encountered a series of technological problems, first delaying initial production and then reducing capacity. Cuban authorities have also complained recently about delays in the arrival of Soviet oil and other inputs.[17]

Table 9.6. 1985 Cuban Import Prices of Selected Products (pesos)

Product	U.S.S.R.	World market[a]
Wheat grain (per ton)	189.4	126.1
Tires (per unit)	115.1	43.3
Buses (per unit)	23,125	12,000
Trucks (per unit)	13,715	12,785
Automobiles (per unit)	3,207	2,259
Cut lumber (per cubic meter)	151.3	108.8
Tin plates (per ton)	641.2	559.6
Butter (per ton)	1,667	1,157
Powdered milk (per ton)	975.1	721.6

Source: CEE/AEC 1985: 444–69.

[a]The "world market" price represents the lowest price Cuba paid for the product from any of its trading partners, or, when this price was not available, it represents the average price paid to all its capitalist trading partners. Per ton prices refer to metric, as opposed to short, tons.

In the end, it cannot be denied that the Soviet aid and special terms of trade offered to Cuba have played a large role in supporting Cuba's economic progress. Yet the existing analyses significantly exaggerate the magnitude of Soviet aid and do not support the claim that Cuba's economic and social successes are entirely attributable to its special relationship with the Soviet Union. Further, before any arguments can be soundly made regarding the Cuban economy's ability to generate self-sustained development, it is imperative that the direct and indirect costs of the U.S. economic blockade and political aggression be taken into account (see Morley 1987; Rich 1988; Smith and Morales 1988; and Jones 1988).

Nor can one overlook Cuba's extensive program of international aid. For instance, in January 1985 Cuba had one civilian international aid worker for every 625 Cuban inhabitants, whereas during 1982 the U.S. ratio was one aid worker for every 36,298 U.S. inhabitants.[18] Cuba had more health workers abroad in 1985 (1,500 in 25 countries) than did the World Health Organization. In 1981, Cuba accounted for 19.4 percent of all Soviet, East European, and Cuban technicians working abroad. During the 1984–85 academic year, Cuba granted scholarships to 22,000 foreign students from 82 developing countries to study in Cuba, 1,800 of these in medicine; whereas during the academic year 1982–83, the United States funded but 9,000 scholarships for foreigners. Although Cuba began to charge for some international assistance programs in 1977, these charges are levied on an ability-to-pay basis. Thus poor countries receive the assistance without charge and middle-income countries pay subsidized prices. Cuba also regularly offers humanitarian aid to Third World countries. One recent example of such support is the June 1988 agreement with Nicaragua. Castro pledged to forgive Nicaragua's $50 million debt to Cuba and to provide free of charge 270,000 tons of oil through 1990. The oil gift will mean that Nicaragua will receive approximately 12 percent of its petroleum gratis and save roughly $8 million a year at current prices (*Latin American Weekly Report*, July 14, 1988: 5).[19]

Lastly, despite the magnitude of Soviet aid to Cuba, there are other economies in Latin American that receive more international aid per capita than Cuba does. For instance, Puerto Rico received $1.82 billion in aid from the United States in 1975, $3.71 billion in 1980, and $4.57 billion in 1983, while Cuba received from the Soviet Union, even according to the inflated CIA estimates, $1.06 billion, $3.46 billion, and $4.1 billion respectively in these years. Thus in 1983, with a population one-third that of Cuba's, Puerto Rico received 1.12 times more aid than Cuba, or 3.34 times more aid on a per capita basis. Yet the Puerto Rican economy can hardly boast of the social or economic achievements of post-1958 Cuba.[20]

TRADE PROSPECTS AND DEBT

At the end of September 1986, Cuba's hard currency debt equaled $4.68 billion and its debt to the U.S.S.R. roughly equaled 7.5 billion rubles.[21] At official exchange rates converted to dollars, the debt to the U.S.S.R. was approximately $10 billion. Again, the official rates are widely recognized to overvalue both the ruble and the peso, so this figure must be interpreted as an upper bound of the market value of Cuba's debt to the Soviet Union. Nevertheless, it lies considerably below the $23 billion estimated by some Western experts (*Cuba Business*, April 1987: 1).

For purposes of comparison, if we sum Cuba's 1986 Western and Soviet debt, it comes to $14.68 billion, or $1,439 per capita. This is below the 1986 per capita debt in several Latin American economies: $2,161 in Panama, $2,030 in Venezuela, $1,822 in Chile, $1,800 in Costa Rica, $1,714 in Argentina, $1,630 in Uruguay, and $1,496 in Nicaragua. It is above the levels in most other Latin American countries, for example: $1,306 in Mexico, $1,000 in Ecuador, $890 in Peru, and $832 in Brazil. If hard currency debt is considered as a percentage of hard currency exports, Cuba's figure of 322 percent falls below the average of 416 percent for Latin America.[22] If debt were considered instead as a share of national income, Cuba would still fall somewhere in the middle of Latin American economies.

The more important point about Cuban debt, however, is that roughly two-thirds of it is with the Soviet Union and is held on very different terms than its Western debt. Cuba's debt payments (principal and interest) to the U.S.S.R. were suspended in 1972 and were to resume in 1986 with a payment equivalent to $125 million. Given Cuba's foreign exchange problems in 1986, however, the U.S.S.R. agreed to delay all payments to 1990 at least. Many observers believe that these payments will be delayed indefinitely as long as Cuba's political alliance with the Soviet Union is maintained.[23]

Despite the extraordinary terms of Cuba's Soviet debt, Cuba's Western debt is sufficiently large and payments on it sufficiently burdensome to create a significant and growing problem in its own right. Until the summer of 1986 Cuba had been a model debtor, making all due service payments punctually. Since that time, most payments on its private debt have not been made and no mutually satisfactory rescheduling has been arranged between Cuba and its private creditors.

Much of Cuba's story is told by the debt experience of the rest of the Third World. Mounting accumulations of petrodollars in the 1970s, commercial banks' presumption that governments were creditworthy, demands for more rapid growth in the Third World, the need for additional foreign exchange to pay for more expensive oil, and so on, all led to growing indebtedness among developing nations. When the unprecedentedly high interest rates arrived in late 1979, world market demand for Third World exports diminished at the same time the interest burden on debt began to soar. By 1982 shrinking markets, growing protectionism, and deteriorating terms of trade had made the problems of debt intractable for many less developed countries as well as for international financial markets.

Cuba's particular situation has been further aggravated by a number of factors. First, the economic blockade by the United States was tightened during the Reagan administration. An early, effective measure was to pressure many foreign companies doing business with the United States not to trade with Cuba. In 1981 the French conglomerate Le Creusot Loire was using Cuban nickel in steel it was shipping to the United States. The steel was banned from entering the United States, and Le Creusot Loire cancelled its contract with Cuba to build two factories, already under construction, for converting bagasse to paper. In early 1982, two Canadian firms negotiating contracts to build a citrus processing factory and a power plant backed down under pressure from the U.S. Department of Commerce. The next measure came in May 1982 when U.S. tourism to Cuba, which had been opened during the Carter administration, was once again prohibited, depriving Cuba of potentially substantial foreign exchange earnings. More recently, the Reagan administration 1) proscribed dollar remittances from Cuban exiles in the United States to relatives in Cuba, 2) forbade U.S. companies to trade with joint Cuban–Panamanian companies operating out of Panama, and 3) refused to pay dollar charges for Cuban exit visas. Reagan also pressured multinational banks and foreign governments not to reschedule Cuba's debt or to impose harsh terms and, generally, to restrict their trade with Cuba; it is difficult to assess what, if any, effect this pressure has had. However, in its March 1986 report to Cuba's creditors, the National Bank claimed that because of "the lack of access to creditor countries' markets, 50 million pesos' worth of nonsugar exports could not be sold in the convertible currency area."[24]

Second, affecting many Caribbean Basin countries, developments in the world sugar market were extremely unfavorable through 1985. World market prices fell steadily from an average of 29 cents per pound in 1980 to 4 cents in 1985.[25] A major influence behind these plummeting prices was the marked reduction in U.S. sugar imports, which in 1986 were approximately 75 percent below their level in 1981. Part of this reduction is attributable to the substitution of high fructose corn syrup for sugar by U.S. soft drink producers, but part is because the U.S. government has allowed U.S. cane producers to increase output (at heavily subsidized prices) even in the face of falling demand.[26] The shrinking U.S. market for sugar imports affects Cuba in two ways: First, it means more sugar production is sold on the world market by other sugar exporters, further depressing prices; and second, it means that many of Cuba's natural trading partners in Latin America (e.g., Costa Rica, Panama, the Dominican Republic, Brazil) do not earn sufficient foreign exchange to expand or even maintain their imports from Cuba. Of course in terms of real purchasing power, the nominally low sugar prices of the world market through 1985 were even lower.

The third factor aggravating Cuba's economic situation concerns climatic conditions. All agricultural exporters are vulnerable to natural cycles, but Cuba has experienced unusually bad times since 1980. At the beginning of the decade, Cuba's sugar crop was decimated by cane rust and the tobacco crop was acutely affected by blue mold. In October 1985 the Cuban countryside was devastated by Hurricane Kate, which, among other things, was estimated to have reduced the 1985–86 cane harvest by over one million tons. Between 1983 and 1986 there was an intensifying drought, with rainfall in 1986 at 35 percent below the annual average. The drought is held responsible for reducing the 1986–87 sugar harvest by another one million tons and for seriously damaging output of several other crops. Finally, torrential rains struck Cuba in December 1986, destroying, among other things, 9,400 acres of tobacco land and severely damaging an additional 20,000 acres. Torrential rains and serious flooding struck Cuba's central provinces in June 1988 and damaged large quantities of stored sugar.[27]

Fourth, as already explained, Cuba has been reexporting Soviet petroleum since 1980. During 1983–85, such exports averaged 41.7 percent of all hard currency earnings. The precipitous drop in world oil prices, beginning in late 1985, lowered 1986 earnings from reexports by an estimated $300 million. In 1986, oil reexports accounted for only 26 percent of Cuba's hard currency earnings BNC, *Informe Económico*, May 1987). The situation improved somewhat in 1987, as oil prices recovered approximately one-third of the previous drop and oil reexports accounted for 29.7 percent of hard currency earnings (BNC, *Informe Económico* 1988: 15).

Fifth, Cuba has been seriously affected by the steady devaluation of the dollar against the currencies of other OECD economies since mid-1985. Many of Cuba's exports are denominated in dollars, corresponding to the dollar's preeminent role on world commodity markets. Yet, since Cuba does not trade

with the United States, most of its imports from the developed market economies are denominated in those currencies that have appreciated against the
dollar. Further, most of Cuba's hard currency debt is denominated in nondollar
currencies (87 percent is in yen and European currencies). Since most of these
currencies have appreciated in value against the dollar by over 40 percent since
mid-1985, the dollar value of Cuba's debt has risen accordingly. The Cuban
National Bank has estimated that the dollar devaluation cost the Cubans over
$150 million in 1986 (BNC, *Informe Económico* 1987: 9).

All told, hard currency availability for imports diminished dramatically by
1986. According to the figures of the Cuban National Bank, hard currency
export earnings plus net credits in 1986 came to $650 million available for hard
currency imports. This sum stands in sharp contrast to the $1.5 billion that was
available in 1984. The 1986 predicament is even bleaker in comparative terms
when the figures are put in constant 1984 dollars: 1986 available hard currency
was worth only $500 million in 1984 purchasing power.

Although Cuba's hard currency problem is experienced to varying degrees
by all Latin American countries, and Cuba's condition has been exacerbated by
the special factors enumerated above, it should not be overlooked that Cuba's
long-term foreign trade performance has left much to be desired. With overall
(hard and soft currency) balance of trade deficits in all but two years since 1959,
Cuba's external economy had been able to avoid crisis until mid-1986 in large
measure due to the cushion provided by the CMEA.

Cuba was first forced to ask for debt rescheduling in August 1982, in the
wake of a sharp reduction in short-term credits and deposits, rising interest
rates, and falling sugar prices. At the time, the Cubans requested a rescheduling
of all their medium-term obligations falling due between September 1982 and
December 1985, including stretching out payments over ten years with a three-
year grace period. Eventually Cuba accepted less favorable terms (rescheduling
of obligations maturing between September 1982 and December 1983 only,
amortization periods of seven to eight years, and higher rates of interest than
requested) (BNC 1986b). These terms forced Cuba back to the bargaining table
to renegotiate its debt in 1984, in 1985, and again in 1986. Agreements were
reached with Cuba's private and public creditors both in 1984 and 1985.[28] In
1986, however, although agreement with Cuba's public creditors from among
the Paris Club was reached after several months' delay in July, no agreement
was forthcoming between Cuba and its private creditors (which held 57 percent
of Cuba's $4.68 billion foreign debt in September 1986.)[29]

The Economist Intelligence Unit described Cuba's 1986 negotiations with
its private creditor banks as follows:

Negotiations with private banks have continued without yet reaching a final agreement. In response to Cuba's original request for $300 million, the group of creditor
institutions headed by Credit Lyonnais made an offer at the end of last year which

involved rescheduling the debt and "recycling" the interest payments with an $85 million loan (in Deutschemarks) to cover obligations on short and medium term debts due between June 1986 and June 1987. The banks are also said to have drafted an offer to reschedule payments of principal falling due in 1987 over a ten year period.

It seems probable that talks will continue to drag on for a while longer, and may well overlap with the 1987 round of talks with the Paris Club on Cuba's government to government debt. (EIU 1987: 12)

Cuba's acute hard currency shortage compelled it to reject the private banks' offer in 1986. Medium-term debt service payments have been halted and short-term service payments have become irregular. As of June 1988, no new accord has been reported with Cuba's private creditors. Although Cuba has neither taken a principled stand against paying its debt, nor declared a suspension of payments, nor set limits on its servicing obligations as has Peru, Cuba does seem to have entered the ambiguous terrain of debt muddling along with many of its Latin neighbors.

The lack of bank financing and export credit underwriting forced Cuba to resort increasingly during 1986–87 to suppliers' credits, which are shorter term and carry higher interest charges. This prevented Cuba from benefiting from the falling international interest rates of 1986. Suppliers' credits in Cuba's hard currency debt grew from 27 million pesos (0.8 percent of hard currency debt) in 1980 to 1.2 billion pesos (21.3 percent) in September 1987.

With hard currency trade surpluses from 1979 to 1985, it has been the large deficit in services (interest on debt, shipping, insurance, tourism, international construction, etc.) that has produced Cuba's current account (hard currency) deficits during the 1980s. These deficits, in turn, are primarily responsible for Cuba's growing foreign debt.

Hard currency trade surpluses were 367 million pesos in 1980, 285 million in 1981, and 624 million in 1982. These surpluses permitted the reduction of Cuba's foreign debt from 3.3 billion pesos in 1979 to 2.7 billion in 1982. Between 1982 and 1985, however, shrinking trade surpluses and growing interest payments led to the debt build-up. Nineteen eighty-six brought the first hard currency trade deficit of the decade, and this was compounded by the rapid dollar devaluation. By the end of September 1986, the hard currency debt in pesos stood at 3.87 billion, up 44 percent from 1982.

Despite increases in tourism revenue, earnings from construction overseas, and the growth of the national merchant fleet, Cuba's large debt service payments and the effects of exchange rate variation kept the 1986 service balance negative. Excluding the interest payments on the debt, however, Cuba's 1986 service balance in hard currency turned to a positive 26.4 million pesos from a negative 308.9 million pesos in 1985.[30]

Notwithstanding Cuba's success in turning its 1986 hard currency trade deficit of 289.3 million pesos into a trade surplus of 34.2 million pesos in 1987, Cuba's hard currency foreign debt had continued to climb (BNC, *Informe*

Económico 1988: 5). On September 30, 1987, it stood at 5.55 billion pesos, or 1.68 billion pesos above its level in December 1986.[31] Most of this increase in the peso value of the debt, however, is attributable to exchange rate variation. According to the Economist Intelligence Unit (1988 no. 1: 10), 567 million pesos of this increase is due to the dollar's devaluation against other OECD currencies. An additional 790 million pesos of the increase is due to a procedural change in Cuban accounting: namely, the February 1987 decision of the Cuban National Bank to put the commercial peso/dollar exchange rate at parity (a devaluation of 20.5 percent).

With or without accounting adjustments, however, the magnitude of Cuba's hard currency debt is mounting and the service obligations are unpayable. At the beginning of 1988, Cuba had accumulated arrears of 2.1 billion pesos in principal and 356 million pesos in interest. An additional 1.2 billion pesos in principal and 505 million pesos in interest were due in 1988. The total of debt service obligations in 1988, then, came to 4.18 billion pesos, a sum 400 percent above projected hard currency export earnings. At its meeting with Paris Club creditors in January 1988, Cuba requested that all bilateral credits due in 1988 be extended for fifteen years with a 5-year grace period. As of June 1988, no agreement had been reached between Cuba and its public creditors.

For its part, Cuba, without recourse to the World Bank or the International Monetary Fund, has drastically curtailed hard currency imports, imposed a domestic austerity program, and reduced planned growth from the 5 percent range down to 1 to 1.5 percent. In contrast to the usual Latin American austerity strategy of depressing overall economic activity, Cuba's 1987 program specifically targeted foreign exchange-sensitive activities. Among the salient measures were: reduction of monthly kerosene rations (mainly used for cooking) in order to reduce imports by 256,500 barrels from hard currency areas; diversion of 10 million square meters of textiles from domestic consumption to exports; diversion from domestic sugar consumption to exports; reduction of television programming by 29 hours a week to save oil and allow exports to increase by 130,000 barrels; reduction by 20 percent of gasoline allocations for state administrative activities; and tightening of diplomatic expense accounts and diminution of officials' perquisites (BNC 1987b). Although not fully implemented, the program did generate 33 million pesos' worth of hard currency during the year (ibid.: 1). It is also noteworthy that concern for the impact of the program on low-income family budgets prompted substantial wage increases for the lowest wage groups. Further, although there was some increase in temporary worker furloughs and a decrease in worker productivity because of input shortages, general full employment was maintained.

The partial recovery of world sugar prices in 1986–87 and of petroleum prices in 1987 helped Cuba somewhat, but unfavorable weather patterns brought considerable harm to Cuba's crops. Hard currency earnings for 1987 were approximately one-third their real level three years earlier and real gross social product fell by 3.5 percent. During the first half of 1988, petroleum prices were basically stable, but sugar prices jumped to over 13 cents a pound by the end of June in response to a number of factors . One important reason for the price spurt, however, was severe flooding that spoiled tens of thousands of tons of stored Cuban sugar, making it unclear to what extent Cuba would be able to take advantage of this favorable development in sugar prices.[32] In any event, sugar prices settled back into the 9 to 10 cents a pound range by the end of the summer.

Nevertheless, there are some reasons for optimism regarding Cuba's merchandise trade balance. Barring major natural or political disruptions, it appears that Cuba's exports are poised for a period of strong growth. Investments have been made to allow for significant jumps in nickel, copper, sugar, and refined petroleum exports. Healthy growth can be expected in many of the new manufactured exports mentioned above. Further, Cuba has begun to revise its pricing methods for international trade with the goal of bringing foreign and domestic prices in line with each other. If Cuban authorities hold to this policy, it should help to stimulate greater efficiency in export production as well as to curtail imports. It should also help in selecting new export products and in remedying the anomalous situation that exists for several export products that use up more foreign exchange in their production than they generate in their sale.[33]

With the rectification campaign (discussed in the last chapter) still ongoing and the difficult foreign debt situation unresolved, it is perilous to make projections for the Cuban economy over the coming years. The lingering effects of the debt overhang and the generally inauspicious world market conditions, however, suggest slow growth—well below the original 5 percent annual target of the 1986–90 five-year plan—for the remainder of the quinquennium. To be sure, early reports suggest a real GSP growth for 1988 of around 2.5 percent, leaving the GSP at roughly the same level at the beginning of 1989 as it was at the beginning of 1986. The longer-term prospects appear more sanguine, but intervening structural reforms and political changes (both domestic and international) will play a central role in determining the trajectory for Cuba's socialist economy in its fourth decade.[34]

CHAPTER 10   *Conclusion: Cuban Development in Comparative Perspective*

The first nine chapters of this book have concentrated on the dynamics of the Cuban economy. Chapters 2 through 5 attempted to establish the quantitative record of Cuban economic performance since January 1959. Chapters 6 through 9 provided interpretive discussions of sectoral development experience, overall development strategy, Cuba's system of planning and management, and Cuba's changing relationship to the world economy.

In this chapter we consider aspects of the post-1959 Cuban development experience in a comparative perspective. As discussed in chapter 2, making statistical comparisons among countries is fraught with difficulties. Drawing lessons for other countries from one country's development history is even more problematic, given the vast differences in social and economic contexts. A few qualified comparisons and judgments, however, can be hazarded.

CUBA'S COMPARATIVE PERFORMANCE: EQUITY AND GROWTH

A Comparison with Latin America

In Part One, we established that the Cuban economy has experienced creditable growth since 1959 and strong growth since 1970. Accompanying this growth there has been a consistent and successful policy of income redistribution. The trend toward redistribution was clearly discernible through the 1970s (Brundenius 1984b: ch. 5). Questions may, however, be raised as to whether this trend has continued, especially in view of the 1976–86 development of material incentives and the introduction of new wage scales in 1980. Following the income distribution estimates for Cuba made by Brundenius (1984b), we have made a new estimate for 1986 based on the same method. Briefly, we use the wage scales arranged by type of occupational category as the basis, with a partially hypothetical distribution of the workforce over the wage scale for each occupational category (based on wage scale data and employment statistics supplied by the State Statistical Committee).

A comparison of the 1986 estimate with estimates for earlier years is shown in Table 10.2. The data clearly indicates that there has been a continuation of the trend toward income equality after 1978. It is true that the 1986 estimate does not reflect possible effects of the introduction of bonus payments in the 1970s

Table 10.1.   Estimates of Income Distribution in Cuba, 1986

Deciles	Percentile share	Cumulative share
0–10	5.23	5.23
11–20	6.06	11.29
21–30	7.19	18.48
31–40	7.52	26.00
41–50	7.80	33.80
51–60	9.20	43.00
61–70	11.10	54.10
71–80	12.10	66.20
81–90	13.70	79.90
91–100	20.10	100.00
Top 5 percent	10.12	
Gini coefficient		0.22

Sources: CEE/AEC 1986 and unpublished information supplied by CEE.

Table 10.2.   Income Distribution in Cuba (various years)

Deciles	1953 PS	1953 CS	1962 PS	1962 CS	1978 PS	1978 CS	1986 PS	1986 CS
0–10	0.6	0.6	2.5	2.5	5.1	5.1	5.2	5.2
11–20	1.5	2.1	3.7	6.2	5.9	11.0	6.1	11.3
21–30	1.9	4.0	4.8	11.0	6.5	17.5	7.2	18.5
31–40	2.5	6.5	6.2	17.2	7.3	24.8	7.5	26.0
41–50	4.3	10.8	6.8	24.0	8.0	32.8	7.8	33.8
51–60	6.8	17.6	9.5	33.5	8.5	41.3	9.2	43.0
61–70	10.6	28.2	12.0	45.5	9.9	51.2	11.1	54.1
71–80	13.9	52.1	13.1	58.6	12.8	64.0	12.1	66.2
81–90	19.1	61.2	18.4	77.0	14.9	78.9	13.7	79.9
91–100	38.8	100.0	23.0	100.0	21.1	100.0	20.1	100.0
Top 5 percent	26.5		12.7		11.0		10.1	
Gini coefficient	0.55		0.35		0.25		0.22	

Note: PS stands for percentile share and CS for cumulative share.
Sources: CEE/AEC 1986, unpublished information supplied by CEE; and Brundenius 1984b: tables 5.1, 5.3, and 5.6.

(see Chapter 8), but total payment of bonuses (*normas*, *primas*, and *premios*) only amounted to 10.6 percent of worker income in 1985.[1] The estimate here implicitly assumes that these bonus payments have been distributed equally among the income groups. This might seem to be an unrealistic assumption, but a criticism of the existing bonus system has been precisely that the norms have been set so low that practically every wage earner can exceed them. It is also true that payment for overfulfillment of norms and, generally, *primas* have only been available to production workers.

In January 1987 a new decree closed the income gap even further, upgrading all wage earners in wage categories below 100 pesos per month to 100 pesos and in some cases to 106.74 pesos. In all, 186,000 people were affected by this decree. The overall effect of this reform on income distribution turned out to be rather modest, mainly affecting the share of the bottom 10 percent, which increased its share of total income from 5.2 percent to 5.7, and of the bottom 20 percent, whose share rose from 11.3 percent to 11.8 percent.

It appears that the main force behind the equalization of Cuba's size distribution of income has been income leveling across sectors. This strong leveling is depicted in Table 10.3.

In Table 10.4, we compare the estimated income distributions in Cuba with that for the rest of Latin America. It is important to underscore that the Cuban

Table 10.3. Income Equalization in Cuba, 1975–86 (average annual wage)

	1975		1980		1986	
	Pesos	Index	Pesos	Index	Pesos	Index
Industry	1,758	100.0	1,883	107.1	2,280	129.7
Construction	1,794	100.0	1,969	109.7	2,407	134.2
Agriculture	1,297	100.0	1,520	117.2	2,180	168.1
Transport	2,048	100.0	2,169	105.9	2,616	127.7
Commerce	1,464	100.0	1,611	110.0	2,017	137.8
Education	1,593	100.0	1,763	110.7	2,214	139.0
Cultural activities	1,762	100.0	2,036	115.6	2,696	153.0
Science and technology	2,251	100.0	2,147	95.4	2,514	111.7
Public administration	2,123	100.0	1,952	91.9	2,471	116.4
Total economy	1,616	100.0	1,774	109.8	2,255	139.5

Source: CEE/AEC 1986: 196.

Table 10.4. Income Distribution in Latin America and in Cuba

	Share in total income					
	Latin America[a]		Cuba			
Income strata	1960	1975	1953	1962	1978	1986
Poorest 20%	2.8	2.3	2.1	6.2	11.0	11.3
Next poorest 20%	5.9	5.4	4.4	11.0	13.8	14.7
Poorest 40%	8.7	7.7	6.5	17.2	24.8	26.0
Next 30%	18.6	18.1	21.7	28.3	26.4	28.1
Next 20%	26.1	26.9	33.0	31.5	27.7	25.8
Richest 10%	46.6	47.3	38.8	23.0	21.1	20.1

Sources: For Cuba, Table 10.2. For Latin America, Iglesias 1981.

[a]Estimates by ECLAC on the basis of national surveys for seven countries (Argentina, Brazil, Chile, Colombia, Mexico, Peru, and Venezuela.) It is interesting to note that the results also hold when Cuba is compared to Costa Rica, which is widely reputed to have the most equal distribution of income among the market-oriented countries in Latin America. In 1971, for instance, the poorest 20 percent of Costa Rican households received only 3.3 percent of income, while the top 20 percent received 54.8 percent (World Bank 1987: 253.)

distribution of money income overestimates inequality in the distribution of purchasing power. This is because health care and education in Cuba are provided gratis and basic goods are heavily subsidized by the state. Although a variety of perquisites are available for government officials, most observers agree that they are rather modest in scope (certainly so in comparison with Eastern Europe). In any event, it seems unlikely that they exceed the perquisites offered to public and private employees elsewhere in Latin America. Not only is the distribution of income much more unequal in the rest of Latin America than in Cuba, but the trend in Latin America has been toward greater inequality. Although income distribution estimates for the 1980s are not available, it seems very likely that IMF-mandated programs, with their high unemployment and wage controls, have not reversed this trend.[2]

Cuban equity performance also compares favorably with the rest of Latin America if we consider common social indicators such as life expectancy, infant mortality, illiteracy, and unemployment (see Table 10.5).

Cuba has also had a strong growth record since 1959 when compared to the rest of Latin America. According to our estimates from chapter 4, Cuban GDP per capita grew at an average annual rate of 3.1 percent between 1960 and 1985. GDP per capita growth in Latin America over the same period was 1.8 percent. The only Latin American country with a higher rate of growth over these

Table 10.5.   Social Indicators in Latin America, Mid-1980s[a]

	Life expectancy at birth	Infant mortality[b]	Illiteracy rate[c]	Urban unemployment
Argentina	70	36	6.1	6.1
Brazil	63	71	25.5	5.3
Chile	71	24	8.9	17.2
Costa Rica	73	20	6.4	6.6
Dominican Rep	63	63	27.0	20.3
El Salvador	64	70	38.0	30.0
Haiti	54	107	77.0	40.0
Jamaica	70	28	12.0	25.9
Mexico	66	53	9.7	11.8
Nicaragua	58	84	12.9	16.3
Peru	59	82	17.4	11.8
Uruguay	70	38	6.1[d]	13.1
Venezuela	69	39	15.3	14.3
Cuba	74	13	3.9	3.4[e]

Sources: World Bank 1987; ECLAC, *Statistical Yearbook of Latin America,* 1986; Brundenius and Bye 1986:
    table 7.
[a]Latest available figure.
[b]Dead before 1 year of age per 1,000 born, rounded to nearest integer.
[c]Above 15 years of age.
[d]1975.
[e]Urban and rural unemployment (1981 census).

Table 10.6. Real Income Growth Per Capita in Latin America, 1960/85 (average annual rates of growth, percentages)

	1960/65	1965/70	1970/75	1975/80	1980/85	1960/85
Argentina	2.8	2.8	1.1	0.4	−4.1	0.6
Brazil	1.5	5.0	6.9	4.3	−0.3	3.4
Chile	1.4	2.7	−3.6	5.5	−1.9	0.8
Costa Rica	2.8	3.7	3.2	2.1	−2.4	1.9
Mexico	3.8	3.5	3.1	3.9	−0.9	2.7
Peru	3.4	0.9	1.8	−0.7	−3.2	0.4
Uruguay	−0.3	1.5	1.5	4.1	−4.1	0.5
Latin America[a]	2.5	3.2	2.8	2.6	−1.8	1.8
Cuba	−1.1[b]	1.9	4.8	3.2	6.8	3.1

Sources: ECLAC *Statistical Yearbook of Latin America*, 1984 and 1986 and data for Cuba in chapter 4.
[a]Excluding Cuba.
[b]Global social product per capita in constant 1965 prices, as reported in CEE, *Indicadores Seleccionados, 1950–81*, 1983.

twenty-five years was Brazil. Cuba, however, had the highest rate of growth in Latin America between 1970 and 1985 (see Table 10.6).

Although our formal estimates only go through 1985, it is important not to minimize the 1986–87 downturn in the Cuban economy (the conjunctural circumstances of which are discussed in chapter 9). Data on Cuban national income is not yet available for 1987, but, according to preliminary official figures, gross social product per capita in Cuba in 1981 constant prices grew by 0.1 percent in 1986 and fell by 4.4 percent in 1987.[3] That is, the 1986–87 annual rate of per capita growth in Cuba was −2.0 percent. By contrast, real per capita growth in Latin America averaged 0.9 percent during these two years.[4] If we include the preliminary data from 1986–87, then, the real annual growth rates during 1960–87 for Cuba and Latin America are 2.70 and 1.78 percent, respectively. The conclusion stands: Cuba has outperformed the rest of Latin America in terms of both equity and economic growth.

A Comparison with Taiwan

What happens if Cuban economic performance is compared to that in a rapidly growing, low-income country? Gary Becker has suggested the comparison of Cuba and Taiwan (*Business Week*, June 16, 1986). Both countries are islands that have been isolated economically for long periods of time, supported by a distant superpower, and historically dependent on cane sugar as their primary export. Table 10.7 summarizes the record of economic growth and structural change of the two countries.

It is estimated that Taiwanese GDP per capita was as low as $160 at the beginning of the 1950s, compared to $430 in Cuba (estimates in current dollars

Table 10.7.   Growth and Structural Change in Cuba and Taiwan

	Cuba	Taiwan
GDP per capita 1980 (official exchange rate)	$2,325[a]	$2,668
GDP per capita growth		
1955–65	1.7%	4.8%
1965–85	4.2	6.7
1980–85	6.2	2.0
Shares of GDP		
Agriculture		
1965	24	24
1985	10	6
Manufacturing		
1965	23	26
1985	36	41
Shares of capital goods in manufacturing value added		
1961	1.9	8.4
1970	4.6	25.2
1975	14.7	29.1
1980	19.9	29.6
1986	28.6	35.7

Sources: Cuba: chapter 4; ECLAC, *Economic Survey of Latin America 1963;*
    CEE/AEC 1986: table III.27. Taiwan: *Statistical Yearbook of the Republic
    of China,* various years.
[a]Rudimentary PI estimate on the K_v scale, from Table 5.9.

at official exchange rates). In Taiwan economic growth had accelerated already in the 1950s, while growth was sluggish in Cuba until the beginning of the 1970s. Taiwanese per capita growth accelerated further in the 1960s and 1970s, but tapered off in the first years of the 1980s, a period when growth in Cuba reached unprecedented levels. It should, however, be stressed that growth in Taiwan has regained momentum in the last two years (an impressive 12 percent rate of annual growth between 1985 and 1987), while, as noted above, the rate of growth of the Cuban economy during 1986–87 was negative.

In both countries the leading sector has been manufacturing, the growth of which has outstripped agriculture by a wide margin. The role of capital goods has been instrumental in the growth strategies of both countries. Capital goods production started earlier in Taiwan and had by 1970 reached 25 percent of manufacturing value added, while the corresponding figure in Cuba was still less than 5 percent. The output of capital goods in Cuba has since grown steadily, and its share in manufacturing value added had reached nearly 29 percent by 1986—not far from the Taiwan figure.

Yet there is a clear distinction in the growth strategies of the two countries. Capital goods production has mainly been import substitution-oriented in Cuba until recently, while capital goods production in Taiwan has mainly been export-oriented (Amsden 1984).

Taiwan's strategy of promoting industrial exports has led to a thorough restructuring of exports. The major export of Taiwan in the early 1950s was sugar, which accounted for 84 percent of total exports in 1952. That share has since drastically decreased and was in 1986 only 5 percent. Instead, light industry exports grew rapidly in the 1960s and 1970s, reaching 38 percent of total exports in 1975 and then declining to an export share of 26 percent in 1986. The export share of capital goods went from zero in 1952 to 5 percent in 1965, then expanded to 23 percent in 1985 and reached 36 percent in 1986 (*Statistical Yearbook of the Republic of China*, various years).

Taiwan has also performed remarkably well with regard to equity, although not as well as Cuba. It should also be added that the trend toward increasing equality in Taiwan has been reversed since 1980, and, according to economists at the Chung-Hua Institute for Economic Research in Taipei, this reversal has accelerated since 1985 partly as a result of a speculative boom in urban land rents.[5] Table 10.8 compares the distribution of income and its trend in Taiwan and Cuba.

Taiwanese performance in the areas of education and health is less impressive than Cuba's, as shown in Tables 10.9 and 10.10. Perhaps the sharpest difference is with respect to social welfare. Cuba has an insurance program that covers 100 percent of the population. A similar program (although less extensive) covers only about 60 percent of the workforce in Taiwan. While all Cuban workers are guaranteed one month of vacation each year, Taiwanese workers are guaranteed only one week and are often discouraged from exercising even this prerogative (but with double pay in that case as an incentive). Regarding other socio-economic indicators, overall performance in the two countries is similar. In the mid-1980s, for instance: life expectancy in Cuba was 74.4 years (1987) and in Taiwan, 73.5 years (1986); unemployment has been in the 2–3

Table 10.8. Income Distribution in Cuba and Taiwan

Income strata	Cuba				Taiwan				
	1953	1962	1978	1986	1953	1959	1964	1981	1986
0–20	2.1	6.2	11.0	11.3	3.0	5.7	7.7	8.8	8.3
21–40	4.4	11.0	13.8	14.7	8.3	9.7	12.6	13.8	4.5
41–60	11.1	16.3	16.5	17.0	9.1	13.9	16.6	17.6	17.4
61–80	24.5	25.1	22.7	23.2	18.2	19.7	22.1	22.8	22.6
81–95	31.4	28.7	25.0	23.7	28.8	26.3	24.8	24.7	38.2[a]
96–100 (top 5%)	26.5	12.7	11.0	10.1	32.6	24.7	16.2	12.3	na
Decile ratio	64.7	9.2	4.1	3.9	30.4	13.7	8.6	6.4	na
Gini coefficient	0.55	0.35	0.25	0.22	0.56	0.44	0.33	0.28	na

Sources: Cuba: Table 10.2; Taiwan: Kuo et al. 1981; Directorate-General of the Budget n.d.; Kuo 1988.
[a]Refers to the top 20 percent.

Table 10.9.   Students Enrolled by Level per 1,000 Inhabitants

	Primary	Secondary	Higher	Other	Total
Cuba					
1958	106.1	13.0	3.8	1.0	123.9
1980	163.6	120.0	15.6	28.5	327.6
1985	143.0	151.0	21.5	18.5	334.0
Taiwan					
1958	146.6	27.0	2.6	1.3	177.5
1980	126.1	89.0	18.5	12.7	246.3
1985	117.6	86.7	21.4	14.1	239.8

Sources: CEE/AEC 1985; Brundenius 1984b; *Statistical Yearbook of the Republic of China*, various years.

Table 10.10.   Medical Personnel per 10,000 Inhabitants

	Cuba		Taiwan	
	1958	1985	1958	1985
Physicians	9.3	19.7	6.5	11.4
Dentists	3.1	4.2	1.2	2.9
Nurses	7.4	28.7	4.0	17.5

Sources: Cuba: Brundenius 1984b: ch. 4; CEE/AEC 1986; Taiwan: Council for Economic Planning and Development 1985.

percent range in both countries, although Cuba's labor force participation rate is approximately 6 percentage points higher (Zimbalist 1988c: 7, 15);[6] infant mortality in Taiwan was among the lowest in the world at 6.6 per thousand (1986) while Cuba's rate was 13.3 (1987), though methodological quirks bias Taiwan's official rate downward;[7] illiteracy in the population over 15 years of age was 9.1 percent in Taiwan (1986) and 3.9 percent in Cuba (1981).

The forgoing is, of course, only a partial comparison of economic performance. Many variables, such as current account balance, debt, and price and cyclical stability, have not been discussed. The point is not that one economy or economic system is superior to another, but that Cuban development performance in terms of both growth and equity has much to commend it. This observation leads naturally to the question: Can any general insights about the development process be gleaned from the Cuban experience?

"LESSONS" FROM THE CUBAN EXPERIENCE

A perennial issue of debate among development economists as well as policymakers is the relative importance of "getting prices right," or put differently, the role of markets versus the role of government in the development process. This ongoing debate has taken place in different disguises: structuralism vs. monetarism; Friedmanism vs. liberalism; orthodoxy vs. heterodoxy; private enterprise vs. nationalization; import substitution vs. export promotion; and so on. The polar positions in these contests are maintained by ideologues who never come to grips with the essential question for most developing economies: namely, what is the appropriate mix of plan and market or price and nonprice policies in different countries, at different points in time. Anyone who holds that state action, on the one hand, or the market, on the other, is always the best promoter of development is out of touch with the profound complexity of the development process.

It is clear that many of the positive attributes of Cuban economic performance during the past three decades are based on the leading role played by the state in capital accumulation and redistribution. It is equally clear to those who have studied the economic development of Japan, Taiwan, and South Korea that active state policy has been an essential ingredient to these success stories. The manifestations of state involvement in the East Asian NICs and in Cuba, of course, are very different, but the nature of the state role in the development process in these countries also contains interesting similarities.

Economic development entails the massive mobilization of human and capital resources. With appropriate cultural and political forms, and in a world without industrial giants, the industrial revolution was able to take place gradually in Western Europe and the United States. As Alexander Gerschenkron noted, however, the latecomers would depend upon an increasing economic involvement of the state (Gerschenkron 1965).

Most low-income countries have lacked some or all of the ingredients for a sustained "take-off": Social and productive infrastructure has been insufficient, financial institutions have been undeveloped, requisite political stability has been absent, entrepreneurial groups have been inchoate or have lacked access to political power, market integration has been thin, and so on. In the absence of necessary institutional support, the task of capital accumulation has been too large and too risky for private national groups. The state has been needed to provide this support and minimally to nurture initial projects. Nurturance has been likely to include, *inter alia*: infant industry protection; technical, managerial, financial, and marketing assistance; tax credits or production subsidies; interenterprise coordination; and assistance in labor-management relations. It also might have extended to state ownership and management of enterprises and various forms of economic planning.

Although the state is not necessarily "smarter" than the private sector, its perspective and potential command over resources often allows it to take a longer-run view, to invest in projects with large capital requirements and long payback periods, and to undertake complementary projects simultaneously.[8] The state's role in development has been elaborated theoretically often enough. Naturally the role differs with the circumstances and, generally, tends to diminish as the economy develops and becomes more complex. Whether or not the state can fulfill its role in a particular country depends on an intricate matrix of historical forces, for example: whether a traditional landed class retains significant sway over government decision-making; whether a military imperative exists; whether the government elite is well educated and whether it maintains cooperative relations with other well-educated groups, and so on.[9]

Albeit in a more pervasive and heavy-handed manner than the East Asian NICs,[10] the post-1959 Cuban state has fulfilled many of the basic development functions just outlined. As in Korea in the late 1940s and Taiwan in the early 1950s, the 1959–63 land reforms in Cuba enabled the channeling of resources for industrialization and the progressive integration of rural areas into the national market. Massive social infrastructure investments by the Cuban state have not only created a relatively highly educated and healthy labor force, but also a national health industry that has few, if any, rivals in the developing world (Feinsilver 1987; Santana 1987, 1988).

The sine qua non of any industrialization process of course is capital accumulation—the generation and productive channeling of savings. Following the initial agrarian reforms in South Korea and Taiwan, surplus was generated at the expense of small landholders and urban workers, and investment rates rose to levels considerably above those in post-1959 Cuba. Unlike in other centrally planned economies, accumulation proceeded gradually in Cuba, and investment rates increased slowly. The early priority in Cuba was fulfilling basic needs and human capital development. Given this priority and without a harsh collectivization drive or the colonization of agriculture for surplus appropriation—and without aid, trade, or foreign investment from the United States—substantial funds were not available initially for extensive investments in large-scale industrial projects. Nevertheless, the virtual elimination of luxury imports and sumptuous consumption left enough saving to increase investment above the pre-1959 levels. The eventual increases in Soviet aid and the shift away from consumer goods production allowed investment expenditures to increase steadily (see Table 10.11). The investment ratio (gross investment as a share of national income[11]) rose gradually from 20.3 percent during the period 1962–65 to 23.2 percent during 1966–70, 24.3 percent during 1971–75, 29.2 percent during 1976–80, and to 28.0 percent during 1981–85.[12]

Cuban state control over investment allocation also brought rapid growth in capital goods production (see chapter 6). Approximately one-quarter of invest-

Table 10.11. Average Annual Investment (millions of pesos)

1953–58	400
1960–65	650
1966–70	850
1971–75	1,500
1976–80	2,600
1981–85	3,304

Source: Figueras 1985: 50; CEE/AEC 1987: 215.

ment spending on machinery and equipment in the 1980s has been on capital goods produced in Cuba. Similar to the Asian NICs and apparently spurning the conventional wisdom of a static comparative advantage view, the state opted for an expanded industrial development, eventually encompassing capital-intensive sectors.[13] After initial development of labor-intensive manufacturing, domestic production of capital goods for local light industry was explicitly promoted by state policy. As suggested by Albert Hirschman in 1968, a major attraction of capital goods is the potential learning experience they offer (Hirschman 1968). The production of capital goods denotes production of the means of production and, hence, of technology. Not only does this allow technological adaptation to local conditions, but, in the words of Henry Bruton, it opens the prospect for "the creation of technological capacity and the capacity to develop a more or less continuous flow of new technological knowledge" (Bruton 1988: 49; also see Rosenberg 1976).

In a sense, Cuba's choice to develop the capital goods sector was forced upon it. Between 80 and 90 percent of Cuba's industrial machinery and equipment park was of U.S. origin in 1959 (Figueras 1985: 36). The U.S. blockade compelled Cuba to design and produce needed spare parts. Trade with the Soviet bloc helped a bit in this regard, but lower levels of technological development and the use of the metric system within the CMEA placed a heavy burden on Cuba to make its own adaptations.[14]

Two keys to Cuba's eventual success in capital goods were the early emphasis on 1) general and technical education, and 2) research and development institutes. Together these resource commitments provided Cuba with the potential for autonomous technological development as well as the ability to manage and operate related production activities. By 1980, on a per capita basis Cuba was actually graduating 40 percent more students from universities than was Czechoslovakia and 31 percent more than the German Democratic Republic (Figueras 1985: 45). In the mid 1980s, Cuba had over 175 major R&D institutes with over 17,000 specialists (CEE/AEC 1987: 512, 515). Cuba's access to scientific training in the U.S.S.R. and Soviet generosity in sharing technology and engineers with Cuba have been vital elements to this process.

Cuba's technological capacity has begun to yield increasingly obvious benefits. The introduction of state-of-the-art techniques with homegrown innovations in medicine and biotechnology, world leadership in technology for the sugar industry, the adaptation of production methods in electronics, and the growth of many nontraditional exports are all linked to the development of the capital goods sector.

In chapter 9, we detailed Cuba's strong performance in nontraditional exports since 1980, particularly in comparison to the rest of Latin America. Here again, the potential significance of the state is apparent. The nations of the Caribbean Basin are prospective beneficiaries of favorable tariff treatment and geographically easy access to the U.S. market. The exports of these nations receive additional fillips from foreign investment and resource diversion toward the external economy. Yet nontraditional export performance in this region has been uneven at best, and certainly far below the Cuban performance.

The recent history of nontraditional exports in Central America and the Caribbean is tainted not by inadequate will or inaccurate prices, but by insufficient institutional support to confront the many obstacles of export promotion. Feasible new export products must first be identified. Then they must be produced. Production requires finance, which is usually not available to local producers, or when it is, only at very high rates of interest. It also requires technical assistance, market knowledge, and time. Gestation periods for new products, industrial or agricultural, often vary between one and four years. Once a quality product is being produced, it must be packaged, shipped, and marketed. But packaging facilities are generally poor, transportation networks and auxiliary equipment (e.g., refrigeration) are woefully insufficient and expensive, and marketing ties are absent or minimal. For nations in the Caribbean Basin, the U.S. Agency for International Development (USAID) frequently offers support for one or two steps of the process for a limited time period. Local entrepreneurs and their capital become invested in new projects that are promising at first but then become encumbered at later stages and ultimately fail. This failure denotes not only a waste of human and financial capital, but also the likely dispiriting of other prospective exporters.[15]

Comprehensive support packages need to be designed for the entire gestation period of new projects. Inadequate amounts of private capital, the presence of high risk at each stage, inadequate capital markets, and insufficient auxiliary structures all suggest a possible role for the state in promoting new exports. The Cuban state, whatever its inefficiencies, has committed sufficient resources to new export projects and has bargained effectively with foreign trading companies for market access and fair prices. The governments in South Korea, Taiwan, and Japan have provided similar support, particularly during the early periods of new export promotion. It is also common to the Cuban and East Asian experiences that export promotion and import substitution have been pursued together as part of the overall development strategy (Bruton 1988; Ranis 1987; Sachs 1987).

Another potential advantage of centralized control over resources has been highlighted by the Third World debt dilemma of the 1980s. During the first half of this decade, Cuba was largely insulated from the effects of the debt crisis by its favorable terms of trade with and debt relief from the Soviet Union. But as the terms of trade with the Soviet Union deteriorated, petroleum prices and the dollar dropped, poor weather decimated the harvest, and Western debt accumulated, Cuba by 1985 was facing the same foreign exchange crunch as the rest of Latin America. Similar to other countries in the region, Cuba introduced an austerity package. The social and economic impact of the Cuban package, however, was dramatically different from that of austerity packages introduced elsewhere. In Cuba, activities related to use or generation of foreign exchange (e.g., fuel, electricity, television programming, transportation, sugar) were either directly curbed or promoted (see chapter 9). Elsewhere in Latin America the approach was, among other things, to curb aggregate demand and thereby lower imports. The market economy austerity package, hence, brought with it deeper recession, more unemployment, lower wages, and acutely aggravated social conditions. The Cuban package isolated particular sectors and succeeded in maintaining high levels of economic activity and low unemployment. There were greater shortages in Cuba and some contraction of economic activity, but the ensuing social costs were distributed evenly and lower-income groups actually received wage increases and consumption subsidies.

To be sure, the desirability of active state intervention in economic affairs diminishes as an economy develops. Not only does the supply of skilled labor increase over time, allowing for more effective decentralization of decision-making, not only do the requisite infrastructure and support institutions evolve, but the economy grows and becomes more complex. Greater size and complexity place insurmountable hurdles in the way of centralized information gathering and processing, and modern technology demands greater flexibility. Thus the governments of the East Asian NICs have used fewer direct levers of control, and the centrally planned economies have been experimenting with extending the scope of market transactions. As discussed in chapter 8, Cuba also followed a limited market-type decentralization strategy from 1976 to 1986, but, for a variety of reasons, has since April 1986 entered into a phase of reevaluation and relative deemphasis of material incentives. Cuba has already resumed efforts at administrative decentralization, and an eventual return to experimentation with aspects of a market-oriented decentralization seems inevitable.

The need for some coordination of economic activity, however, persists even in the most developed economies. As technology changes more rapidly, investments become riskier and inter-enterprise partnerships, whether national or international, become more attractive. Further, issues of market failure seem to become more pressing as industrial growth proceeds. Concerns with the preservation of the environment or of cultural values and social structures also suggest an ongoing imperative for state involvement.

From this perspective, it is both ironic and disturbing that USAID, the World Bank, and the IMF are conditioning new loans and debt relief packages on the liberalization of economic policy. The weight of the historical evidence does not support the case for universally applied packages of tariff reduction, exchange rate devaluation, privatization of enterprise, and market pricing. Sometimes it makes as much sense to encourage raising the quality of public management as it does to privatize public enterprise. Sometimes, particularly in smaller countries, market pricing is monopoly pricing and is not conducive to either static or dynamic efficiency. Sometimes exchange rate devaluation will yield much more price instability than it will export growth (Rodríguez and Schydlowsky 1988). Sometimes tariff reduction will reduce fledgling industry to its knees rather than stimulate competitiveness.

Monolithic or ideological approaches that call for the same set of policies for all countries at all times are not the answer to the development dilemma. The Cuban experience not only underscores the important potential role of the state in development but, in comparative perspective, it points to the different ways this role can be fulfilled. It is perhaps paradoxical to conclude, then, that post-1959 Cuba supports the case for nonideological, eclectic, and pragmatic approaches to development policy.

Notes

1. Among the more interesting studies in this new wave of scholarship are: Benglesdorf 1985; Fuller 1985; Pérez-Stable 1985; Feinsilver 1987; Meurs 1988; Santana 1987; and Hamburg 1986.

Chapter 2. Statistical Methods and Meanings

1. Mesa-Lago (1981: 33) erroneously states that GMP excludes "material services," i.e., transportation, trade, and communication. "Material services" are excluded from the concept total material product (TMP) but they are included in GMP. Borrowing Mesa-Lago, Azicri (1988: 258) repeats this error.

2. The MPS system considers transportation, communications, and commerce to be "productive" services and includes their value in national income measurements.

3. In the SNA system, NNP is net national product. It is equivalent to GNP minus depreciation. NNP minus indirect business taxes equals the SNA category of national income. The latter should not be confused with the MPS category of national income, which does not include nonproductive services.

4. The 2.25 billion peso depreciation figure for 1984 is estimated on the basis of data on capital stock provided by the Cuban State Statistical Committee and data on gross investment from CEE/AEC 1984, both in current prices. Since price changes subsequent to the 1981 wholesale price reform have been very minor, there is unlikely to be any major distortion from using a current price figure for depreciation along with a 1981 constant price figure for NMP.

5. One reason for this difference is the importance of foreign trade to the Cuban economy. Imports of intermediate goods are registered as part of the gross value of output. Such imports amounted to approximately 12.5 percent of Cuban GSP in 1984.

6. Imports of intermediate goods as a share of total imports fell from 58.9 percent in 1970 to 44.7 percent in 1983 (*Cuba Business*, April 1987: 9).

7. To be sure, this is a conservative assumption since the share of the state budget going to social services has increased from 33 percent in 1978 to 40 percent in 1982, and to 46 percent in 1985. Caution is still necessary, among other reasons, because the share of other service-related expenditures has diminished in recent years.

8. See, for example, the polemic between Zimbalist and Brundenius, on the one side, and Mesa-Lago and Pérez-López, on the other, appearing in the journal *Comparative Economic Studies* 27: 1 & 3 (Spring and Winter 1985).

9. See the aforementioned debate and CEE/AEC 1984 (83c, 95).

10. This point is developed in Brundenius and Zimbalist 1987.

11. The figure of one million plus products includes all intermediate and final goods. A large share of these, perhaps as large as 40 or 50 percent, is imported. Fixing prices for imported goods, although not always straightforward, is considerably easier than for domestic goods. Basically, there are two procedures for fixing imported goods' prices. For products without a "stabilized" price, the CEP essentially takes the c.i.f. price, converts it at the relevant exchange rate, and adds domestic trade expenditures. For products with a "stabilized" price, the CEP usually fixes the price as the average c.i.f. converted price for the previous three years, state subsidies or turnover taxes making up the difference.

12. Since 1986 it has become fashionable in Cuba to refer to the system as simply SDE. *Dirección* is considered to encompass *planificación*.

13. There does appear to be a tendency, however, for the number of yearly price adjustments to increase since 1984. According to a 1986 article in the journal of the State Price Committee, there were price modifications in 51 product groups in 1985, and there were planned price modifications in 96 product groups (B. Hernández 1986: 98).

14. The first general price freeze began on November 15, 1961. There were several subsequent modifications before the major price reform of 1965. For an interesting history of Cuban price policy since 1959, as well as some data on early prices and price changes, see Santiago 1986.

15. We were informed in May 1987 by one official at the CEP that the 1989 reform will be pushed back at least a year. After the 1965 Soviet reforms, which introduced enterprise self-financing, there was a major reform of wholesale prices in 1967, and the next price reform did not come for fifteen years. For an excellent discussion of Soviet pricing institutions and methods, see Feygin 1983.

16. In the 1981 reform the percent markup above cost varied by economic branch, according to priorities assigned in the economic plan. The intention for the 1989 price reform is to have the same percent markup throughout the economy. There is a growing awareness among Cuban economists and planners that product prices, particularly for tradeables, need to reflect scarcity value or opportunity cost to avoid resource waste. The proposal to have a common percent markup is consistent with this appreciation of scarcity pricing, but it is unlikely to generate relative prices that approximate scarcity values as long as prices are based on average cost plus principles, ignoring movements in product demand. Profitability in Cuba is measured as a percent of *costo de elaboración*, which basically is total cost minus raw material, transport, and storage costs. Prices were set in 1981 so that average profitability in the economy would equal 9.2 percent; actual realized profitability, however, averaged 5.3 percent in 1981, 1982, and 1983. In 1983, out of 2,098 enterprises analyzed, 58 percent earned profits and 42 percent earned losses (Salom 1985a: 34).

17. For simplicity here we ignore the distinction between total costs and *costo de elaboración*.

18. For an excellent discussion of this issue and the tensions of a market-oriented reform of a centrally planned economy, see Kornai 1980a.

19. To cite some other examples: The price of rationed chicken was 1.54 pesos per kilo and the parallel market price was 8.80 pesos; the price of rationed beans was 66 centavos per kilo and the parallel market price was 3.30 pesos; the price of rationed cooking oil was 88 centavos per kilo and the parallel price was 6.60 pesos; the price of

rationed sugar was 24 centavos per kilo and the parallel price was 88 centavos; and the price of rationed coffee was 3.48 pesos per kilo and the parallel price was 52.80 pesos per kilo (Instituto de Demanda Interna 1988).

20. The reported percentage of work centers violating official prices rose from 3.0 percent in 1979 to 3.9 percent in 1981, 5.2 percent in 1984, and 13.9 percent in 1985 (Padron 1985: 102). According to one source, by the end of 1986 four of ten enterprises had been found guilty of price violations, and between April and September of 1986 alone 21.4 million pesos were confiscated from enterprises for overpricing their products. Again, the principal culprits were restaurants (EIU 1986: 9). An excellent discussion of Cuba's food distribution system and the circumvention of official prices is available in Benjamin et al. 1986.

21. Many of the related difficulties in interpreting Cuban statistics from this period have been described by Carmelo Mesa-Lago in a variety of his publications. See, for instance, Mesa-Lago 1969, 1979, 1985.

22. See Mesa-Lago 1969, 1979, 1985, 1988.

23. Ironically, the Soviets have been willing to provide figures to Western researchers. See chapter 9.

24. Pérez-López 1986 (18). Pérez-López bases his claim on a limited sample of consumer goods. Among other problems here, this claim is a non sequitur since Cuban national income measures are based on wholesale, not retail, prices. Wholesale and retail prices are separated by an extensive system of subsidies and turnover and taxes and do not generally track each other very closely. The Cubans have published their own implicit GSP deflators in the 1984 *Statistical Yearbook* and explicit GSP and consumer goods deflators in the 1985 yearbook. These deflators are based on virtually complete product coverage.

25. We refer here primarily to economic statistics. A similar conclusion has been reached regarding Cuban health statistics by Santana 1988 and regarding sugar statistics by James Fry (1988), managing director of the British consultancy firm Landell Mills Commodities Studies.

CHAPTER 3. INDUSTRIAL GROWTH

1. Calculated from CEE/AEC 1985 (102, 148). Constant price industrial value added, however, decreased in both 1986 and 1987 during Cuba's recession (to be discussed in later chapters). See CEE/AEC 1986 (102) and CEE 1988a (3).

2. The actual range of techniques is rather broad. Mongrel and makeshift methods are also prevalent because of the frequent irregularity and paucity of data. Some of the more important studies are: A. Becker 1969; Bergson 1950 and 1961; Converse 1982; Greenslade 1976; Hodgman 1954; Kaplan and Moorsteen 1960; Montias 1967; Pitzer 1982; Staller 1962; and Treml and Hardt 1972.

3. For a critique of this study, see Brundenius and Zimbalist 1985a and 1985b.

4. The 1985 paper was presented at the Latin American Studies Association meetings in Albuquerque, New Mexico. It was revised and published in the *Journal of Developing Areas* 20 (January 1986): 151–72.

5. That is, following the findings of Grossman 1960, Nove 1977 (ch. 13), and others, WEFA accepts the official physical production data as reliable.

6. Since WEFA sectoral weights are from a 1974 conversion study by the Cuban State Statistical Committee and 1974 is the base year, the branch GVO distribution in 1975 was used to proxy for the same in 1974. Cuba changed its branch classification system in 1977 and has published consistent series for the new system only back to 1975. See CEE/AEC 1977 and G. Rodríguez 1987.

7. Disaggregated information on individual products is available for other branches in Brundenius and Zimbalist 1985a and 1985b.

8. The Cuban State Statistical Committee provided us with physical output data from 1959 through 1965. The data for 1959 through 1962, however, was spotty, with many entries unavailable. If these entries are assigned a zero value, the resulting estimate is biased upward. The estimate for 1959–62 industrial growth using this procedure is 27.7 percent annually—obviously an unrealistic figure. From 1963 the data is basically complete.

9. The Peruvian prices are from the Ministerio de Industria y Comercio (1969). The Chilean prices are from the Instituto Nacional de Estadísticas, División de Encuesta Muestrales 1986.

10. The output index for each year in this branch was then interpolated based upon an annual growth rate of 8.9 percent during 1965–84, with 1974 = 100.

11. The one product covered, aluminum shapes, is insignificant in its contribution to the branch relative to the four excluded products: three varieties of nickel compounds and copper concentrate.

12. The data necessary to calculate export prices for all but copper concentrate is available in the Cuban statistical yearbook.

13. Strictly speaking, this downward bias would be in comparison to Chilean prices from an earlier year, rather than in relation to Cuban prices from an earlier year.

14. Conversations with officials at the Cuban State Statistical Committee in October 1985, March 1986, and May 1987.

15. The official value added growth rate in constant 1981 *precios de empresa* is 25.1 percent for 1981 (CEE/AEC 1985: 114–35). The possibility that Cuban real industrial output actually increased by 25 percent in a single year seems remote. We do not have an explanation for this figure, but it does suggest that the full effect of the price reform of that year might not be captured in the official constant price figures.

16. For discussions of the new product pricing issue see, *inter alia:* Greenslade 1972 (181–86) and Pitzer 1982 (13).

17. Calculated from Brundenius 1985 (table 1, appendix).

18. Basically, the regression growth rate identifies a growth trend over a given period and reduces the potential bias of unrepresentative end points. Specifically, the regression growth rate for each branch is estimated using the following equation:

$$\ln Y = \ln A + rt$$

where Y stands for the estimated value of branch output in each year, A is a constant term, r is the exponential rate of output growth, and t is a time variable (equaling one in year one, two in year two, etc.).

19. Cohn (1972) considers different but overlapping categories from those in the present study in analyzing the sources of difference in Western and official estimates of Soviet national income growth. Nevertheless, our procedure was inspired by Cohn.

20. In the comparison of the two estimates under consideration, it is important to recall that the WEFA weights are based on value added estimates from the early 1960s for most branches, but are distorted by the inclusion of turnover taxes in the weight estimates for other branches.

21. Disaggregated data on individual products and estimated branch output for each year, 1962–85, will be furnished by the authors upon request.

CHAPTER 4. GROSS DOMESTIC PRODUCT: RATE OF GROWTH

1. For a discussion of other differences in the two concepts, see, for one, Naciones Unidas 1982.

2. Net value added, as distinct from value added as used in the West, does not include depreciation. That is, net value added is the sum of payments to labor plus surplus.

3. There are a few curious aspects to the Cuban presentation of this data, but, if anything, they give greater force to the view that the Cubans are reporting statistics accurately, without embellishment. Perhaps the most striking oddity is the series on net value added in the industrial sugar products branch, which reports negative figures for 1975 through 1980 (CEE/AEC 1984: 137). When questioned about this and other apparent anomalies, officials at the State Statistical Committee explained that they were the result of price distortions, production inefficiencies, and heavy capital investments (e.g., cane harvesters, conversion of milling to use of bagasse as energy source, etc.). Although we were unable to quantify the impact of these factors, the explanations themselves appeared logical.

4. Calculated from Codina 1987 (131, 135).

5. Calculated from data in CEE/AEC, various years; Brundenius 1984b (134); and Mesa-Lago 1978 (44).

6. Although the table itself is still classified in Cuba, much relevant information from it has been published in the statistical yearbooks (cf., CEE/AEC 1985: 177).

7. See CEE/AEC 1985 (177). The industrial share based on labor payments plus surplus is substantially different from that based only on labor. We cannot explain this discrepancy to our satisfaction.

8. Information about other commodities from the journals of the State Price Committee, the State Finance Committee, and JUCEPLAN (central planning board) confirms this view. These journals are: *Teoría y Práctica de los Precios*, *Finanzas y Crédito*, and *Cuba: Economía Planificada*, respectively, various issues, 1985–87.

9. Chilean data from 1981 was not available to us. The 1981 weights are derived from the Inter–American Development Bank 1982 Report and the ILO Year Book.

10. The estimates have varied from a low of 13.3 percent to a high of over 30 percent. See Brundenius and Zimbalist 1987.

CHAPTER 5. GROSS DOMESTIC PRODUCT: DOLLAR LEVEL

1. Typically, a variety of functional forms (log, semilog, etc.) are tested and the best fit is then used.

2. The various indicators have significantly different elasticities with respect to per

capita GDP at different levels of development. See, for one, Economic Commission for Europe 1980.

3. Factor analysis has the additional advantage of allowing a confidence interval based on the standard error of the estimate to be established. There is no straightforward way to generate such an interval using the simple regression technique.

4. See, for instance, Santana 1987 and 1988.

5. Measurements of static efficiency for an economy are notoriously difficult. See the essays by Bergson and Domar in A. Eckstein 1971. Anecdotal evidence is easier to come by, but more difficult to interpret. Mesa-Lago and Pérez-López, for instance, cite evidence to the effect that Cuban tractors were utilized at 25.2 percent of planned capacity during the 1969–70 sugar harvest (1985b: 300). This surely is strong specific evidence of inefficiency, but it must be qualified due to the peculiar nature of the 1969–70 harvest in Cuba. Among other things, Cuba had just imported a large stock of combines from the Soviet Union that did not work. Utilization of tractor capacity more than doubled in the ensuing ten years; see chapter 7 on agriculture.

6. The Ehrlich method is also described in her working paper (1985: 7). Here Ehrlich writes that the iterations procedure "corrects the various inexactnesses of the exchange rates."

7. Here we follow the convention in the existing literature. Strictly speaking, a direct comparison of tightness of fit cannot be properly made since the dependent variable in the double logarithmic form is different.

8. Rounding off to the nearest integer, Mesa-Lago and Pérez-López had 18 such equations.

9. Estimates are from United Nations, Commission of the European Communities, *World Comparisons of Purchasing Power and Real Product for 1980* (part I, pp. 7–9).

10. Economic Commission for Latin America and the Caribbean, *Economic Survey of Latin America and the Caribbean, 1982* (88, 99, 101).

11. This is also true to a lesser degree for middle-income countries. The 1980 exchange rate deviation index (or ERDI, i.e., the ratio of estimated GDP per capita on the K_x scale to estimated GDP per capita on the K_v scale) for Ireland is estimated to be 1.24, for Spain 1.32, and for Greece 1.41 (Marer 1985b: 90).

12. Of course, when using exchange rates to gauge living standards it is also important to bear in mind that (generally short-run) distortions related to capital movements and expectations are possible as well. On the other hand, purchasing power parity estimates are also subject to distortions related *inter alia* to differential product quality across countries and the weighting scheme used to determine "international prices."

13. To our knowledge, factor analysis was employed in physical indicators estimation once before by Szilagyi (1978), although his inquiry was more exploratory. Szilagyi concluded cautiously that factor analysis held promise for use in international comparisons.

14. The larger discrepancy on the K_v (than the K_x) scale is arguably desirable since it appears to result from corrections to acute exchange rate bias, e.g., the exchange rate converted GDP per capita for Argentina is $5,453 while the factor analysis prediction (on the K_v scale) is the more realistic $3,265 (see Table 5.2, columns 2 and 3).

15. A box plot is a graphic display invented by Tukey (1977). Box plots are not standardized, but their basic structure is as follows. Vertical lines are drawn at the median and the upper and lower quartiles and are joined by horizontal lines to produce

the box. A horizontal line is drawn from the upper quartile to the most extreme data point that is within a distance of 1.5 IQR (interquartile range) of the upper quartile. A similarly defined horizontal line is drawn from the lower quartile. Each data point beyond the ends of the horizontal lines is marked with an asterisk or a plus sign.

16. The estimates in Table 5.8 are based upon our output index for GDP1 from chapter 4, which, for reasons explained in the text, we believe to be more reliable. Briefly, GDP2 is less reliable in early years due to limited output data for products in our industrial list and in later years due to the increasing underrepresentation of new products in our industrial list.

17. Mathematical proofs for the arguments in this section can be found in Joglekar and Zimbalist 1989.

18. These properties of the underlying system of equations obtain whether arithmetic or geometric averages are taken to derive the predicted per capita GDP for each country in each iteration. When we carried out the same empirical exercise using arithmetic averaging, the convergence still occurred, with numbers above the mean approaching the mean more slowly and numbers below the mean approaching the mean more rapidly.

CHAPTER 6. CAPITAL GOODS: DEVELOPMENT AND PROSPECTS

1. Capital goods are often used as a categorization of ISIC group 38 (ISIC = International Standard Industrial Classification of all Industrial Activities), which comprises "manufacture of fabricated metal products, machinery, and equipment." That is not entirely correct since ISIC 38 also includes durable consumer goods (such as radios, televisions, refrigerators, stoves, etc.). A better label for ISIC 38 is the *engineering goods* industries, and this is also the label given to it in this study. Thus the term capital goods is reserved for goods that are used as means of production.

2. For an account of U.S. economic warfare against Cuba in the 1960s, see, among others, Adler-Karlsson 1968 (ch. 17), Morales and Pons 1987–88, and Morley 1987.

3. Information given to the authors during visit to the Santa Clara mechanical plant on September 18, 1984. On the history of capital goods production in Cuba, see Figueras 1985 and Chaviano et al. 1988.

4. See note 1.

5. Survey of capital goods industries prepared for the authors by CEE in September 1984.

6. On the even geographical distribution of industry in Cuba, see G. Rodríguez 1987.

7. Quoted in the daily *Trabajadores*, November 3, 1982.

8. For a detailed account of the trial-and-error process of developing a Cuban-designed sugar combine-harvester, see CICMA 1983 and Edquist 1985.

9. KTP is the Russian abbreviation for Kombain Trostnikouborochny Pryamotochny ("straightforward cane harvesting combine").

10. Interview with Jorge Abreu, Deputy Director of Research of CICMA (see Table 6.7) on September 19, 1984.

11. UNIDO 1979, for instance, claims that a plant producing tractors should have an annual capacity of 10,000 units in order to be economical.

12. CMEA is the Council of Mutual Economic Assistance (often referred to as

COMECON); Cuba has been a member since 1972.

13. Interview with Jorge Abreu, September 19, 1984.

14. These figures are in GVO. In value added terms the shares would be higher (see chapter 10). A similar projection indicates that the DPR of capital goods would reach 43 percent in 1990 and 66 percent in 2000, compared with 32 percent in 1984 (see Table 6.8).

15. To be sure, output in the engineering branches declined in both 1986 and 1987.

16. One peso is equal to U.S. $1 at the official exchange rate in 1988.

17. The machine park figure is given by Figueras (1985: 39). The figures on imports of machine tools were calculated by the authors from DEC/BEC 1968, 1970, 1971; and CEE/AEC 1974, 1979, 1981, 1984, and 1986.

CHAPTER 7. AGRICULTURE: ORGANIZATION AND PERFORMANCE

1. Estimates of percent of irrigated and fertilized land vary by year and source. For the mid-1940s, it appears that only 3 percent of land was irrigated and 7.4 percent fertilized. Some estimates report the percent of irrigated land rising to near 10 percent by the mid-1950s—still a very low share. This data as well as data on the backward application of modern techniques and undermechanization are discussed in Bianchi 1964 (90–95).

2. The 1953 census reported that 41.7 percent of the rural population was illiterate, and a mid-1950s survey reported that 44 percent of rural workers had never attended school; of those who had, 88 percent did not go beyond the third grade (Bianchi 1964: 97).

3. Alternatively, the top 28 sugar companies controlled over 83 percent of the sugar land (Bianchi 1964: 77). An earlier agricultural census (1946) revealed that the 1.4 percent of farms with more than 500 hectares controlled 47 percent of agricultural land, and the 7.9 percent with more than 100 hectares controlled 71.1 percent of the land (see Bianchi 1964: 75).

4. The comparative yields are reported in Bianchi 1964 (91), based upon a 1961 U.N. Food and Agriculture Organization study.

5. The same study found the share of cultivated land to be 46.4 percent in Chile and 75.5 percent in Costa Rica. These and other estimates are presented in Bianchi 1964 (84, 400).

6. This data is from J. L. Rodríguez 1987 (26) and Chonchol 1963.

7. See Benjamin et al. 1986 (8–14). The share of food in imports in 1958 was 21.7 percent (CEE/AEC 1986: 425).

8. Cited in J. L. Rodríguez 1987 (27).

9. Brundenius 1984b (14); J. L. Rodríguez 1987 (26). Also see Benjamin et al. 1986 (ch. 1); MacEwan 1981 (ch. 3); O'Connor 1970 (ch. 4); and Rodríguez and Carriazo 1987 (24–34).

10. Not surprisingly, the introduction of price controls and rationing of basic foodstuffs (in March 1962) led to the emergence of black markets. Free market sales, however, were permitted throughout the 1960s, although cars entering cities were limited to 25 pounds of produce (Gilly 1964: 22). Such sales were made illegal with the Fourth Congress of ANAP in the fall of 1971. They were, of course, legalized again in

1980, brought under tighter regulations in 1982, and finally abolished again in May 1986. The experience with free farmers' markets is analyzed in chapter 8.

Among the more significant problems with labor incentives were growing labor shortages, particularly in sugar. Manual cane cutting is difficult and extremely arduous work, and with guaranteed jobs elsewhere in the economy many *macheteros* fled to the cities. The official response to this shortage was to push ahead with mechanization, to develop voluntary labor, and eventually to raise wages for cane cutters.

11. Bianchi 1964; Gilly 1964; Dumont 1970a and 1970b; O'Connor 1970; Karol 1970; Boorstein 1968; Morley 1987; Rich 1988; Jones 1988; Smith and Morales 1988; etc.

12. See, for instance, MacEwan 1981 (117–20). Since there is more than one output series for the 1960s and official data includes only output sold to the state, growth estimates for the decade differ according to the methodology employed. J. L. Rodríguez (1987: 37), for instance, estimates higher agricultural output in 1969 than in 1970 and 4.2 percent yearly growth between 1962 and 1969. Most observers, however, seem to agree that output stagnated during the 1960s and probably fell in per capita terms.

13. Between 1959 and 1961 there was an all-out drive to diversify Cuban agriculture and move away from sugar. Hectarage planted in cane was reduced by 15 percent over these years. In 1962, however, the Cubans decided that they were attempting to diversify too rapidly, and 74,340 hectares were added for cane planting; 1963 and 1964 also witnessed increased cane planting with 78,640 and 80,400 hectares added, respectively (C. R. Rodríguez 1983: 229). It was during Castro's trips to the U.S.S.R. in April–May 1963 and again in January 1964 that the commitment was made to significantly increase sugar output over the long run and to pursue gradual diversification.

14. Pérez-López (1987a: 53) reports that by 1958 there were 48 distilleries in the country, but that only half were operating.

15. Daily per capita consumption of proteins was 66.4 grams in 1965 and 79.7 grams in 1986. Daily calorie consumption was around 2,700 in 1958, 2,552 in 1965, and 2,948 in 1986 (CEE/AEC 1986: 175). Comparisons to the pre-1959 period are more problematic both because of data reliability and very unequal consumption patterns across income groups. For instance, in the countryside malnutrition rates were as high as 91 percent even though agricultural workers were supposed to consume over 3,000 calories per day (Leyva 1972: 458–59). The overall improvement in the Cuban diet is discussed in detail by Benjamin et al. (1986) and by Rodríguez and Carriazo (1987).

The extent to which the Cuban government remains committed to ongoing import substitution in food production is not clear. As long as the Cubans continue to emphasize increases in sugar output, one major constraint on continuing diversification will be land. Yet, as pointed out earlier, it is difficult to assess the costs and benefits of agricultural crop policies because, *inter alia*, of the ambiguous meaning of Cuban prices.

16. This is why we have not included output figures and growth rates for these products from the 1960s.

17. Falling capital productivity in agriculture is analyzed in Nova González 1986.

18. There are two ways of accounting value added. One is to add together labor costs, profits, and depreciation (although the Cubans more commonly exclude depreciation in estimating *net* value added). The other is to take gross output and subtract intermediate consumption. Presumably because of pricing irregularities, the two methods do not always yield the same figure, and net value added figures are negative for

some crops for certain years. Although we were constrained to use value added measures for agricultural production in chapter 4 to avoid double counting in estimating GDP growth, we feel that gross output gives a more accurate picture of the trends in agricultural production and, hence, we rely primarily on gross output measures in this chapter.

19. As measured by gross value of output in constant 1981 enterprise prices divided by the average number of laborers per year.

20. Private farmers working for their own account are not covered by state social security. They do, however, have the right to incorporate their land into a state farm or to sell their land to the state. The corresponding revenues serve as a form of proxy pension.

21. See, for instance: J. L. Rodríguez 1987; MacEwan 1981; Ghai et al. 1988; Boorstein 1968; C. R. Rodríguez 1983; Benjamin et al. 1986; Dumont 1970a and 1970b; O'Connor 1970; among others.

22. See, for instance, the discussion of C. R. Rodríguez (1983: 391–92). Szulc (1986: 576) writes that the counterrevolutionary activity in the Escambray Mountains alone accounted for more than 300 deaths and "economic losses calculated at around $1 billion in ruined crops, burned houses, destroyed rolling stock, roads and bridges—and the military cost of the 'antibandit' operations."

23. As a share of total agricultural and forestry land in June 1987, the state sector occupied 81.4 percent of the land, production cooperatives occupied 9.3 percent, and private farmers occupied 9.3 percent. Calculated from CEE 1988b (7). That is, the so-called private sector (individual farmers plus production cooperatives) accounted for 18.6 percent of total land.

24. Sale of agricultural land to private individuals is prohibited. Although land sales to the state are voluntary, it should also be added that through its control over services and resources generally the state makes it attractive for individual farmers to move out of private farming.

25. Karol (1970: 30), for instance, wrote: "The whole program was run on a purely voluntary basis, with no pressure of any sort and amid much popular enthusiasm." Dumont (1970a: 96) wrote: "Unlike the majority of the other socialist countries, *no* [emphasis his] political, moral, administrative or even tax pressure has been applied to oblige the peasants to join cooperatives [read state farms] against their will." And Ghai et al. (1988: 137) wrote: "This policy to create and sustain a peasantry for over two decades remains a distinctive feature of Cuban agriculture."

26. This data comes from the CEE/AEC 1986 (299–301) and from private discussions with Cuban officials. In 1985 there were 109,300 private farmers working for their own account and 69,900 farmers belonging to the producer cooperatives (CEE/AEC 1986: 192). In June 1987, there were 69,174 cooperative members (CEE 1987 and 1988c).

27. Self-provisioning, or *autoconsumo*, was introduced as official policy on state farms in 1980. Collective plots were set aside for the production of a variety of staples. This policy not only simplified central tasks of allocation and improved local diets, it also expanded possibilities for land rotation, balancing labor requirements throughout the year and attracting private farmers to integrate into state farms.

28. Although climatic and soil conditions are different, it is perhaps appropriate to lend some perspective to the size of Cuban state farms by noting that state farms in the U.S.S.R. average approximately 18,000 hectares (Zimbalist et al. 1988: 296). Accord-

ing to Ghai et al. (1988: 58), some agricultural experts in Cuba believe the optimum size to be 26,480 hectares. Given that Cuba has chosen to integrate sugar fields and mills in agro-industrial complexes, it is relevant to note a recent study by Willard Radell, Jr., that finds less efficiency in larger mills than in smaller ones (Radell 1987: 141–58).

29. Brigades are also being introduced on the production cooperatives. See Meurs 1988 (ch. 4).

30. See the sources for Table 7.11.

31. These figures are based on gross output. The trend is similar. albeit more pronounced, when net output is used.

32. The hurricane of October 1963 brought more rainfall and flooding, but overall destruction from the winds of Hurricane Kate in 1985 was more severe.

33. For a fuller discussion of these benefits, see Benjamin et al. 1986 (175–78) and Ghai et al. 1988 (74–87). Also, see Stubbs 1987.

34. Actually, the average hectarage and number of members on the production cooperatives have fallen slightly since 1985; see CEE 1987 (5).

35. Typically these farmers previously belonged to the same credit and service cooperative.

36. The question of management, participation, and incentives on the production cooperatives is addressed at length by Meurs (1988: ch. 4).

37. In 1986, according to preliminary data, the average cost per peso of output on cooperatives increased to 82 centavos. The corresponding figure for state farms was over 100 centavos (one peso).

CHAPTER 8. INCENTIVES AND PLANNING

1. See, for one, Espinosa and Zimbalist 1978. Also see Carnoy and Shearer 1980; Jones and Svejnar 1982; and Brus 1973.

2. C. R. Rodríguez (1988: 15) states that *el plus* was also an earlier term for *salario histórico* (historical wage).

3. In theory, self-financed enterprises are supposed to cover all their expenditures with their own revenues, without subsidies from the state budget. Generally, self-financed enterprises are also expected to turn a profit. The alternative form is enterprises that are budget financed. Such enterprises have their expenditures covered by the state budget and are not judged by the existence of profits or losses. In practice, self-financed enterprises in Cuba and other centrally planned economies generally do receive state subsidies and are not allowed to go bankrupt.

4. On the history of piece payments in Cuba, also see L. Domínguez 1987 (96–103).

5. Two interesting sources on this debate are Bernardo 1971 and Silverman 1973. The Silverman volume contains translations of several original articles from the debate. An excellent Cuban source on this period is Montadas and Rodríguez (n.d.).

6. In a July 1987 speech at a heavy industry conference, leading Politburo member Carlos Rafael Rodríguez emphasized the flexibility in Guevara's position at the time. Rodríguez, Guevara's antagonist in the 1960s debate, quotes Guevara as acknowledging the necessity of material incentives in the short run yet stressing the importance of gradually reducing their scope over time (Rodríguez 1988: 21).

7. Zimbalist (1975: 45–54) details the failure to develop worker participation in the

1960s. Other negative factors were, of course, at work to constrain the effectiveness of Cuban economic policy during this period.

8. Mesa-Lago is one such author. He reports that economywide output per worker jumped 21 percent in 1972 (Mesa-Lago 1978: 39).

9. Castro's speeches to the 1975 and 1980 Party Congresses.

10. Pérez-Stable's sample of 57 workers was selected nonrandomly and disproportionately represented more highly educated and politically conscious workers.

11. The share of norms that were elementary actually increased between 1982 and 1987. See L. Domínguez 1987 (90).

12. JUCEPLAN 1985 (52); and Meurs 1987 (30).

13. The adoption of the SDPE occurred in 1976, but this year was designated as a year of study and preparation. The actual implementation began in 1977. Since mid-1986, it is more commonly referred to as simply the SDE.

14. The establishment of the *Grupo Central* in December 1984 is pointed to by some analysts as the beginning of the current rectification period. The *Grupo Central* is composed of the vice-presidents of the Council of Ministers, all the ministers, the president of JUCEPLAN, provincial heads of Popular Power, and heads of departments of the Communist Party. The raison d'être of the *Grupo Central* is too complex for a full analysis here. Suffice it to suggest that its formation in part was an effort to weaken ministerialism (both sectoral chauvinism and excessive tutelage over enterprises), in part to facilitate lines of command and communication between the Council of Ministers and JUCEPLAN, and in part to deal with the worsening foreign exchange crisis as effectively and expeditiously as possible. Finally, it was an element of the larger effort to reinvigorate and rationalize the planning apparatus as well as to renovate its personnel.

15. The latest round of planning reforms, urging administrative decentralization and simplification, were announced in early 1988 and are detailed in Comisión Nacional del Sistema de Dirección de la Economía 1988.

16. Additional data through 1984 and analysis is provided in U-Echevarria et al. 1986 (110–39). The hoarding of inputs by enterprises, however, is still a major problem in Cuba, as it is in other CPEs. See, for example, C. R. Rodríguez 1988 (24).

17. This decision was reinforced in 1988 by the planning reforms announced by the study commission appointed by the *Grupo Central*. See Comisión Nacional del Sistema de Dirección de la Economía 1988.

18. This system was actually begun on an experimental basis in 1979 in the province of Pinar del Rio and was not implemented until 1986 in Havana. The Soviet Union, of course, has had this system for many years.

19. The rectification campaign is the name given to the current period of reevaluating the balance of material and moral incentives, redressing the perceived excesses connected to material incentives and private sector activity, and addressing other problems of economic and political management.

20. A very clear indication of the decentralizing inclinations at the time came in the speech by then-JUCEPLAN president Humberto Pérez before the closing session of the Fourth Plenary. A typical line from Pérez's remarks follows (our translation): "We do material balances, we assign material resources, we set output targets, basing our decisions in technical consumption norms and inventory levels, we attempt to do all this at the most centralized level when, in fact, these things are only feasible to do at the decentralized level of the enterprise" (H. Pérez 1985: 25).

21. It is clear that, at the time of this writing, the direction of policy change in Cuba is different from that in the Soviet Union. Some analysts have predicted that this discrepancy will produce political conflict between the two countries or, at least, discomfort. They have pointed to the sparse coverage in the Cuban press of the details of Gorbachev's economic reforms and statements by Castro that Cuba must find its own path. In fact, Castro has made such statements repeatedly during the course of the revolution, and Gorbachev's reforms, while not highlighted in daily newspapers, have been given serious analysis in the popular biweekly *Novedades de Moscú.* For various reasons, the Cuban government does not see the Gorbachev reforms as appropriate for mass discussion in Cuba at this time, but if there were true discomfort and potential conflict involved, it does not seem that the coverage in *Novedades de Moscú* and elsewhere would be tolerated. This is especially the case since *Novedades* sells out within a few hours of appearing at the kiosks.

Further, there is not only the question of the direction of change, but also the issue of where along the spectrum of centralization and rigidity each economy finds itself. At least some Cuban leaders see their economy as more flexible and decentralized at present than the Soviet economy. For example, the Economist Intelligence Unit report recently observed: "The Vice President, Carlos Rafael Rodríguez, in Bucharest for a closed session of COMECON representatives, recently drew specific attention to what he called the mood of imaginativeness and flexibility now abroad among the Moscow allies, with which he associated the Cuban process" (EIU 1986: 10). If the Gorbachev reforms, as approved at the CPSU Central Committee Plenary in June 1987, are actually carried out, then the Soviet Union will have traveled significantly beyond Cuba's 1987 point on the road toward decentralization.

22. Since two of Cuba's market-oriented reforms (the free farmers' markets and the direct sale of private housing) were actually ended, the reader might object to the characterization of the decentralization process being "put on hold" rather than "reversed." The farmers' market and free direct housing sales represented a particular aspect of the decentralization process in food distribution and housing. The farmers' markets never amounted to more than 3.2 percent of reported retail sales and by 1985, their last full year of operation, represented only 1.2 percent of reported retail sales. The more substantial process of decentralization in food distribution has occurred through the expansion of the parallel markets that are state-run but charge prices approximating supply and demand conditions. The growth of parallel market sales quantitatively have more than made up for the disappearance of the peasant markets, although certain perishable and specialty items such as garlic are more difficult to obtain. (For an interesting discussion of the problems of the state's food distribution system, see Geldof 1988.) Similarly, the major change in housing policy came with the reform to eventually convert all tenants into homeowners and to allow the private exchange and sale of houses. The private sale of houses is still permitted, but now it cannot take place directly between the buyer and seller. In order to avoid speculation and exorbitant prices, the state now regulates such sales. The basic change, however, is still in place.

This explanation is not intended as an endorsement of the new policies. It is, rather, to argue that there has not been a reversal to the centralization of the 1960s and early 1970s. Decentralization in a centrally planned economy is a very complex process. It has many aspects, assumes different forms depending on the time and place, and never progresses linearly.

To say "put on hold" is not to deny that there has been some backsliding or retrenchment; there has. It is to say, however, that this retrenchment is normal and has occurred in other countries that eventually went on with their reform process. It seems to us that it is much more likely that the Cuban reform process will again move toward greater decentralization in the near future (further efforts at administrative decentralization are already under way) than that the reform will move toward a return to the centralization of earlier periods. Our phraseology, then, is chosen to convey this analytical judgment.

23. These efforts are highlighted in the planning reforms promulgated in early 1988 and are outlined later in the text; see Comisión Nacional 1988.

24. A second wage increase in June 1987 benefited an additional 208,343 low-income workers (see Table 8.1). The austerity measures, among other things, curtailed various perquisites of officials. Personal use of official state cars, for instance, was prohibited. Other measures, however, such as retail price increases on various goods and the reduction of the monthly kerosene ration, disproportionately affected low-income budgets, and this was a basic reason for the wage increases.

25. There are actually five different systems in Cuba of pay according to output, all of which are based on norms and are referred to generally as *sobrecumplimiento de las normas*. According to the number of workers covered, these systems in order are: *destajo individual* (individual piece rates with specially set rate); *acuerdo o campo terminado* (pay according to number of tasks fulfilled where direct output quantification is not feasible); *destajo colectivo* (collective piece rates where technology mandates group evaluation); *sistema del 1 x 1* (individual piece rates with pay increasing 1 percent for every 1 percent increase in production above the norm, and vice versa); *destajo indirecto* (mostly for auxiliary workers, where direct output cannot be measured, so pay is a function of total output of the workers who are supported by the auxiliary worker).

26. H. Pérez, closing speech at the Third Plenary evaluating the SDPE, October 1982, p. 2.

27. An excellent article on the difficulty of applying rational norms and prices to construction work, given its highly variegated and specialized nature, is Salom 1985b. Another article based on a December 1986 survey of 471 enterprises observes that in one construction enterprise, norm overfulfillment as high as 2,447 percent was reported (L. Domínguez 1987: 95).

28. See, for instance, Whyte 1955; Espinosa and Zimbalist 1978; Ouchi 1982; and Braverman 1974.

29. Interesting case studies on the perverse effects of piece rates can be found in Zimbalist 1979.

30. There is also indirect evidence that the rectification campaign brought intensification of work. The number of work-related injuries rose from 63,467 in 1986 to 71,244 in 1987, and the number of work fatalities rose from 316 in 1986 to 370 in 1987 (CEE/BEC 1988: 117).

31. A useful background article on the *prima* is Aristides Pérez 1984.

32. *Primas* for overfulfillment of quantity targets primarily have been used in agriculture. These are for enterprise plan fulfillment, not the fulfillment or overfulfillment of work norms as has been argued incorrectly by Sergio Roca; see, for instance: Roca 1986, 1987. Also see Zimbalist 1987b.

33. Calculations on the basis of figures provided to the authors by the Cuban State Statistical Committee.

34. See, for instance, the analysis of *primas* in the *Dictamenes* of the Fourth Plenary JUCEPLAN (1985: 53).

35. In viewing this differently, Cuban economist Ileana Diaz (1987: 34) reports that in 1986 stimulation funds were employed in 50 percent of all enterprises and in approximately 75 percent of all enterprises in industry, construction, and agriculture.

36. Calculated from data provided to the authors by the State Statistical Committee.

37. The problem is aggravated by the fact that actual payment is typically delayed an additional three to five months after year's end (Velázquez and Shvidanenko 1988: 23).

38. Among others, recent Cuban analyses of these problems include Cejas 1988; Velázquez and Shvidanenko 1988; Diaz 1987; and Vilarino and Ma. Domenech 1986.

39. This point is corroborated by Velázquez and Shvidanenko (1988: 23).

40. This change in determining the normative adjustment coefficient began in 1985 and has not been applied uniformly to all sectors of the economy. Among others, see Diaz 1987.

41. For the tenacious reader, a more detailed description of the system with numerical examples can be found in Carlos Martínez 1986 (157–202).

42. This problem, of course, had solutions other than the abolition of the farmers' markets. But the government was unwilling to let the price mechanism work freely to offer the incentives necessary to avoid this cropping pattern.

The farmers' markets were also seen as an impediment to the expansion and healthy functioning of the production cooperatives. Indeed, membership on the cooperatives after 1983 first fell and then stagnated until after the markets' abolition. In 1987, cooperative membership increased for the first time in four years. The causality here is complex and other factors may have been at work. Finally, the farmers' markets had also inspired substantial public criticism for their high prices. There has been no concerted outcry over their abolition, despite considerable evidence of inconvenience.

43. In a sense, the motivation issue is all the more pressing in 1986–88 because Cuba's young workers today are a new generation. They did not experience the revolutionary struggle or the early romantic years of the revolution.

44. See, for instance, *Granma*'s coverage of Roberto Veiga's speech before the Plenary of the CTC National Council (January 11, 1987).

45. For an excellent theoretical discussion on the vital role of worker participation in CPEs, see the work of Wlodimierz Brus, particularly his book *The Economics and Politics of Socialism* (Brus 1973). Also see Zimbalist 1984.

46. Some workers have been lauded in the Cuban press for denouncing bureaucratic managers. One such worker, Silvia Spence, from a cement factory in Santiago, Cuba has been made something of a national hero. See the detailed and fascinating coverage of her case in *Granma*, December 25 and 26, 1986.

47. *Trabajadores*, June 6, 1986 (1). Cited in Meurs 1988.

48. Cited in Meurs 1988.

49. See the review of this literature in Espinosa and Zimbalist 1978 (ch. 5). Also see Pateman 1970.

50. See White 1987. For a discussion of the sweeping mandate of the Study Commission (Comisión Nacional del Sistema de Dirección de la Economía), see *Cuba: Economía Planificada* 1986. For the reform proposals emanating from the commission, see Comisión Nacional 1988.

51. The purpose and evolution of *uniones de empresas* is discussed in G. D. Martínez 1983 (74–107).

52. The planning reforms proposed by the Commisión Nacional call for further amalgamation of enterprises into *uniones* as part of the ongoing thrust toward plan simplification and procedural decentralization.

53. The practice of brigade members selecting their own chief has also developed unevenly. Without the custom of exercising such authority, it often takes time before worker attitudes and behavior adapt to their new, augmented prerogatives. In early 1987, for instance, it appears that most brigade chiefs in agriculture were still appointed by the state farm administration and approved by the Ministry of Agriculture (communication from Mieke Meurs). On the internal structure of the brigades, see Ghai et al. 1988 (ch. 4.1).

54. This conclusion is supported by three separate studies as well as our own interviews. See Kay 1987; Meurs 1988; Codina 1987 (127–38). It is also supported in the case of nonsugar agriculture by two detailed studies of the Cuban Ministry of Agriculture (1985, 1986).

CHAPTER 9. FOREIGN SECTOR: DEPENDENCE, AID, AND DEBT

1. Shares are calculated from data in the 1985 statistical yearbook of Cuba. The reader will recall from the discussions in chapters 2 and 4 that net material product is basically equal to gross domestic product minus depreciation and the value of all nonproductive services in the economy. Gross social product, on the other hand, is generally greater than gross domestic product for Cuba even though it too excludes nonproductive services. This is because it is based on the gross value, rather than value added, of output.

2. For a review of some of this literature, see Brundenius and Zimbalist 1987 and Turits 1987. Also see Roca 1988.

3. This is accomplished by taking the share of petroleum reexports in total exports in 1980 and 1985 and diminishing constant-price exports by this percentage. The constant-price value of raw sugar exports was then divided by this diminished constant-price total export value. Since there were no petroleum reexports in 1965, 1970, or 1975, the reported shares in the last two columns are identical for these years.

4. This data is calculated from CEE/AEC 1985 and BNC, *Informe Económico* 1986.

5. According to the *Wall Street Journal*, Cuba's foreign investment code will be changed in 1988 to allow 100 percent foreign ownership in the tourist industry. Reportedly, this change is part of an effort to upgrade the quality of tourist services (Berkowitz 1988: 18).

6. Revenue from tourist services itself more than doubled from 1984 to 1985, increasing from 8.5 million pesos to 17.6 million.

7. 90.8 percent of all tourism revenues in 1986 came from visitors from market countries. Abraham Maciques, head of Cuba's new tourism company Cubanacan S.A., projects that the number of tourists will increase to two million by the end of the century (*Cuba Business*, June 1988).

8. These service exports are discussed in S. Eckstein 1987 and Feinsilver 1987.

9. See discussion in chapter 6. There are several other sources on the development of

Cuba's heavy industrial branches. Among them: Figueras 1985; Garcia 1987a and 1987b; O. Pérez 1987.

10. In its overall trade (convertible and nonconvertible currencies) Cuba has run a balance of trade deficit every year since the revolution, except in 1960 and 1974 (CEE/AEC 1985: 376).

11. Since no methodology is provided, this figure is cited only as illustrative of the magnitudes involved. Also, according to recent reports released by Cuba, the CIA has persisted in its political destabilization and assassination efforts against Cuba in recent years. See the issues of *Granma Weekly Review* during August 1987.

12. The Soviet price has varied between roughly 22 and 39 centavos per pound over the last ten years. There have been several reports that the 1986–90 trade protocol agreement with the Soviet Union calls for a seven to ten percent reduction in the average sugar price. Cf. Economist Intelligence Unit 1986, Staff of Radio José Martí 1986, and Brezinski 1986 and 1988. Castro, speaking at the Third Party Congress on November 30, 1986, also alluded to the Soviet price as falling and below 30 centavos per pound. Cf. *Granma Weekly Review*, December 14, 1987 (part 2, p. 4). The *Quarterly Economic Report* of March 1987 of the Cuban National Bank lists the quantity and value of Cuban sugar exports to the U.S.S.R. for the first quarter of both 1986 and 1987; this comparison suggests that the Soviet purchase price for Cuban raw sugar fell 7.3 percent in 1987.

Since the onset of *perestroika* there has been considerable speculation regarding growing tension and diminishing aid between the Soviet Union and Cuba. Although sugar price subsidies appear to have fallen and new efficiency measures on Soviet projects have been demanded, Soviet project aid to Cuba seems to have increased (reportedly by 50 percent) for the present quinquennium.

Castro has reported that Gorbachev does not expect the direction of economic reform in Cuba to follow that in the U.S.S.R., but since July 1988 Castro has issued strong criticism of the Gorbachev reforms. Interestingly, exiled Cuban economist Pérez Cott has maintained that having a socialist ally in the Western Hemisphere is too important to the Soviet Union to squabble over domestic policy differences. Pérez Cott has also been quoted as saying that Gorbachev promised Castro that the Soviet reforms would not lead to less aid (Staff of Radio José Martí, first quarter 1988: II–2).

13. In chapter 5 we note that Cuba's exchange rate deviation index is probably over one; that is, for purposes of estimating Cuban GDP per capita, a straight exchange rate conversion would likely understate the dollar value. This observation, however, does not contradict the fact that for purposes of obtaining international equilibrium (and measuring the free market value of Cuban transactions), the Cuban peso is overvalued. The discrepancy arises because of the behavior of the relative prices of tradeables and nontradeables (particularly basic goods that are often subsidized and labor intensive).

In his new book, Jorge Domínguez (1989) recognizes the problems with the CIA estimates and makes his own estimates using the price Cuba receives for its sugar from Spain, Canada, and Japan as the opportunity cost. Domínguez's method improves little on that of the CIA, however, because Canada and Japan, and Spain since 1979, have bought Cuban sugar at residual world market—not preferential—prices. Hence it is not surprising that Domínguez produces estimates similar to the CIA's.

14. Conversation with Zimbalist, May 1987. This pricing pattern has affected several East European economies as well (Pérez-López 1988: 134).

15. These figures are based on those products reported in the 1985 statistical year-

book and include 88.5 percent of the value of Cuba's exports to the U.S.S.R. and 72.5 percent of the value of the imports. If the different coverage were adjusted for, the percent increase in import prices would be 3.1 times greater than the percent increase in export prices, as opposed to the unadjusted figure of 2.6, based on the percentages given in the text.

16. It is, of course, also possible that there are other products where the Soviet Union offers Cuba a positive subsidy. Although we were not able to confirm or quantify this, it appears that such a subsidy exists for Canadian wheat, which is bought by the Soviet Union for hard currency but is shipped directly from Canada to Cuba. Cuba apparently pays for the wheat in transferable rubles.

17. These examples are cited in Staff of Radio José Martí 1987 (second quarter: II–5). This report also claims: "In addition, former Cuban officials have stated that the Soviet Union hardly ever provides its less developed trading partner with up-to-date technology or adequate supplies of goods, parts and services." The reference for this statement, however, mentions only one former official, Luis Negrete. Interestingly, this report further suggests that although actual debt repayment to the U.S.S.R. has been put on hold, the Cubans might be expected to perform other services for the Soviets, such as exporting manpower for Soviet-conceived projects. No evidence is adduced, however, to back up this speculation.

18. This and other figures in this paragraph come from Feinsilver 1987 unless otherwise noted. Also see S. Eckstein 1987 and Erisman 1985.

19. Other recent examples include: $2.5 million to Mexico for earthquake relief; donation of 50,000 doses of Dengue fever vaccine and additional doses of meningitis vaccination to Brazil; construction and educational materials for two schools in Uruguay; and construction and equipping of an intensive care unit for a hospital in Santa Cruz, Bolivia. The last two examples were cited in the Staff of Radio José Martí 1987 (second quarter: II–16). The first is cited in *Granma Weekly Review*, December 14, 1986 (part 2, p. 4).

20. Soviet aid figures are from the CIA (1984: 40). These CIA estimates have apparently been increased and updated through 1985, though no explanation of method is provided (Fogarty and Tritle 1987: 540). Puerto Rico aid figures are from various publications of the U.S. Department of Commerce, cited in Feinsilver 1987. The subject of aid to, and underdevelopment in, Puerto Rico is analyzed in interesting detail by Wesskopf 1986.

21. Cuba's hard currency debt figure is from the BNC, *Informe Económico* (May 1987: 27) (annual report to its creditors). We convert the reported peso value into dollars at the average 1986 official exchange rate. The ruble debt figure is from A. Bekarevich, a Cuba specialist at the Latin American Institute of the Soviet Academy of Sciences, in a communication to Brundenius. Of the 7.5 billion rubles, 6 billion originated as trade aid and 1.5 billion as project aid. The Economist Intelligence Unit's *Country Profile: Cuba, 1986–87* reports Cuba's debt to the U.S.S.R. to be $7.5 billion in 1985. This figure appears to come from the same source as Bekarevich's, but it is not stated what conversion factor was used to put the estimate in dollars.

22. If total debt (hard currency plus ruble) to total exports is considered, the Cuban figure falls to 215 percent (Ritter 1988: Table 4).

23. It might be argued that the forgiven interest is implicit aid and should be imputed and added on to estimates of Soviet aid.

24. BNC, *Informe Económico* (March 1986a: 4). Legislation has been introduced in both houses of the U.S. Congress that would extend the blockade further, essentially by punishing countries that continue to lend aid or trade with Cuba.

25. World sugar prices increased slowly during 1986 and 1987, but then shot up in mid-1988. In early July 1988, the world market price was approximately 13.5 cents per pound. By December 1988, however, prices were back to around 9 cents per pound. The residual character of the world sugar market helps to explain the volatility of sugar prices.

26. Another strong influence on the world sugar market has been the rapid expansion of subsidized beet sugar production in the European Economic Community, which turned from being a significant net importer of sugar in the late 1970s to being a net exporter of around 4.5 million tons annually (roughly one-quarter of free market trade).

27. This was an important reason behind Cuba's inability to meet many of its Western sugar contracts in 1988. Cuba was bailed out by a special loan from the Soviet Union that was used to purchase sugar on the world market.

28. In the 1985 renegotiations the Cuban proposal contained two unusual and interesting points. First, Cuba requested the reduction in tariff and nontariff trade barriers from its creditor nations in order to facilitate export diversification. Second, Cuba proposed the establishment of a $60 million fund (half financed by Cuba) to finance 120 different feasibility studies for a variety of nontraditional exports.

29. Of this privately held debt 61.4 percent was medium term; the rest was short term (BNC, *Informe Económico*, May 1987: 28).

30. This and other data on debt comes from the Banco Nacional's annual reports to Cuba's creditors.

31. By December 31, 1987, Cuba's hard currency foreign debt stood at 5.657 billion pesos (BNC, *Informe Económico* 1988: 18).

32. According to preliminary figures, industrial production during the first quarter of 1988 was 7.6 percent above its level a year earlier (CEE/BEC 1988: 16).

33. The distortions and waste in foreign trade connected to Cuba's price system are discussed in González and Menéndez 1986.

34. Of course, other factors will be at play as well, including the gradual reintegration of 50,000 Cuban soldiers returning from Angola and the favorable demographic development of lower dependency ratios. On the latter, see Díaz-Briquets 1988.

CHAPTER 10. CONCLUSION: CUBAN DEVELOPMENT IN COMPARATIVE PERSPECTIVE

1. The 10.6 percent figure also includes overtime pay. As pointed out in chapter 8, available information suggests that this share fell in both 1986 and 1987. Private-sector income is also excluded from our estimate.

2. We do know, however, that average real wages were lower in all but three Latin American countries in 1985 than they were in 1980 and that open unemployment in large Latin American cities in 1985 was 21 percent higher than in 1980 (ECLAC 1987: 23, 38).

3. 1986 data is from CEE/AEC 1986 (102); 1987 data is preliminary and is from CEE, *La economía cubana, 1987*, with our estimate that population growth was 0.9

percent in 1987. Preliminary data for the three quarters of 1988 indicates a return to positive growth (CEE/BEC 1988).

4. The 1987 figures for Latin America are also preliminary and are from the Inter-American Development Bank.

5. Interview, September 2, 1988 at CIER, Taipei.

6. The last officially published unemployment rate for Cuba is from 1981, the year of the last population census. The rate for that year was 3.4 percent. The previous census, 1970, estimated unemployment at 1.6 percent (see discussion in Brundenius 1984b (126–28). Between 1981 and 1985, employment in Cuba grew at an average annual rate of 3.0 percent and in 1986 at 2.35 percent. These high rates of employment growth suggest that the unemployment rate would have tended downward after 1981. This, of course, is not to deny either that much labor in Cuba is used inefficiently or that temporary layoffs (*interruptos*) increased during the 1987 downturn. The official unemployment rate in Taiwan in 1986 was 2.7 percent. Although published statistics do not permit a rigorous comparison, it is probably also the case that Cuba has less involuntary part-time employment than does Taiwan.

7. For instance, according to the Taiwanese Statistical Yearbook (1987: 411), the Taiwan figure only includes deaths of infants born in the same calendar year in which they died. The Cuban figure, following general practice, includes all infant deaths in a calendar year whether or not they were born in that year. Also, it seems that there is less than 100 percent registration of births and deaths in Taiwan because the regulations stipulate mandatory reporting within 15 days. Among other things, this implies that infants who die within the first several days of birth may never be registered. Over 99.3 percent of births in Cuba take place in hospitals and are registered immediately. Any infant death in Cuba is recorded from the moment of delivery. The bias in the official Taiwan infant mortality figure, then, might be rather substantial. Cuban infant mortality and birth data is from MINSAP 1988 (5, 19).

8. It should go without saying that we do not intend to imply that an active state role is a sufficient condition for promoting development. The experience of African nations over the past twenty years should be adequate to convince anyone of this.

9. For extended treatments of this subject, see: Amsden 1985; Rueschemeyer et al. 1985; Johnson 1982, 1984; Zimbalist et al. 1988; and Bardhan 1984.

10. On the role of the state in Taiwan, South Korea, and Japan, see, among others, Amsden 1984, 1985, 1989 and Kuznets 1988.

11. The reader will recall that national income, or net material product, in the MPS national income accounts roughly equals net national product in the SNA or Western system minus "unproductive" services.

12. Figures are calculated from Brundenius 1984b (33); CEE/AEC 1982 (102) and 1986 (100). It would be preferable to take gross investment as a share of gross material product, but a consistent series of gross material product is not available. If these rates were taken as a share of gross national product, they would probably range from the mid-teens to the low-twenties. That is, they are appreciably below the investment rates of over 30 percent that have been attained in Japan, Taiwan, and South Korea. Due to different relative prices accounting methodologies, however, it is not clear whether the official investment series between Cuba and the Asian NICs are commensurable.

13. Viewed dynamically, specializing in labor-intensive products can consign a country to low productivity and low income in the long run. Further, since endowments

of many factors are maleable, comparative advantage can be created.

14. A fascinating nuts-and-bolts discussion of these problems is provided in Boorstein 1968, especially chapter 3.

15. These arguments are developed and illustrated in Paus 1988.

References

Acosta, José. *Teoría y Práctica de los Mecanismos de Dirección de La Economía*. Havana: Editorial de Ciencias Sociales, 1982.

Adler-Karlsson, Gunnar. *Western Economic Warfare, 1947–1967*. Stockholm: Almqvist & Wiskill, 1968.

Amsden, Alice. "Exports of Technology by Newly Industrializing Countries," *World Development* (May/June 1984).

———. "The State and Taiwan's Economic Development." In Peter Evans et al., eds. *Bringing the State Back In*. New York: Cambridge University Press, 1985.

———. *Asia's New Giant: Late Industrialization in South Korea*. New York: Oxford University Press, 1989.

Azicri, Max. *Cuba: Politics, Economics and Society*. London: Pinter Publishers, 1988.

Banco Nacional de Cuba (BNC). *Informe Económico*, 1982, 1986, 1987, 1988.

———. *Informe Económico*, trimestral reports, 1985–88.

———. *Quarterly Economic Report*, March 1986a.

———. *Cuba: Foreign Debt and Its Rescheduling Process*. Havana, December 1986b.

———. *Highlights of the Balance of Payments, 1986–87*. Havana, 1987a.

———. *Report on the Implementation of the Program of Measures Adopted on December 26, 1986*. Havana, 1987b.

Bardhan, P. *The Political Economy of Development in India*. Oxford: Basil Blackwell, 1984.

Becker, Abraham. *Soviet National Income, 1958–1964*. Berkeley and Los Angeles: University of California Press, 1969.

Becker, Gary. "The Lessons of Cuba and Taiwan." *Business Week*, June 16, 1986.

Bengelsdorf, Carollee. "Between Vision and Reality: Democracy in Socialist Theory and Practice." Ph.D. diss., Department of Political Science, Massachusetts Institute of Technology, 1985.

Benjamin, M., J. Collins, and M. Scott. *No Free Lunch: Food and Revolution in Cuba Today*. New York: Grove Press, 1986.

Bergson, Abram. "Soviet National Income and Product in 1937." *Quarterly Journal of Economics* 64 (1950).

———. *The Real National Income of Soviet Russia Since 1928*. Cambridge: Harvard University Press, 1961.

———. "Comparative Productivity and Efficiency in the USA and the USSR." In A. Eckstein, ed. *Comparison of Economic Systems: Theoretical and Methodological Approaches*.

Berkowitz, Peggy. "Cuba Is Seeking Another Rescheduling of Its Loans from Governments, Banks." *Wall Street Journal*, January 13, 1988 (18).

Bernardo, R. *The Theory of Moral Incentives in Cuba*. University, Ala.: University of Alabama Press, 1971.

Bianchi, Andrés. "Agriculture." In Dudley Seers et al. *Cuba: The Economic and Social Revolution*. Chapel Hill: University of North Carolina Press, 1964.

BNC. *See* Banco National de Cuba.

Boorstein, Edward. *The Economic Transformation of Cuba*. New York: Monthly Review Press, 1968.

Bohemia, May 29, 1985; May 9, 1986; July 4, 1987.

Braverman, H. *Labor and Monopoly Capital*. New York: Monthly Review Press, 1974.

Brezinski, Horst. "Economic Relations Between European and the Less-Developed CMEA Countries." In Joint Economic Committee, *East European Economies: Slow Growth in the 1980s*. Washington, D.C.: U.S. Government Printing Office, 1986.

————. "Cuba's Economic Ties with the Soviet Union and the CMEA in the Mid-Eighties." Working Paper no. 13. Universität-Gesamthochschule, Paderborn, West Germany, August 1988.

Brown, James G. *The International Sugar Industry: Developments and Prospects*, World Bank Staff Commodity Working Papers, no. 18. Washington, D.C.: World Bank, 1985.

Brundenius, Claes. "Capital Goods in Economic Thought—Some Notes From Selected Readings." Discussion Paper Series, no. 164, Lund, Sweden, December 1984a.

————. *Revolutionary Cuba—The Challenge of Economic Growth with Equity*. Boulder, Colo.: Westview Press, 1984b.

————. "The Role of Capital Goods Production in the Economic Development of Cuba." Paper presented to conference on technology policies for development, Research Policy Institute, University of Lund, Sweden, May 29–31, 1985.

————. "The Role of Capital Goods Production in the Economic Development of Cuba." *Political Power and Social Theory: A Research Annual* 6. Greenwich, Conn.: JAI Press, 1986.

————. "Development and Prospects of Capital Goods Production in Revolutionary Cuba." *World Development* 15:1 (January 1987a).

————. "Development and Prospects of Capital Goods Production in Cuba." In A. Zimbalist, ed. *Cuba's Socialist Economy Toward the 1900s*. Boulder, Colo.: Lynne Rienner Publishers, 1987b.

Brundenius, Claes, and Vegard Bye. "Towards Economic Relations between the Nordic Countries and the Caribbean Basin." Peace Research Institute, Oslo, Norway, 1986.

Brundenius, Claes, and Andrew Zimbalist. "Recent Studies on Cuban Economic Growth: A Review." *Comparative Economic Studies* 27:1 (Spring 1985a).

————. "Cuban Economic Growth One More Time: A Response to 'Imbroglios.'" *Comparative Economic Studies* 27:3 (Fall 1985b).

————. "Cuban Growth: A Final Word." *Comparative Economic Studies* 27:4 (Winter 1985c).

————. "Cubanology and Cuban Economic Performance." In A. Zimbalist, ed. *Cuban Political Economy: Controversies in Cubanology*. Boulder, Colo.: Westview Press, 1987.

Brus, Wlodimierz. *The Economics and Politics of Socialism*. London: Routledge and Kegan Paul, 1973.

Bruton, Henry. "Import Substitution." Paper delivered to the Northeast Development

Consortium Conference at Harvard University, April 29–30, 1988.

Bulnes, Carlos Fernández, and Miguel Alejandro Figueras. "La producción de bienes de capital en Cuba." Paper presented to the Congress of Latin American Economists, Havana, November 1987.

Bureau of Labor Statistics. *Producer Prices and Price Indexes*. Washington, D.C.: U.S. Government Printing Office, various years.

Carnoy, M., and D. Shearer. *Economy Democracy*. New York: Sharpe, 1980.

Carnota, Orlando de. "La aplicación de las computadoras en el campo económico y social en un pais de desarrollo." *Economía y Desarrollo* 9 (1972).

Castro Tato, Manual, and Arturo Bas Fernández. *The Development of the Capital Goods Industry in the Republic of Cuba*. Vienna: UNIDO, November 2, 1982.

CEE/AEC. *See* Comité Estatal de Estadísticas.

CEE/BEC. *See* Comité Estatal de Estadísticas.

Cejas, Francisco. "El abastecimiento técnico-material: un nuevo enfoque." *Economía y Desarrollo* (January/December 1988).

Central Intelligence Agency (CIA). *The Cuban Economy: A Statistical Review*. Washington, D.C.: National Technical Information Service, 1984.

Centro de Investigaciones de Construcción de Maquinaria Agrícola (CICMA). *Desarrollo perspectivo de las combinadas cañeras y sus limitaciones*. Havana, 1983.

Centro de Investigaciones de la Economía Internacional (CIEI). *Aspectos Sobresalientes de la Economía Cubana (VI)*. Havana: Centro de Estudios Demográficos, 1986.

Chaviano, Noel, Angel Rico, and Manuel López. "Características del sistema financiero-crediticio la República de Cuba." *Finanzas y Crédito* 6 (1986).

Chaviano, Pablo, Auturo Rua, and Tania Tolezano. "Desarrollo y perspectivas de la industria de maquinarias en Cuba revolucionaria." *Cuba: Economía Planificada* 3:3 (July/September 1988).

Chonchol, Jacques. "Análisis crítico de la reforma agraria cubana." *El Trimestre Económico* (January/March 1963).

CICMA. *See* Centro de Investigaciones de Construccion de Maquinaria Agrícola.

Clausura de la IV Plenaria Nacional del Chequeo del SDPE (May 25, 1985).

Codina, Alexis. "Worker Incentives in Cuba." *World Development* (January 1987).

Cohen, Roger. "Inflation's Resurgence in Brazil Triggers Disillusionment and Statistical Warfare." *Wall Street Journal*, March 31, 1987a.

———. "Brazil Erred on Trade Figure by $1.2 Billion." *Wall Street Journal*. May 29, 1987b.

Cohn, Stanley. "National Income Growth Statistics." In Vladimir Treml and John Hardt, eds. *Soviet Economic Statistics*. Durham, N.C.: Duke University Press, 1972.

Comisión Nacional del Sistema de Dirección de la Economía. *Decisiones adoptadas sobre algunos elementos del sistema de dirección de la economía*, I and II. Havana, March and June 1988.

Comité Estatal de Estadísticas (CEE). *Anuario Estadístico de Cuba* (AEC). Havana, 1973 through 1987.

———. *Algunas conceptiones sobre el desarrollo de Cuba en la década de 1950—Recopilación de textos, Tomos 1–4*. Havana, 1981a.

———. *Cuba: Desarrollo económico y social durante el período 1958–1980*. Havana, 1981b.

———. *Cuba en cifras*. Havana, 1981c.

————. *Cuba: Conversión de los principales indicadores macroeconómicos del sistema de balances de la economía nacional al sistema de cuentas nacionales, 1974*. Mimeographed. Havana, 1982.

————. *Indicadores Seleccionados, 1950–81*. Havana, 1983.

————. *Proceso de creación y crecimiento de las CPA*. Havana, September 1987.

————. *La economía cubana, 1986, 1987*. Havana, 1988a.

————. *Distribución y uso de la tierra en las CPA*. Havana, March 1988b.

————. *Distribución y uso de la tierra del fondo agrícola y forestal por formas de tenecia*. Havana, June 1988c.

————. *Selected Statistical Information of the Cuban Economy*. Havana, June 1988d.

————. *Boletín Estadístico de Cuba* (BEC). Havana, November/October 1985, January/December 1987, March/February 1988.

Converse, Ray. "An Index of Industrial Production in the USSR." In Joint Economic Committee, *USSR: Measures of Economic Growth and Development, 1950–80*. Washington, D.C.: U.S. Government Printing Office, 1982.

Council for Economic Planning and Development. *Statistical Data Book*. Taipei, 1985.

Cuba Business, various issues, 1987–88.

Cuba: Economía Planificada 1:3 (July/September 1986).

Cuban Delegation. "The Development of Research in the Field of Industrial By-products of Sugar Cane." International Symposium on Industrial Development, 1967.

DEC/BEC. *See* Dirección Central de Estadística.

Diaz, Ileana. "Análisis críticos sobre los fondos de estimulación material." *Economía y Desarrollo* 99 (July/August 1987).

Díaz-Briquets, Sergio. "Age-Structure, Fertility Swings, and Socioeconomic Development in Cuba." In S. Roca, ed. *Socialist Cuba: Past Interpretations and Future Challenges*.

Dirección Central de Estadística (DEC). *Boletín Estadístico de Cuba* (BEC). Havana: Junta Central de Planificación, 1968–1971.

Directorate-General of the Budget, Accounting, and Statistics, Republic of China. *Report on the Survey of Personal Income Distribution in Taiwan Area 1981*. Taipei, n.d.

————. *Statistical Yearbook of the Republic of China*. Taipei, 1987.

Domar, Evsey. "On the Measurement of Comparative Efficiency." In A. Eckstein, *Comparison of Economic Systems: Theoretical and Methodological Approaches*.

Domínguez, Jorge. "Cuba: Charismatic Communism." *Problems of Communism*. (September/October 1985).

————. *Cuba: Order & Revolution*. Cambridge: Harvard University Press, 1979.

————. *To Make a World Safe for Revolution*. Cambridge: Harvard University Press, 1989.

Domínguez, L. "Para un análisis de las deficiencias en la normación del trabajo en Cuba." *Cuba Socialista* 4:7 (July 1987).

Dumont, Rene. *Cuba: Socialism and Development*. New York: Grove Press, 1970a.

————. *Cuba: es socialista?* Caracas: Editorial Tiempo Nuevo, 1970b.

Eckstein, Alexander, ed. *Comparison of Economic Systems: Theoretical and Methodological Approaches*. Berkeley and Los Angeles: University of California Press, 1971.

Eckstein, Susan. "Why Cuban Internationalism." In A. Zimbalist, ed. *Cuba's Socialist*

Economy Toward the 1990s. Boulder, Colo.: Lynne Rienner Publishers, 1987.

ECLAC. *See* Economic Commission for Latin America.

Economic Commission for Europe. "International Comparisons of Real Incomes, Capital Formation, and Consumption." *Economic Survey of Europe, 1969*, Part 1. New York: United Nations, 1970.

———. "Comparative GDP Levels." *Economic Bulletin for Europe* 31:2 (1980).

Economic Commission for Latin America and the Caribbean (ECLAC). *Economic Survey of Latin America and the Caribbean*. New York: United Nations, various years.

———. *CEPAL Review 25* (April 1985).

———. *Economic Survey of Latin America and the Caribbean, 1985*. Santiago, Chile: United Nations, 1987.

———. *Statistical Yearbook of Latin America*. Santiago, Chile: United Nations, various years.

Economist Intelligence Unit (EIU). *Country Report: Cuba, Dominican Republic, Haiti, and Puerto Rico* 4 (1986).

———. *Country Report*, nos. 1–4 (1987) and no. 1 (1988).

———. *Country Profile: Cuba, 1986–87*.

Edquist, Charles. *Capitalism, Socialism, and Technology—Comparative Study of Cuba and Jamaica*. London: Zed Books Ltd., 1985.

Ehrlich, Eva. "Economic Development, Levels, Proportions, and Structures, 1960–80." Unpublished manuscript, May 1985.

Erisman, Michael. *Cuban International Relations*. Boulder, Colo.: Westview Press, 1985.

Espinosa, J., and A. Zimbalist. *Economic Democracy*. New York: Academic Press, 1978.

Feinsilver, Julie. "Cuba as a World Medical Power: The Politics of Symbolism." Ph.D. diss., Yale University, 1987.

Feygin, Bella. *The Theory and Practice of Price Formation in the USSR*. Falls Church, Va.: Delpic Associates, 1983.

Fiandor Rosario, Héctor. "Desarrollo Actual de los Derivados de la Caña." *Compendio de Investigaciones* (JUCEPLAN) 4 (January 1988).

Figueras, Miguel Alejandro. *Producción de maquinarias y equipos en Cuba*. Havana: Editorial Científico-Técnica, 1985.

Fogarty, Carol, and Kevin Tritle. "Moscow's Economic Aid Programs in Less-Developed Countries: A Perspective on the 1980s." In Joint Economic Committee, *Gorbachev's Economic Plans*, vol. 2. Washington, D.C.: U.S. Government Printing Office, 1987.

Fry, James. *Sugar: Aspects of a Complex Commodity Market*. Division Working Paper no. 1985-1, Washington, D.C.: World Bank, 1985.

———. "Cuba's Sugar Statistics: How Reliable Are They?" *Cuba Business* 2:2 (April 1988): 8–10.

Fuller, Linda. "The Politics of Workers' Control in Cuba, 1959–1983." Ph.D. diss., Department of Sociology, University of California, Berkeley, 1985.

———. "Power at the Workplace: The Resolution of Worker–Management Conflict in Cuba." *World Development* (January 1987).

Garcia, Hugo. "La indústria siderúrgica en Cuba." *Economía y Desarrollo* 97 (March/April 1987a).

———. "La indústria mecánica." *Economía y Desarrollo* 100 (September/October 1987b).

Garcia, Silvia. "La Indústria de los Derivados de la Caña de Azúcar." Unpublished manuscript, CIEI, Havana, n.d.

Geldof, Lynn. "Huge Product Waste." *Cuba Business* 2:3 (June 1988).

Gerschenkron, Alexander. *Economic Backwardness in Historical Perspective*. New York: Praeger, 1965.

Ghai, Dharam, Cristobal Kay, and Peter Peek. *Labour and Development in Rural Cuba*, London: Macmillan, 1988.

Gilly, Adolfo. *Inside the Cuban Revolution*. New York: Monthly Review Press, 1964.

González, Armando Nova. "Apuntes preliminares sobre el proceso inversionista en la actividad agropecuaria." In JUCEPLAN, *Compendio de Investigaciones*: Resúmenes de los Trabajos Presentados en la Jornada Científica Sobre Planificación de las Inversiones. Havana, July 1986.

González, L. R. "Revisión de la normas de trabajo." *Bohemia*, March 6, 1987.

González, R., and C. Menéndez. "La evaluación de la efectividad de las exportaciones y su vinculación con el sistema de precios." *Teoría y Práctica de los Precios* 2 (April/June 1986).

Granma, January 1, 1984; December 25, 1986; December 26, 1986; January 1, 1987; January 11, 1987; January 14, 1987.

Granma Resumen Semanal, October 5, 1982; January 1, 1984; December 14, 1986; January 11, 1987; January 14, 1987; August 12, 1987; December 14, 1987.

Greenslade, Rush, "Industrial Production Statistics in the USSR." In Vladimir Treml and John Hardt, eds. *Soviet Economic Statistics*. Durham, N.C.: Duke University Press, 1972.

———. "The Real Gross National Product of the USSR, 1950–75." Joint Economic Committee, *Soviet Economy in a New Perspective*. Washington, D.C.: U.S. Government Printing Office, 1976.

Grossman, Gregory. *Soviet Statistics of Physical Output of Industrial Commodities*: *Their Compilation and Quality*. Princeton: Princeton University Press, 1960.

Gustafsson, Hans. "Is Agriculture Mechanization a Point of Entry into Capital Goods Production in LDCs?—A Critique of the UNIDO Approach." Lund, Sweden: Research Policy Institute, University of Lund, 1986.

Hamburg, Jill. *Under Construction: Housing Policy in Revolutionary Cuba*. New York: Center for Cuban Studies, 1986.

Hernández, B., "La Planificación de los precios en las condiciones de la economía cubana." *Teoría y Práctica de los Precios* 2 (1986).

Hernández, D'Angelo, and Armengol Rios. "Aspects de los procesos de comunicación y participación de los trabajadores en la gestión de las empresas." *Economía y Dessarrollo* 42 (July/August 1977).

Herrera, A., and H. Rosenkranz. "Political Consciousness in Cuba." In J. Griffiths and J. Griffiths, eds. *Cuba: The Second Decade*. London: Britain–Cuba Scientific Liaison Committee, 1979.

Hirschman, Albert O. "The Political Economy of Import Substituting Industrialization in Latin America." *Quarterly Journal of Economics* 82 (1968).

Hodgman, Donald. *Soviet Industrial Production, 1928–1951*. Cambridge: Harvard University Press, 1954.

Hoffman, Stanley. "Power Unshared and Total." *New York Times Book Review*, November 30, 1986.

Instituto Cubano de Investigaciones de los Derivados de la Caña de Azúcar (ICIDCA). "La Indústria de los Derivados de la Caña de Azúcar." Havana, 1986.

Iglesias, Enrique. "Development and Equity: The Challenge of the 1980s." *CEPAL Review* (December 1981).

Instituto de Demanda Interna. *Nivel y modo de vida de la población cubana*. Havana, 1988.

Instituto Nacional de Estadísticas, División de Encuesta Muestrales. *Indice de Precios al Por Mayor*. Santiago, Chile, 1986.

Inter-American Development Bank. *Economic and Social Progress in Latin America: 1982 Report*. Washington, D.C., 1982.

International Labour Office. *Year Book of Labour Statistics*. Geneva, 1982.

Joglekar, G., and A. Zimbalist. "Using Physical Indicators to Estimate GDP Per Capita in Cuba: An Estimate and a Critique." *Journal of Comparative Economics* 13:1 (March 1989).

Johnson, Chalmers. *MITI and the Japanese Miracle*. Stanford, Calif.: Stanford University Press, 1982.

————, ed. *The Industrial Policy Debate*. San Francisco: Institute of Contemporary Studies, 1984.

Jones, Derek, and Jan Svejnar, eds. *Participatory and Self-Managed Firms*. Lexington, Mass.: Heath, 1982.

Jones, Kirby. *Opportunities for U.S.–Cuba Trade*. Washington, D.C.: Cuban Studies Program, Johns Hopkins University School of Advanced International Studies, June 1988.

JUCEPLAN, *Segunda Plenaria Nacional de Chequeo de la Implantación del SPDE*. Havana, July 1980.

————. *Dictámemes de la IV Plenaria Nacional de Chequeo del Sistema de Dirección y Planificación de la Economía*. Havana, 1985.

Kalecki, Michal. "Hypothetical Outline of the Five Year Plan (1961–1965) for the Cuban Economy." In Michal Kalecki, ed., *Essays on Developing Economics*. London: Hassocks, 1976.

Kaplan, Norman, and Richard Moorsteen. "An Index of Soviet Industrial Output." *American Economic Review* 50 (June 1960).

Karol, K. S. *Guerrillas in Power: The Course of the Cuban Revolution*. New York: Hill and Wang, 1970.

Kay, Cristobal. "New Developments in Cuban Agriculture: Economic Reforms and Collectivization." Occasional Paper no. 1, Centre for Development Studies, University of Glasgow, 1987.

Koont, Sinan, and A. Zimbalist. "Incentives and Elicitation Schemes: A Critique and an Extension." In A. Zimbalist, ed. *Comparative Economic Systems: An Assessment of Knowledge, Theory and Method*. Boston: Kluwer-Nijhoff, 1984.

Kirsch, L. *Soviet Wages*. Cambridge: MIT Press, 1972.

Kornai, Janos. "The Dilemmas of a Socialist Economy: The Hungarian Experience." *Cambridge Journal of Economics* 4 (1980a).

————. *The Economics of Shortage*. Amsterdam: North Holland, 1980b.

Kuo, Shirley. "Development of the Tiawanese Economy." Paper presented at the Chung-Hua Institute for Economic Research (CIER), Taipei, August 31, 1988.

Kuo, Shirley, Gustav Ranis, and John C. H. Fei. *The Taiwan Success Story: Rapid Growth with Improved Distribution in the Republic of China*. Boulder, Colo.: Westview Press, 1981.

Kuznets, Paul. "An East Asian Model of Economic Development: Japan, Taiwan, and South Korea." *Economic Development and Cultural Change* 36:3 (April 1988).

Latin America Weekly Report, January 3, 1986; July 14, 1988.

Lenin, V. I.. "The Immediate Tasks of the Soviet Government." *Pravda*, no. 83 (April 28, 1918).

Leyva, Ricardo. "Health and Revolution in Cuba." In R. Bonachea and N. Valdes, eds. *Cuba in Revolution*. New York: Anchor, 1972.

MacEwan, Arthur. *Revolution and Economic Development in Cuba*. New York: St. Martin's Press, 1981.

Marer, Paul. "Alternative Estimates of the Dollar GNP and Growth Rates of the CMEA Countries." In Joint Economic Committee, *East European Economies: Slow Growth in the 1980s*. Washington, D.C.: U.S. Government Printing Office, 1985a.

————. *Dollar GNPs and Growth Rates of the USSR and Eastern Europe*. Baltimore: Johns Hopkins University Press for the World Bank, 1985b.

Martínez, Carlos. "El perfeccionamiento del mecanismo de estimulación material en Cuba." *Cuba: Economía Planificada* 1:1 (January/March 1986).

Martínez, Gilberto Diaz. "El sistema empresarial estatal en Cuba." *Cuba Socialista* 8 (September/November 1983).

Martínez, Ramon, *La Comparabilidad de las Estadísticas*. Havana: Comité Estatal de Estadísticas, 1985.

Mata, Nelson. "Los gastos de presupuesto de los Organos Locales del Poder Popular." *Finanzas y Crédito* 5 (1986).

Mejías, Aledio. "El precio como criterio de eficiencia en la exportación e importación de mercancías." *Cuba: Economía Planificada* 1:3 (July/September 1986).

Mesa-Lago, Carmelo. "Availability and Reliability of Statistics in Socialist Cuba." *Latin American Research Review* 4: 1 & 2 (Spring and Summer 1969).

————. *Cuba in the 1970s*. Rev. ed. Albuquerque: University of New Mexico Press, 1978.

————. "Cuban Statistics Revisited." *Cuban Studies* 9:2 (July 1979).

————. *The Economy of Socialist Cuba: A Two Decade Appraisal*. Albuquerque: University of New Mexico Press, 1981.

————. "Review." *Cuban Studies* 15:2 (Summer 1985).

————. "Cuba's Centrally Planned Economy: An Equity Tradeoff for Growth." In J. Hartlyn and S. Morley, eds. *Latin American Political Economy: Financial Crisis and Political Change*. Boulder, Colo: Westview Press, 1986.

————. "The Cuban Economy in the 1980s: The Return of Ideology." In S. Roca, ed. *Socialist Cuba: Past Interpretations and Future Challenges*.

Mesa-Lago, Carmelo, and Jorge Pérez-López. "Study of Cuba's MPS, Its Conversion to SNA, and Estimation of GDP/Capita and Growth Rates." Paper presented at Second Workshop on CPE National Income Statistics, the World Bank, Washington, D.C., October 1982.

————. "Imbroglios on the Cuban Economy: A Reply to Brundenius and Zimbalist." *Comparative Economic Studies* 27:1 & 3 (Spring and Winter 1985a).

————. "Estimating Cuban Gross Domestic Product Per Capita in Dollars Using Physical Indicators." *Social Indicators Research* 16 (1985b).

Meurs, Mieke. "Planning, Participation and Material Incentives: Motivating Efficiency in Socialist Cuba." Paper presented to the Third Annual Workshop on Soviet and East European Economies, Washington, D.C., 1987.

————. "Planning, Participation and Incentives in Socialism: The Case of Cuban Agriculture." Ph.D. diss., University of Massachusetts, Amherst, 1988.

Miami Herald, December 11, 1986.

Ministerio de Agricultura (MINAG). *Evaluación de la experienca sobre la introducción de la Brigada permanente de producción y el cálculo económico interno en las empresas del Ministerio de la Agricultura*. Havana, November 1985.

————. *Informe: Resultados Económicos de las Empresas Constituídas en BPP*. Havana, 1986.

Ministerio de la Indústria Azucarera (MINAZ). *Development of the Cuban Sugar Industry*. Havana, n.d.

Ministerio de Indústria y Comercio. *Estadísticas Industrial, 1967*, 21. Lima, 1969.

Ministerio de Salud Pública (MINSAP). *Informe Anual, 1987*. Havana, 1988.

Montadas, E., and R. Rodríguez. *Evolución Histórica de la Planificación en Cuba*. Havana: Facultad de Planificación de la Economía Nacional e Indústrias, University of Havana, n.d.

Montias, John M. *Economic Development in Communist Rumania*. Cambridge: MIT Press, 1967.

Morales, Esteban, and H. Pons. "Embargo o bloqueo? Compensación? Aspectos económicos del conflicto bilateral Cuba-EU." *Economía y Desarrollo* (November/December 1987; January/February 1988; March/April 1988).

Morley, Morris. *Imperial State and Revolution: The United States and Cuba, 1952–1986*. New York: Cambridge University Press, 1987.

Naciones Unidas, Consejo Economico y Social. *Comparabilidad de los sistemas de cuentas nacionales y del producto material en America Latina*. E/CEPAL/SEM, 5/L.2, April 1982.

Neuberger, Egon, and L. Tyson, eds. *The Impact of International Economic Disturbances on the Soviet Union and Eastern Europe: Transmission and Response*. New York: Pergamon, 1980.

Nove, Alec. *The Soviet Economic System*. London: George Allen and Unwin, 1977.

O'Connor, James. *The Origins of Socialism in Cuba*. New York: Cornell University Press, 1970.

Oshima, Harry. "A New Estimate of the National Income and Product of Cuba in 1953." Food Research Institute Studies 2:3, Stanford University, November 1961.

Ouchi, W. *Theory Z*. New York: Avon, 1982.

Padron, M. "Un método para medir la eficacia del plan de inspecciones minoristas y su proyección óptima." *Teoría y Práctica de los Precios* 3 (1985).

Palacios, B., G. Solaún, L. Acosta, and L. Miranda. "Posibilidad de aplicación del balance intersectorial físico valor al proceso de elaboración del plan anual de la economía cubana." *Cuba: Economía Planificada* 1:2 (April/June 1986).

Partido Comunista de Cuba (PCC). *Socioeconomic Guidelines for the 1976–80 Period.* Havana, 1976.

———. *Socioeconomic Guidelines for the 1981–85 Period.* Havana, 1981.

———. *Lineamientos económicos y sociales para el quinquenio 1986–90.* Havana: Editora Política, 1986.

Pateman, Carole. *Participation and Democratic Theory.* Cambridge: Cambridge University Press, 1970.

Paus, Eva, ed. *Struggle Against Dependence: Nontraditional Export Growth in Central America and the Caribbean.* Boulder, Colo.: Westview Press, 1988.

Pérez, Aristides. "La prima como forma de estimulación material." *Economía y Desarrollo* 80 (May/June 1984).

Pérez, Humberto. "La plataforma programática y el desarrollo económico de Cuba." *Cuba Socialista* 3 (June 1982).

———. *Intervención a la Clausura de la III Plenaria Nacional del Chequeo de SDPE.* Havana: JUCEPLAN, October 1982.

———. *Intervención a la Clausura de la IV Plenaria Nacional del Chequeo de SDPE.* Havana: JUCEPLAN, May 1985.

Pérez, Omar. "La indústria de materiales de construcción," *Economía y Desarrollo* 98 (May/June 1987).

Pérez-López, Jorge. *Construction of Cuban Economic Activity and Trade Indexes.* Washington, D.C.: Wharton Econometric Forecasting Associates, November 1983.

———. "Real Economic Growth in Cuba, 1965–82." Paper presented at the Latin American Studies Association Meeting, Albuquerque, New Mexico, April 1985.

———. "Real Economic Growth in Cuba, 1965–82." *The Journal of Developing Areas* 20 (January 1986a).

———. "Cuban Economy in the 1980s." *Problems of Communism* (September/October 1986b).

———. "Sugar and the Cuban Economy: A Survey of the Literature." Unpublished manuscript, 1986c.

———. *Sugar and the Cuban Economy: An Assessment.* Coral Gables, Fla.: Research Institute for Cuban Studies, University of Miami, 1987a.

———. *Measuring Cuban Economic Performance.* Austin: University of Texas Press, 1987b.

———. "Cuban Hard Currency Trade and Oil Reexports." In S. Roca, ed., *Socialist Cuba: Past Interpretations and Future Challenges.*

Perez-Stable, Marifeli. "Institutionalization and Workers' Response." *Cuban Studies* 6 (1976).

———. "Politics and Conciencia in Revolutionary Cuba, 1959–1984." Ph.D. diss., Department of Sociology, SUNY–Stonybrook, 1985.

Pisani, Francis. "La rectificación cubana." *Nexos* (Mexico), December 1987.

Pitzer, John. "Gross National Product of the USSR, 1950–80." In Joint Economic Committee, *USSR: Measures of Economic Growth and Development, 1950–1980.* Washington, D.C.: U.S. Government Printing Office, 1982.

Purcell, Susan Kaufman. "Was Communism an Afterthought?" *New York Times Book Review,* October 19, 1986.

Radell, Willard. "Cuba-Soviet Sugar Trade, 1960–1976." *The Journal of Developing Areas* 17:3 (April 1983).

———. "Comparative Performance of Large Cuban Sugar Factories in the 1984 Zafra," *Cuban Studies* 17 (1987).

Ramírez Cruz, Jose. "El sector cooperativo en la agricultura Cubana." *Cuba Socialista* 11 (1984).

Ranis, Gustav. "Challenges and Opportunities Posed by Asia's Superexporters: Implications for Manufactured Exports from Latin America." In J. Dietz and J. Street, eds. *Latin America's Economic Development: Institutionalist and Structuralist Perspectives*. Boulder, Colo.: Lynne Rienner Publishers, 1987.

Rich, Donna. *The U.S. Embargo against Cuba: Its Evolution and Enforcement*. Washington, D.C.: Johns Hopkins University School of Advanced International Studies, July 1988.

Ritter, Archibald. *The Economic Development of Revolutionary Cuba*. New York: Praeger, 1974.

———. "Cuba's Convertible Currency Debt Problem, 1980–1988." Unpublished manuscript, School of International Affairs, Carleton Univeristy, Ottawa, Canada, March 1988.

Roca, Sergio. "State Enterprise in Cuba under the New System of Planning and Management. *Cuban Studies* 16 (1986).

———. "Planners in Wonderland: A Reply to Zimbalist." *Cuban Studies* 17 (1987).

———, ed. *Socialist Cuba: Past Interpretations and Future Challenges*. Boulder, Colo.: Westview Press, 1988.

Rodríguez, Carlos Rafael. *Letra Con Filo 2*. Havana: Editorial de Ciencias Sociales, 1983.

———. "Sobre la contribución del Che al desarrollo de la economía socialista." *Cuba Socialista* 33 (May/June 1988).

Rodríguez, Gonzalo. *El proceso de industrialización de la economía cubana*. Havana: Editorial de Ciencias Sociales, 1980.

———. "Apuntes sobre el desarrollo industrial de Cuba, 1976–85." *Economía y Desarrollo* 99 (July/August 1987).

Rodríguez, José Luis. "Agricultural Policy and Development in Cuba." In A. Zimbalist, ed. *Cuba's Socialist Economy Toward the 1990s*. Boulder, Colo.: Lynne Rienner Publishers, 1987.

Rodríguez, J. L., and G. Carriazo. *Erradicación de la Pobreza en Cuba*. Havana: Editorial de Ciencias Sociales, 1987.

Rodríguez, Martha, and Daniel Schydlowsky. "The Effectiveness of Devaluation to Achieve Industrial Competitiveness in Latin America: A Simulation Analysis." Paper presented to the conference of the Northeast Development Consortium at Harvard University, April 29–30, 1988.

Rodríguez, Santiago. "La industria del combustible." *Economía y Desarrollo* 99 (July/August 1987).

Rosenberg, Nathan. *Perspectives on Technology*. Cambridge: Cambridge University Press, 1976.

Rueschemeyer, D., and P. Evans. "The State and Economic Transformation: Toward an Analysis of the Conditions Underlying Effective Intervention." In Peter Evans et al., eds. *Bringing the State Back In*. New York: Cambridge University Press, 1985.

Sachs, Jeffrey. "Trade and Exchange Policies in Growth-Oriented Adjustment Programs." National Bureau of Economic Research Working Papers, no. 2226, April 1987.

Salazar-Carrillo, Jorge. "Is the Cuban Economy Knowable?" *Caribbean Review* 15:2 (1986).

Salom, J. "Los Precios, los costos y la gestión empresarial en la rama de construcción y montaje." *Teoría y Práctica de los Precios* 2 (1985a).

———. "Influencia del exceso de rentabilidad en las empresas de construcción civil y montaje en el proceso inversionista." *Teoría y Práctica de los Precios* 2 (1985b).

Santana, Sarah. "The Cuban Health Care System." *World Development* (January 1987).

———. "Some Thoughts on Statistics and Health Status in Cuba." In A. Zimbalist, ed. *Cuban Political Economy: Controversies in Cubanology*. Boulder, Colo.: Westview Press, 1988.

Santiago, Armando. "La formación planificada de los precios y su papel en el perfeccionamiento de las relaciones del cálculo económico de la empresa industrial cubana." Ph.D. diss. in economics, University of Havana, 1986.

Silva, Arnaldo. *Cuba y el mercado internacional azucarero*. Havana, 1986.

Silverman, B. *Man and Socialism in Cuba: The Great Debate*. New York: Atheneum, 1973.

Smith, John T. "Sugar Dependency in Cuba: Capitalism versus Socialism." In M. Seligson, ed. *The Gap Between Rich and Poor*. Boulder, Colo.: Westview Press, 1984.

Smith, Wayne. *The Closest of Enemies*. New York: Norton, 1987.

Smith, Wayne, and Esteban Morales, eds. *Subject to Solution: Problems in Cuban-U.S. Relations*. Boulder, Colo.: Lynne Rienner Publishers, 1988.

SRI International. *Nontraditional Export Expansion in the Central American Region*. Report prepared for the Bureau of Latin America and the Caribbean, U.S. Agency for International Development, Arlington, Va., March 1987.

Staff of Radio José Martí. *Cuba: Quarterly Situation Report*. Washington, D.C.: U.S. Information Service, 1986, 1987, and 1988 (quarterly).

Staller, George. "Czechoslovak Industrial Growth: 1948–1959." *American Economic Review* 52:3 (1962).

Statistical Yearbook of the Republic of China. See Directorate General of the Budget.

Stubbs, J. "Gender Issues in Contemporary Cuban Tobacco Farming." In A. Zimbalist, ed. *Cuba's Socialist Economy Toward the 1990s*. Boulder, Colo.: Lynne Rienner Publishers, 1987.

Szilagyi, Gy. "Factor-Analytical Comparison of Economic Level and Structure." *Acta Oeconomica* 21:4 (1978).

Szulc, Tad. *Fidel: A Critical Portrait*. New York: Morrow, 1986.

Taylor, F. W. *Scientific Management*. New York: Harper and Row, 1947.

Theriot, Lawrence. *Cuba Faces the Economic Realities of the 1980s*. Washington, D.C.: U.S. Department of Commerce, 1982.

Toledo, R. "Los precios mayoristas y el uso racional de la energía." *Teoría y Práctica de los Precios* 2 (1985).

Torres, Olga Ester. "El desarrollo de la economía cubana partir de 1959." *Comercio Exterior* 31:3 (1981).

Trabajadores. November 3, 1982; June 6, 1986; September 9, 1986.

Treml, Vladimir, and John Hardt, eds. *Soviet Economic Statistics*. Durham, N.C.: Duke University Press, 1972.

Tukey, J. *Exploratory Data Analysis*. Reading, Mass.: Addison-Wesley, 1977.

Turits, Richard. "Trade, Debt and the Cuban Economy." In A. Zimbalist, ed. *The Cuban Economy Toward the 1990s*. Boulder, Colo.: Lynne Rienner Publishers, 1987.

U-Echevarria, Oscar, L. Ramos, and A. Díaz. "Consideraciones metodológicas para el cálculo de la demanda de piezas de respuesto." *Cuba: Economía Planificada* 1:2 (April/June 1986).

United Nations. *Statistical Yearbook 1980, 1981.* New York: 1980, 1981.

United Nations Commission of the European Communities. *World Comparisons of Purchasing Power and Real Product for 1980*. New York, 1986.

United Nations Conference on Trade and Development (UNCTAD). *The Capital Goods Sector in Developing Countries: Technology Issues and Policy Options*. New York, 1985.

United Nations Industrial Development Organization (UNIDO). *World Wide Survey of the Agricultural Machinery Industry* (ICIS. 119). Vienna, 1979.

————. *Conditions of Entry into the Capital Goods Sector and Integrated Manufacture* (ID/WG. 442/3). Vienna, 1985.

————. *Cuba* (IS.615). Vienna: Industrial Development Review Series, UNIDO, March 1986.

United States Senate, Committee on Foreign Relations, Staff Report. *Report on Cuba*. Washington, D.C.: U.S. Government Printing Office, 1975.

Vega, J. J., B. Sánchez, L. Ramos, and A. O. Díos. "El desarrollo de la industria electrónica hasta el año 2000." *Revista Cuba: Economía Planificada* 2 (April/June 1987).

Velázquez, Rafael, and F. Shvidanenko. "Cálculo económico: realización de sus principios en la economía cubana." *Economía y Desarrollo* (January/February 1988).

Vilarino', Andres, and S. Ma. Domenech. *El sistema de dirección y planificación de la economía: historia, actualidad y perspectiva*. Havana: Editorial Pueblo y Educación, 1986.

Weisskopf, Richard. *Factories and Food Stamps: The Puerto Rican Model of Development*. Baltimore: Johns Hopkins University Press, 1986.

World Bank. *World Development Report* (various years).

White, Gordon. "Cuban Planning in the Mid-1980s: Centralization, Decentralization, and Participation." In A. Zimbalist, ed. *The Cuban Economy Toward the 1990s*. Boulder, Colo.: Lynne Rienner Publishers, 1987.

Whyte, W. F. *Money and Motivation*. New York: Harper, 1985.

Zimbalist, Andrew. "Worker Participation in Cuba." *Challenge* 18:5 (November/December 1975).

————, ed. *Case Studies on the Labor Process*. New York: Monthly Review Press, 1979.

————. "Soviet Aid, U.S. Blockade and the Cuban Economy." *Comparative Economic Studies* 24:4 (Winter 1982).

————, ed. *Comparative Economic Systems: An Assessment of Knowledge, Theory, and Method*. Boston: Kluwer-Nijhoff, 1984.

————. "Cuban Industrial Growth, 1965–84." *World Development* (January 1987a).

————. "Analyzing Cuban Planning: A Response to Roca." *Cuban Studies* 17 (1987b).

————. "Interpreting Cuban Planning: Between a Rock and a Hard Place." In A. Zimbalist, ed. *Cuban Political Economy: Controversies in Cubanology*. Boulder, Colo.: Westview Press, 1988a.

————. "Cuba's Statistical and Price Systems: Interpretation and Reliability." *Latin American Perspectives* 15:2 (Spring 1986b).

————. "Labour Markets: Another View." *Cuba Business* 2:2 (April 1988c).

————. "Incentives and Planning in Cuba." *Latin American Research Review* 23:1 (January 1989).

Zimbalist, Andrew, H. Sherman, and S. Brown. *Comparing Economic Systems: A Political-Economic Approach*. San Diego: Harcourt Brace Jovanovich, 1988.

Index

Andrew Zimbalist is professor of economics at Smith College and at the Five-College Graduate Faculty. **Claes Brundenius** is the associate director of the Research Policy Institute at the University of Lund, Sweden.

Books in the Series

Designed by Chris L. Hotvedt
  Composed by The Composing Room of
  Michigan, Inc.,
  in Times Roman text and display
  Printed by BookCrafters on 50-lb. Natural
  Booktext paper and
  bound in Holliston's Roxite A